D0849062

AFRICAN AMERICAN POLITICS IN RURAL AMERICA

Theory, Practice, and Case Studies from Florence County, South Carolina

E. Ike Udogu

University Press of America,® Inc.
Lanham · Boulder · New York · Toronto · Oxford

Copyright © 2006 by
University Press of America,® Inc.
4501 Forbes Boulevard
Suite 200
Lanham, Maryland 20706
UPA Acquisitions Department (301) 459-3366

PO Box 317
Oxford
OX2 9RU, UK

Library of Congress Control Number: 2006927253
ISBN-13: 978-0-7618-3540-0 (clothbound : alk. paper)
ISBN-10: 0-7618-3540-7 (clothbound : alk. paper)
ISBN-13: 978-0-7618-3541-7 (paperback : alk. paper)
ISBN-10: 0-7618-3541-5 (paperback : alk. paper)

This book is dedicated to political actors in rural America and elsewhere for their invaluable contributions to the political, social, religious and economic well-being of a majority of citizens in society.

Contents

Preface

The motivation to write this book began after I was invited, as the only black political scientist teaching at a college in the area, to chair the campaign committee of a young African American lady running for a seat in the South Carolina Legislature. The political campaign was conducted in 1996. The political process was tough and challenging, but the experience was both exciting and educational. Indeed, after over two decades of studying, reading and observing American politics, it was stimulating to finally enmesh myself in grassroots politics. As a scholar, one important lesson learned participating in legislative elections was the contradictions between theoretical idealism and practical realism in politics.

The research for this book took me over eight years to complete. The number of years taken to put this manuscript together reflects the uniqueness of the project, and the necessary adjustments I have had to make in order to contextualize the study within a broader framework than just the politics of a County in the south and South Carolina in particular.

As a student of politics, my interest in local, state and national politics has always remained high. After all, there is so much truth to the cliché that "all politics are local." Besides, I am a registered voter and this fact made it all the more fascinating to examine some of the factors that influence voter turnout in rural America, particularly among African American electorate in small towns and communities.

Moreover, after so many years of living, teaching and becoming actively involved in the electoral process in rural America, one of my concerns was on how to boost minority political participation as a strategy for addressing the issues that affect Blacks in the polity. In order to confront some of these concerns, I tried political activism by joining some local African American groups in hopes that collectively, and as members of the informed public, we could contribute toward political and economic empowerment of African Americans in the area within the context of the democratic theory of politics. In other words, the assumption is that those who participate in a democratic process are likely to derive the benefits that sometimes flow from it. One such organization was the Coalition of Black-networking (CBN) in which I also served as president. To be sure, there were and are several local organizations including the NAACP working equally hard to promote the welfare of minorities in the community, such as the campaign to provide more adequate public housing projects, jobs and encouragement of more political participation. To me, however, the progress was frustratingly slow in the 1990s. Generally, rural folks tend to be apolitical when political issues don't affect their immediate interests. Indeed, they are more likely to be laid back and concerned with family matters and places of worship. As a result, I directed my energy and efforts toward teaching and research.

In 2002, after about six years of examining the theoretical dimensions of the project, I went to the public library to see what was available on African American politics in the region. I discovered that the political and social issues in the black community were covered in the *Community Times*, one of the area's excellent African American-oriented newspapers and to an appreciable level by the city's newspaper: The *Florence Morning News*. Through my subscription to the *Community Times*, I was able to keep abreast with matters and political developments that affected African Americans in the region. There were few, if any, available books detailing the politico-historical or historical and political activities of Black political actors in the area.

After mulling over what I perceived to be the deficiency of works on African American politics in rural America, I decided to redouble my efforts on the work. Moreover, the sizable population of African American political actors in the region dictated that a political book of this sort was necessary so that future generations could appreciate the political advancement of black politicos in the south and republic itself. Further, it was my hope that a book that blended political theory with practice could encourage more writers to produce books that deal with the importance of black politics in rural America in order to augment the prodigious volumes on African Americans in urban politics. In this way, an attempt could be made to improve the "lack of balance" between the scholarly concerns for black politics in cities and black politics in rural America—where, in actuality, a majority of African Americans are domiciled. This reality and the group's political character in the periphery of national politics in part informed this study.

My interest in black grassroots politics is not limited to rural America alone; it is borne out of my belief that rural populations globally are, generally, politically marginalized except, of course, if they have powerful interest groups to lobby on their behalf. In virtually all societies, and in every part of the world, rural populations, with a few exceptions, are "regarded" as politically backward, uninformed and those who could be manipulated by political entrepreneurs and their agents who claim, to have their interest at heart—especially during election cycles.

I believe that by writing this very important and concise book, I have in a major way made a significant contribution to black or minority politics in rural America. But more importantly, it is hoped that this study will awaken scholars to the need for such projects and encourage them in particular to undertake more studies on minority politics in the periphery of this and other societies. Such research schemes are likely to give these groups' politics the prominence that they richly deserve.

E. Ike Udogu
Boone, NC
March, 2006

Acknowledgments

The completion of this work would have been impossible were it not for the support of, and encouragement by, my colleagues at Francis Marion University, Florence, South Carolina (1985-2003) and Appalachian State University, Boone, North Carolina where I currently teach. The members of the staff of these excellent universities were extremely helpful. Also, some of the materials cited in this work came from the Florence County Library—a library that has been my home, in a manner of speaking, since 1985.

The staffs of the office of US Congressman Clyburn in Florence and the City/County Councils were very helpful in providing important demographic information some of which are included in the appendices of this volume. Indeed, the information from these sources helped me to sharpen my analyses.

The following were invaluable to the outcome of this volume: Poiette McGill of Marion, whose candidacy for an office in the State of South Carolina spurred this major work and members of her campaign team, viz.: Ivan Williams, Odelia Parsell and supporters who distributed campaign leaflets from house to house and trailer park to trailer park. Others who willingly granted me interviews for this project were Councilman Edward Robinson (Florence City), Councilman Lovith Anderson, Jr. (Lake City) and Mayor Henry Peoples (Timmonsville City Council). I would also like to acknowledge the support of one of my former students, Carolyn Turner.

The Department of Political Science and Criminal Justice at Appalachian State University assigned me three graduate assistants—Ljubica Nedelkoska, Autumn Scarbrough and Jason Grice to work with me on the book. Their help and those of my extremely supportive colleagues and students are greatly appreciated. I am, indeed, especially thankful for their confidence in the project.

My visits to Lake City, Timmonsville, and Florence government complexes and presence at some of the Council meetings were very helpful in clarifying my understanding of how the political actors and institutions worked. The enthusiastic support given me by the administrative staffs of these important institutions—perhaps the most significant institutions given the vast number of citizens that these institutions serve in rural America—were remarkable and also appreciated. Their patience with me as I probed for information was impressive and in great measure made this work possible. To my family and friends who always supported me for spending an inordinate amount of time in the library, I owe a depth of gratitude. Special thanks to Mr. Larry Smith, publisher of the African American newspaper, *Community Times*, with whom I discussed minority politics in the area. My gratitude to Ms. Joyce Marshall, who provided me with useful information relating to Black and Church politic, members of the Coalition of Black-networking (CBN), and all the local African American political actors in the area whose political activities I monitored as long ago as 1985. And to professor Wayne King, the erudite historian at Francis Marion University, Florence who provided invaluable historical information in the region and also directed me to those who might be of help on the project, I say thank you.

Finally, I am delighted to say that my colleagues of the African Studies and Research Forum (ASRF) and Association of Third World Studies (ATWS) have been indispensable "cheer-leaders" of sorts in encouraging me to pursue this study. They have provided me with the forums to share my works and their critiques have been very helpful in improving this and other projects. To these inspiring associates, I say thank you for standing by me through thick and thin.

Introduction

It is challenging, yet exhilarating, to do a book on minority politics with specific emphasis on African American Politics in Rural America. Indeed, as an academic who has a profound intellectual interest in black history and black political "theology," I brought my excitement and expertise to bear in the analyses in this volume—with a strong belief that the study of African American politics in the periphery could add significantly to the literature in American politics and political science in general.

Moreover, let it suffice to say that this book is not just about African American politics in the "margins" of the South; it is to some extent also about minority and ethnic politics in rural America and other democratic societies, globally. And, I am a student of ethnic politics. More importantly, though, this study may be said to be about the politics of everyone with a racial and ethnically diverse rural root—and how the majority versus minority political competition for the control of power is played out in a society.

In the American context, it is safe to argue that without the economic, social and political interactions and contestations of the various collectivities—i.e. European Americans,[1] Jewish Americans, Hispanic Americans, Asian Americans, and so on that make up the United States of America, the study of African American politics may be useless. Moreover, if minority claims on politics and political system in the struggle for the distribution of goods and services were not commonplace, the need for the development of black politics, women's study, ethnic studies, Hispanic studies and other similar programs on university campuses intended to highlight their unique significance in society might be irrelevant.

I have not developed this volume, *African American Politics in Rural America: Theory, Practice and Case Studies from Florence County*, from a structural/institutional approach, which is characteristic of most books on national, state and local governments. In other words, this study does not examine the character and function of the organs of government (such as the Administration, Health Care Department, Law Enforcement Department, Fire Department, and so on in a city) through which decisions and policies are made and implemented in Lake City, Florence and Timmonsville as is often the case in the study of city governments throughout America and other societies. Instead, it is concerned with theory and political actors—particularly their political idiosyncrasies, opinions and strategies with which they tackle constituency problems. In part, this book is about political actor's perceptions, frustrations and sometimes satisfaction with the complex processes of governance at the grassroots level in American politics that this book is all about. In a real sense, one important lesson to be learned from this study is that the complexities and perplexing issues in the governance of a society— especially small cities by those perceived to be minorities are worldwide; it is true in Africa, Asia, Europe, the Middle East and Latin America. It is to this end that this volume is quite useful not just to scholars, but also to political actors at the local, state and national levels.

In a broader context, too, the book is intended to help fill in the void or better yet address an area of study that has been vastly, but unintentionally, "neglected" in the literature—specifically in the study of African American politics in particular and minority politics in general. For example, the literature on urban and inner city politics is very robust[2] while the literature on the study of African American politics in rural America is non-existent or so thin that it requires more attention and research.

A cursory examination of the impressive bibliography in Walters and Smith's volume[3] and elsewhere reveal the dominance of publications in the journals *Urban Affairs Quarterly* and *Urban Affairs Review*. There are no scholarly journals, for instance, titled *Rural Affairs Quarterly, Journal of Rural Politics, et cetera,* that highlight the political importance of African American politics in rural America. But the preceding conjectures by no means imply that African American political activities in the periphery are not covered elsewhere; it is just that they are overshadowed by black politics in Los Angeles, New York, Atlanta, Chicago and Charlotte, for example.

The rationale for publishing manuscripts in mainstream urban journals, not only flows from the high quality of these publications, but also because the cities are where some, if not most, of the African Americans with political, economic, social and intellectual clout are domiciled. So, academic outpouring of works relating to the plights and actions of African Americans in inner city and urban America are preponderant.[4] The studies done on the social and particularly political conditions of African Americans in rural setting are relatively minimal. To this end, this study not only represents an important step in an attempt to augment the literature in African American politics in general, but also rural American politics in particular.

Take, for example, there are excellent studies done on Mayor Marion Barry of Washington, DC, Andrew Young of Atlanta, Thomas Bradley of Los Angeles, Harold Washington of Chicago, Coleman Young of Detroit, Ernest Morial of New Orleans, W. Wilson Goode of Philadelphia, Harvey Gantt of Charlotte, North Carolina and David N. Dinkins of New York City, just to list a few.[5] There are relatively few studies done on elected African American mayors, and legislators for that matter, in small towns and cities in rural America in South Carolina, North Carolina, West Virginia, Alabama, Mississippi, Georgia, Florida, Louisiana, Arkansas, and elsewhere. Yet, there are more Americans and African Americans living in rural America than in metropolitan cities. The question, then, is: why are rural politicos not accorded as much political attention as the urban actors when it came to analyzing their political issues in textbooks? Indeed, what point I am attempting to make here?

It is that the intellectual rigor applied to the study of the political activities of black politics at the rural level is inadequate. Arguably, there are good reasons for this inadequacy. I posit that one of the rationales for the marginalization of the study of black politics in rural America (and for that matter rural politics universally) is due to what I refer to as the "econometrics of politics" or the "politics of econometrics." More African American men and women of political and economic power live in urban areas—New York City, Washington, DC, Atlanta, Detroit, Chicago, Los Angeles, San Francisco, Boston, Dallas, Houston and Charlotte to name a few. They are generally members of the well-informed public. They are well traveled both nationally and internationally and tend to have opinions on major political issues when compared to their kith and kin in rural America. Poverty in the rural periphery where a majority of African Americans live can be sharp and often depressing in a generally affluent society.

Destitution in some rural areas and concerns to take care of problems of daily survival is at the heart of their everyday activity. Such concerns do not always lend themselves to conditions that could further educational pursuits and extra-curricular activities such as reading important journals, let alone concerns with local politics. The econometrics of politics, therefore, implies that since the clash, in politics for the distribution of goods and services, tends to be highly felt in urban areas, analyses of the conflictive politics at the metropolitan level are more likely to affect those who have a lot to gain or lose (in say, Washington, DC, Atlanta and elsewhere). Since these political entrepreneurs often live in urban areas, they are likely to read sophisticated scholarly analyses in *Wall Street Journal, New York Times, Los Angeles Times, Atlanta Constitution, Charlotte Observer* and other newspapers in order to discern social, economic and political trends so that they could position or reposition themselves to take advantage of the prevailing circumstances.

Put another way, there are few rural politicos and African American political actors who might be eager to give up some time out of their laborious and demanding vocation or set aside valuable time for reading a brilliant, or scholarly, paper on the strategies for capturing a mayoral election in rural America. Such an "apathy" issues in part from the fact that a mayoral positions in rural America, is often a part time position and the pay or salary for such an office is not really attractive as that of the mayor of Atlanta, for instance. Compare that, if you will, to a manuscript on the strategies for capturing the mayoral race in San Francisco, California, with its imposing City Hall and the prestige that flows from serving at the helm of city government. Thus, the picture is clear regarding one major reason why the politics of rural areas in America (and worldwide) tend to suffer from "intellectual" marginalization and why this study is intended, in a special way, to bring the political issues in a periphery of American politics to the fore.

Purpose of the Study

For better or worse, and generally for better, rural America remains a political incubator from which political recruits could be harvested for political parties. Rural Americans, especially African Americans, should not be seen only as those whose votes and political activism are significant every biannual and quadrennial presidential elections. Their political activities should be studied beyond the general examination of their voting behavior in national, state and local government textbooks.

It is against the backdrop of the foregoing contentions that this volume rests on the following pillars:

1. Provide some historical context of African Americans in South Carolina that would help bring to the fore the social and political conditions from which the study flows;

2. Attempt to nationalize/universalize the study by situating my analyses on some theories, political behavior patterns, political attitudes, and leadership genre;

3. Contextualize the thrust of the study by examining its root—since politics are activities that occur in a society—and the every character of the environment in which politics are played out generally determines how citizens interact with each other politically and socially.

4. Examine and analyze three case studies aimed at emphasizing the importance of grassroots politics—especially as they bring to light the activities of ordinary, and yet important, politicians whose political activities are often "marginally" discussed in intellectual discourses. The "lack" of interest in the study of rural politicians is problematic because rural mayors and legislators collectively outnumber the political office holders that serve at the national, state and urban levels (and are much closer to the millions of their constituents in America).

The great philosophers, it has been said, tell us that all our past, acclaims the future. Indeed, if this observation is true, a bit of history culled from the illuminating work of Frank J. Klingberg[6] should provide an interesting introduction to this concise work. The assumption is that a better understanding of the history of a group of people—any group of people—in any nation-state and political setting, all over the world, may help explain the character of a collectivity as a unique political or social group. This is the case in any society (worldwide) in which the dominant and privileged group/s find it socially expedient to marginalize the weaker group/s by "demoting" them politically through the sociological ingroup-outgroup competition for the control of power and things of value.

Politics are played out in a larger environment—that might take place in a community, state, national and international, setting. In the struggle for political and social advantage by an individual or group so many strategies are often employed. Population (whether majority or minority) could be peripheral in the struggle for power and advantage since political authority is generally measured by economic wealth, control of natural resources, and the possession and control of the instrument of coercion by an ethnic or a racial cleavage in a polity.

In order to add to the comprehension of the study it is, theoretically, important to examine briefly the history of the area being studied. This approach to the study is important since social and political activities of the past often inform contemporary behavior patterns in all societies.

History

The early history of South Carolina would suggest that the numerical superiority of African Americans were no match to the superior economic, political and military power of the minority European Americans. Moreover, in South Carolina, power politics also determined other forms of relations between African Americans and European Americans during the period of the slave trade. The historic character of the relationship between the two major populations—Blacks and Whites (without reference to Native Americans and other minority groups) was eloquently captured in the following excerpt:

> An analysis of the American population instantly reveals the fact that, of the many racial and nationalistic elements which have fed the main stream of United States history, one of the oldest and largest is that of the Negro, who, according to all available estimates of colonial population, arrived early and in such numbers as to equal, and in many cases, far exceed, the white population. As an involuntary immigrant, living and working in communities where he represented a suppressed majority, his full part in the building of America needs to be brought to light. Indeed, the fact that his contribution has been so largely overlooked by scholars, as compared with European groups: Irish, Germans, Italian, Greek, Polish, Russian, etc. suggests a tacit acceptance of his status as an original settler and founder. Equally indispensable to the mastery of the continent, and fundamentally analogous to other immigrant groups in the problems confronting him, the story of the Negro, when laid bare from the beginning, present clearly the successive stages of Americanization and adaptation to the New World environment.[7]

The agony that followed the forced transplantation of Africans to the new world in the trade in human cargo apart[8] one question that continually baffle students of African and African American history is how come it is that a people who despite their physical presence, work, assimilation, intellect and adaptation became so economically, socially and educationally ostracized in the society? The desire to Americanize African Americans (also once known as Negroes) in colonial South Carolina aside, what about the impressive and towering population of Blacks and the possibility of this group using its share numbers to further the collective interest of the collectivity?

Klingberg and others suggest:

> No other area on the American continent is more rewarding for the study of the relationship between the Negro and the White man, than that embraced under the term, Colonial South Carolina, covering as it did areas not clearly defined. Here the Negro came early, from the West Indies and from Africa, in such numbers that the conflicting estimates show only one constant figure: the Negro in excess of the White man. Of these estimates, that of 1715 seems fairly accurate. In this year the population of South Carolina was given as 6,250 Whites and 10, 500 Negroes. . . . The 1775 figures of approximately 100,000 Negroes to 60,000 Whites show a ratio of ten Negroes to six Whites[9]

In fact, given the overwhelming numbers of Negroes in the area in the 18th century and their labor in developing the economy of the region an observer, Reginald Coupland, was compelled to opine emphatically that as a productive economic unit "America was saved by Africa."[10]

In spite of the growth of the black population and the economic reward that came out of it, why was the group unable to acquire economic power? It was clear at this time that whereas Blacks possessed immense physical power and energy with which they worked the land, the same was not true with education that could have increased their influence. Besides, those who opposed educating Blacks (and other less privileged in society) argued that education was useless; that it was unnecessary and that it took too much time away from manual labor. Education, anti-education proponents further contended, made slaves lazy and proud and that slaves could not interpret what they read so why waste their time on a trivial pursuit.[11] A more important concern, however, was that which the Colonialist feared—and rightly so—that they might not be able to control the political and military power that could possibly come from the impressive and vast number of Blacks. Thus, it was noted

> that the congress bickered over the importation of slaves and for a time, importation was terminated. . . . Congress was concerned that the majority of people living in the South were blacks, because in the event of a mass Negro uprising, the

black dominated South might be able to split with the union and establish a black nation. [However], Southern whites, well aware that satisfied slaves never revolted, made every effort to keep their slaves happy.[12]

In order to avoid the possibility of a secessionist putsch by Blacks several strategies were devised. Some of the measures applied will be discussed in chapter four. Moreover, the fact that black political activities were discouraged for several generations was bound to affect how, as a group, African Americans reacted then, and react now, to politics and government.[13]

These social and political developments in the American polity notwithstanding, the bottom line is that in spite of the economic and social roles played by African Americans in the growth and advancement of America, the character of the group's history, culture and situation that was based on the "master-servant" relationship overall continue to persist—at least psychologically. It was to this end that I stated earlier in this study that the present tends to be informed by the past. Nevertheless, the lessons learned from past experience should induce a people to make a clean break from the social and political mistakes and vices that tended to negate the growth of a people. I must hasten to add that changes in a society are likely to occur if the institutions responsible for the problems are radically changed, too. This is not only true of African Americans; it is also true of minorities and marginalized ethnic groups in Africa, the Middle East, Asia and Latin America.

Generalization

The second pillar of the volume attempts to address the essential dimensions of political participation and politics in all settings—particularly urban and rural. The linkage between the foregoing discussions and proceeding analyses is that an individual's or group's interests (or lack thereof) in politics and political system has their roots in the history and cultural content of a group. For the African Americans, as is true of other majority and minority groups, its experience as a group affects its politics and political behavior. Chapters two and three are intended to bring these assumptions to the fore. The intention in these chapters is to bring up to par, or better yet "accentuate" the politics of rural America over those of urban America, in a manner of expression, and to contextualize rural American politics within the broader parameter of national (and international) politics. This approach to the study is particularly relevant if the political cliché which states that "all politics are local" is to be taken seriously. Come to think and write about it, it is rural America, India, Nigeria, Ghana, Indonesia that truly elect the president and prime minister—not New York, Bombay, Lagos, Accra and Jakarta per se. Yet, the politics of Tugaloo, Mississippi, Kingstree, South Carolina and Americus, Georgia might be less fascinating to study than the politics of the state of Mississippi, South Carolina and Georgia in the American case principally because the governors and legislators command more prestige and control significant resources.

Although the centrality of this study is on African American politics in rural America, it is important to note that its characteristics could also be further understood within the broader context of black politics in America.[14] Thus, chapter two deals with the character of American politics and citizen's right to vote while at the same time situating the discussions within some general theories in political science and sociology. The struggle waged by African Americans to regain the right to vote lasted for about 100 years from the end of the Civil War in 1865 to the 1965 civil rights legislation intended to enlarge the political space to include Blacks. President Lyndon B. Johnson's civil rights initiatives aside, it was clear from black experience that it was one thing to pass legislation that would grant a people their legal rights to participate in the electoral process and quite another for those so given such rights to perform their legitimate functions. It is true that the enthusiasm brought about by the deaths of so many in the civil rights struggle, including its major leader and torch bearer, Dr. Martin Luther King, Jr., galvanized African Americans into action after the late 1960s. The agitation and struggles during the civil rights movement was for Blacks to exercise their franchise in ways that they had not done before. In fact, Perry and Parent noted insightfully:

> In the span of one generation black politics in the United States has advanced from a primary consideration of acquiring the right to vote for Southern blacks to blacks gaining significant representation in the major institutions of American political life. The transformation of black politics is best characterized as moving from protest movement primarily outside normal American political channels to established political behavior inside the political system as the predominant mode of political participation.[15]

It is now over forty years since what might be referred to as the "Second Revolution" occurred, ushering in a "consolidated" or "complete metamorphic democracy" into America.[16] The process of finally granting franchise, albeit after a painful struggle, to African Americans in the 1960s, followed the advancement toward opening up the political space for women in 1920.

The acquisition of the vote and the ability to effectively use it to promote individual as well as group interests may be metaphorically analogous to a marriage; it must be handled and treated delicately otherwise the excitement of going through the ritual could wither away in due course. While the older generations of African Americans who participated in the protest marches, and the spectators who were on the sideline cheering are likely to go to the polls, come hell or high water, the younger or post-civil rights generations tend to be less excited about acquiring the vote. They are not nearly as interested in political participation as their parents, either. The apathy that black youth tend to demonstrate toward political participation in the political process is evident in the politics of rural America. In fact, evidence of the relative lukewarm attitude toward voting of African American youth is illustrated in table 1 of this volume.

But, they should be concerned about the electoral process because they are likely to be more affected by the outcome of policies formulated and initiated by legislators at State Houses, County and City Councils across the country than their parents.

Chapter two also alludes to some important factors that might induce the electorates to vote. These dimensions include, but are not limited to, education, race, gender and age. The chapter further traces the historical developments regarding the political obstacles that African Americans have had to tackle in order to enjoy the same rights as other ethnic groups in the polity. Indeed, the chapter narrates in the words of Preston, Henderson Jr., and Puryear:

> a history not only of political progress [of African Americans] but also of the social progress as well. In a broader context [too], it out-lines the story of a black minority struggling for equality in a white-majority society. And in this context, it is also the story of a democratic society that flaunts and [renders problematic] its theories of equality, fairness and equal justice for all—which is seldom equal in practice. American society is proud to attack the violation of human rights abroad while denying them at home. It is this society that the black politics must operate and in which the struggle for equality for black people must be waged if minority rights are to be practiced and expanded until they are the same as those granted white Americans.[17]

Paradoxically, and by way of comparison, the violation of human rights of minorities is also commonplace in other developed as well as developing nations. The infractions of human rights of citizens—especially those of ethnic minorities in virtually all societies continues to be rampant in spite of governments claim to champion the cause of protecting human rights at home and in their foreign policies.[18]

Context

Chapter three addresses the important aspects of political behavior and attitudes in determining whether an individual participates or not in a political system. Although the central activity of virtually every community is politics, it does not imply that everyone in the community is necessarily enthused about the political struggle for power itself. This is the case in part because politics is by its very character conflictive especially since it, among other things, entails the competition for power that is essential for the distribution of goods and services among contending interest groups and their constituencies. Generally, actors who dare to participate in the political game may have to share certain affinity toward it in spite of the political "bruises" they might sustain during the process of political competition. Moreover, and perhaps more importantly, they must believe that their investment and participation in politics will be rewarding enough to compensate for the strains and stresses they might suffer while actively engaged in politics. In a manner of speaking, politics have become very much like a contact sport—ice hockey, for example. It is entertaining and rewarding to those who play it right. It can also be crippling, and in some societies cause death, if not played right. Also, it is not uncommon for the ego of a losing politician in a political battle to be mercilessly contused and for the bank account to suffer from irreparable damage. Therefore, it tends to take relatively few men and women of political valor, resilience and skill to venture into the "sport" of politics—hence these actors are sometimes referred to as political entrepreneurs or political risk takers.

Chapter three further explains political behavior within the context of both psychological and sociological variables that shape the attitude of those who wish to take the risk in politics. Further, the role leadership plays in uniting a group and galvanizing them into action for causes that are beneficial to the group is discussed drawing extensively from the illuminating works of Walters and Smith.[19] While the procedure for grooming a leader—particularly political leaders—is tough in both dominant and minority groups, overall the process tends to be more problematic within minority groups. In the American situation, African Americans as minorities appear to have had more intricate and perplexing social, economic and political problems than the dominant group. Part of the reason is historic. Having played a subservient role in the system for centuries, the sociological and psychological impact of reversing that role of generally taking orders from the dominant forces in society are relatively difficult though not insurmountable. On the flip side of the equation, too, is that the dominant group having played the role of giving orders to African Americans sometimes finds it difficult to receive orders from Blacks, let alone be led by African Americans—not withstanding the advances Blacks have made in the military, education, sports and other fields.

To be sure, African Americans have produced outstanding leaders, but a majority of these leaders have been in the non-political areas[20] for reasons stated earlier—politics is, and can be, a "dangerous" and expensive endeavor. But in order to be in a position to distribute the national, state, and local wealth (derived from revenues and other resources) may require capturing and controlling the apparatus of government that is used by major political actors to distribute resources. The fact that those who control power often posses the wherewithal to distribute resources has been with humankind from time immemorial. At this juncture, however, African Americans, as minorities, have a long way to go to capture major political power and to use such influence to the group's advantage as dominant groups have traditionally practiced for centuries.

Analyses

The discussions that follow relate to how the analyses and conjectures in chapters two and three, impact African American politics in rural America—especially in Florence County, South Carolina. I specifically examined the politics of the cities of Lake City, Florence and Timmonsville in order to illustrate how African American political actors articulate and implement regimes that impact the society. But before conducting my recorded interviews with three African American political actors, I have had to provide a brief history of the county. Florence County is the political unit or turf on which the political activities are played out in the study. The basic hypothesis is that the character of the larger environment (county in this case) influences the way politics are conducted by its constituent parts. In other words, Florence, Lake City and Timmonsville are less likely to have had their current political contour and geography without the existence, and rich history, of Florence County itself.

Chapter four, *Florence County: the creation and Black politics*, tells the political story that is not all that different from the story of how counties in Alabama, Georgia, Florida, North Carolina, Illinois, Arkansas, Missouri, Maine, Mississippi, Louisiana, Tennessee, Virginia, and elsewhere in America were created. Indeed, it is a story that could be similar to the political history of the founding of local government areas in Venezuela, India, Indonesia, Kenya, France, United Kingdom, and elsewhere in the world; it is the political story of how human beings in a rural area, yet significant portion of the state, of South Carolina in the United States of America attempt to organize themselves in other to further political stability and peaceful coexistence.

The truth of the matter is that politically counties are often treated with great respect during state and national elections by politicians wishing to attract the votes of citizens during gubernatorial and presidential elections, for example. In presidential elections, for instance, candidates for political office have a tendency for rhetorically demonizing the political activities in the center (Washington, DC.) while applauding the peace-loving and genteel periphery (rural America). In fact, Washington, DC and the unique and contentious politics of congressional actors have had its share of "abusers" by politicians dying to represent their local constituency in the same problematic and powerful city. In other words, politicians often applaud rural populations as those representing the moral sanctuary of the polity since there are more votes to be "harvested" in small towns and cities of rural America. But no sooner have political actors been elected to office (Senators, House of Representatives and even Governors) by the rural electorates than they are "abandoned" after state and national elections are over. But what point I am attempting to make here? It is that no matter how political scientists and politicians in particular may "marginalize" the politics of those in the periphery in America by acting as if the electorates are often politically "unsophisticated," it is important to note that rural America is where a majority of Americans reside. Arguably, then, this is where real political power flows from. Voters in rural America are capable of electing senators to serve in Congress until such senators resign, retire or die in office. Thus, the politics of rural America deserve greater attention than has traditionally been given to it. By this I mean beyond the scholarly and academic study of the institutional and structural apparatuses of state and local government. Moreover, the mutual complementarity of the study of micro-and macro- politics that is local and national in this instance could further enrich the literature in political science, sociology, and anthropology just to list a few.

As argued earlier on in this chapter the "politics of econometrics" or "econometrics of politics" has to some extent determined the outpouring of the robust literature in urban African American politics to the chagrin of those who study rural black politics. The investigation of the politics in small cities and towns in America are relatively few and historical. This is the case because political scientists are not nearly as eager to study political actors other than mayors of large cities with national recognition and clout. Academics are also likely to study urban politics because of possible funding they might receive from Foundations. Moreover, some of the highly endowed organizations that support major research projects that impact on black economic and political behavior are often housed in urban settings—New York, Washington, DC., Chicago and Boston, for example.

Little wonder, then, that materials covering African American politics in rural America are understandably few and for obvious reasons—i.e. limited readership, interests and very few publishers wishing to take the risk because of inadequate returns for their investment. Thus, scholarship that does not relate the subject matter to a wider mass or group of readers may suffer from the "politics of econometrics."

The brief history of the area, the founding of Florence County itself, and the political processes that have given the area its unique characteristics are drawn from a number of excellent seminal works including G. Wayne King and Daniel A. Lane and Roy P. Cunningham.[21] Historically, books often provide a rich source from which to understand and appreciate the often complimentary religious, economic and social life, and the antagonistic and adversarial political relationships, in all societies in the struggle to control power.

Chapter four further traces the intricate political jabbing of key actors in Marion, Darlington and Williamsburg counties regarding the usefulness of creating the new county of Florence that was excised from these counties. It addresses the political maneuvers applied by the political heavy weights in the community to undermine black political participation in the area—particularly in the city of Florence that housed the county seat. It narrates the history of the area within the framework of the white's southern strategy following Reconstruction (1867-1878) to depoliticize African Americans in the South. The strategy of "de-politicization" of Blacks by the dominant group was conducted legislatively when feasible and unlawfully when legislative strategies did not work. As a consequence, the majority group was able to enjoy a monopoly on economic and political power. The methods used in South Carolina and Florence itself by some white political activists to thwart black political development in the area are discussed. An analyses of the disillusionment and despair with the political system that politically disenfranchised African American public formed the basis of the concluding paragraphs.

Case Studies

A major analytic dimension in this volume is grounded on the recorded interviews conducted with three African American political actors and lawmakers. The concise analyses in chapters five, six and seven are derived from their responses as articulated and summarized in the appendix.

Chapter five confronts the politics of Lake City, the home of the late Astronaut, Dr. Robert McNair. The City Council was made up of predominantly African American legislators at the time of writing. Indeed, out of the seven council members, only one is White, and the others are African Americans including the mayor, Mr. C. LaRue Alford. My interview and analyses in this chapter covers the major issues that a city of its size anywhere in the republic, particularly in the South of the country, must deal with daily. These are the same issues that inner city African Americans are confronted with, too, except perhaps at a larger scale. These are housing, garbage disposal, law-enforcement issues and so on.

The analysis in chapter six on the city of Florence is identical to chapter five only to the extent that the political actors that I was concerned with were two African American councilmen, and that they represented the interest of the black community as part of their legislative function. They differ, however, from Lake City in that Florence city council is made up of two African Americans and five white councilmen. One of the white members, Mr. Frank E. Willis, is the mayor. The African American councilman Ed. Robinson that I interviewed for this project has had to deal with a Council whose majority membership was not conversant with the kinds of problems that a black legislator confronts in his constituency. As a consequence, the black councilman and the Council had on many occasions appeared to be on a collision course regarding policies intended to address the needs of his predominantly black district. The political confrontations were especially sharp when he first joined the Council. His stance and those of the predominantly white council members eventually improved as the Council later indulged in the politics of bargaining and compromising to resolve conflicting issues. In short, the chapter depicts in part the political depth of the confusions that emanate in a polity from the conflictive character of the politics of who gets what, when and how especially in a divided community or society everywhere.

Chapter seven analyzes the politics of Timmonsville whose Council is made up of two White councilmen and five African American council members one of whom is the mayor. My recorded interview was with the mayor. Some of the lessons that may be learned from this chapter are the extra-ordinary expectations of African Americans from a black mayor—who had captured the mayoral trophy in a city-wide election as a result of black electoral support. Such high expectations for the performance of a black mayor have been splendidly captured in the analyses of scholars who study urban politics. Put another way, the contending debates over the efficacy of black mayors in the governance of their cities—particularly providing substantial goodies, as a result of their victory, to the black constituencies have been articulated by scholars. Indeed, one academic notes rather concernedly:

> The election of a black mayor has generated both elation and conflict among scholars of black politics. On the one hand, a black mayor serves as a symbol that many of the barriers to electoral participation have been dismantled, and that Blacks—often with the help of other racial minorities and Whites—have been able to elect a candidate of their choosing to political office. The thinking was that, once in office, black elected officials would be able to utilize the mechanisms of government to positively [elevate the conditions of] Blacks and other supportive constituents. Yet, it is on this point that many scholars of black politics disagree.[22]

Wilbur C. Rich[23] concurs with the above proposition in his study of the mayoral election in Detroit, Michigan. The outcome of my interview and analyses in chapter seven of this volume also bears the above thesis out. It suggests that the black community in the city of Timmonsville expect "too" much from the black mayor. And, when he did not deliver the bacon, they tended to become irritated, if not indignant, with him for failing to provide their needs. The discomfort on this issue as it concerns the role of the mayor, and the black public, flows in part from the lack of understanding of the complexity of politics and thus confusion on the part of citizens of its processes.

The investigation and analyses in the last three chapters of this work draw upon the conceptual and theoretical constructs in chapters two and three. In so doing, I attempted to establish a fundamental linkage between political theory and practice, and chapter four provided the political theater on which that significant bond (between theory and practice) was made possible.

Whereas my theoretical discussions are sound, my judgment as to the political actors to be interviewed was personal and subjective. In other words, the African American councilpersons that I did not interview probably might have had different opinions regarding the issues that were raised in the questionnaire. Be that as it may, the overall representation of the views of those I interviewed and those that I did not were less likely to be far apart since they shared a common interest on such issues as adequate education for all in the community, and the practice of accountability and transparency in government. In all of the three cases—Florence, Lake City and Timmonsville, the council members and mayor were very forthright in explaining the strengths and weaknesses of the operation of their council including their successes and difficulties in political deliberations with other councilpersons.

Most importantly, too, my explanation to the interviewees that this study was only the beginning of a process that should serve as a springboard from which to launch other studies that would document how African American elected officials conducted themselves in political office was greeted with delight. I must admit that as a black scholar, some of the white council members and administrators during my visits to the City Halls were not quite comfortable—at first. To these individuals, I was like one of those city journalists who had come into the community to probe and pry, if not interfere, in how their local government operated. This attitude was not unexpected. Overall all, however, the cooperation from all of the parties was impressive and greatly appreciated.

Chapter 1. Introduction

1. Vernon, *African Americans at Mars Bluffs, South Carolina*, 2.
2. Preston, Henderson, Puryear, *The New Black Politics: The Search for Political Power*; Alex-Assensoh and Assensoh "Inner City Context: Church Attendance and African-American Political Participation" in *Journal of Politics*, Vol. 63, NO. 3., 886-901; Eisinger, *The Politics of Displacement: Racial and Ethnic Transition in Three American Cities*; Kinfe, *Politics of Black Nationalism: From Harlem to Soweto*; Patterson, *Black City Politics*.
3. Walters and Smith, *African American Leadership*, 277-301.
4. Alex-Assensoh , "Race, Concentrated Poverty, Social Isolation, and Political Behavior" in *Urban Affairs Review*, Vol. 33, No. 2: 209-227; Cohen and Dowson, "Neighborhood Poverty and African American Politics" in American Political Science Review, Vol. 87, No. 2: 286-302; Jencks and Peterson, *The Urban Underclass*; Stack, *All Our Kin: Strategies for Survival in Black Community*.
5. Preston, "The Election of Harold Washington: An Examination of the S.E.S. Model in the 1983 Chicago Mayoral Election" in *The New Black Politics*: 139-163; Rich, "Coleman Young and Detroit Politics" in *The Search for Political Power*: 200-221; Perry, "Politics of Power in the Sunbelt: Morial of New Orleans" in *The New Black Politics*: 222-255; Ransom, "Black Independent Electoral Politics in Philadelphia: The Election of Mayor W. Wilson Goode" in *The New Black Politics*: 256-289.
6. Klingberg, *An Appraisal of the Negro in Colonial South Carolina: A Study of South Carolina, Past and Present*, 1-5.
7. Ibid., 1.
8. Udogu, "African Development and the Immigration of Its Intelligentsia: An Overview" in *Irinkerindo: Journal of African Migration*, Issue 3, p. 12.
9. Klingberg, ibid. 1; Lane and Cunningham, *Notable Blacks of the Pee Dee Section of South Carolina: Past and Present*, 7-13.
10. Ibid., 2.
11. Ibid., 5-7.
12. Lane and Cunningham, *Notable Blacks of the Pee Dee Section of South Carolina: Past and Present*, 9.
13. Walton, *Invisible Politics: Black Political Behavior*, 22.
14. Bailey, *Negro Politics in America*; Dawson, Brown and Allen, "Racial Belief System, Religious Guidance and African-American Participation" in *National Political Science Review*, Vol. 2: 22-44; Gaines, *Uplifting the Race: Black Leadership, Politics, and Culture in the Twentieth Century*; Perry and Parent, *Blacks and the American Political System*; Walters and Smith, *African American Leadership*.
15. Perry and Parent, *Blacks and the American Political System*, 3.
16. Udogu, "Incomplete Metamorphic Democracy as a Conceptual Framework in the Analysis of African Politics: An Exploratory Investigation" in *Democracy and Democratization in Africa: Toward the 21st Century*, 6.

17. Preston, "The Election of Harold Washington: An Examination of the S.E.S. Model in the 1983 Chicago Mayoral Election" in *The New Black Politics*, vi.

18. Udogu "An Examination of Minority Groups and Human Rights in Europe and Africa" in *Journal of Political Science*, Vol. XXVIII, 21-43.

19. Walters and Smith, *African American Leadership*; Walton, *Black Politics: Black Political Behavior* and *Black Politics: A Theoretical and Structural Analysis*; Parent and Stekler, "Black Political Attitudes and Behavior in the 1990s" in *Blacks and the American Political System*, 41-49.

20. West, *Race Matters*, 54-55.

21. King, *Rise Up So Early: A History of Florence County, South Carolina*; Lane and Cunningham, *Notable Blacks of the Pee Dee Section of South Carolina: Past and Present*.

22. Howell, "Racial Polarization, Reaction to Urban Conditions and the Approval of Black Mayors" in *Black and Multiracial Politics in America*, 60.

23. Rich, "Coleman Young and Detroit Politics" in *The Search for Political Power*, 200.

African American Politics:
A Theoretical Analysis

Politics is defined variously as the struggle for power; the authoritative allocation of things of value, and the in the definition of Harold Lasswell who gets what, when and how. Thus, the very character of politics tends to be conflictual as different political cleavages contest and pursue intensely their group interest/s in a polity. The competition for political advantage in a society very often pits contending groups against each other. If the struggle for political influence and profit in a political system is not played out within the context of the rules of the game, or if factions apply illegitimate and extra-legal means to attain superiority over other contestants for political power, the outcome could lead to anarchy. Political instability could be the result of such a scenario since the group/s locked out of power are likely to resist the dominant groups that are subverting the established rules of the game[1].

Generally, in order to avoid anarchy and reduce political conflicts in a system governments or legitimate institutions of governance may be set up within John Locke's political philosophy of liberal democracy. That is to say a government that promotes free choice at the ballot box, encourages freedom of expression, promotes due process of law, and so on. But governments are composed of individuals with diverse and sometimes conflicting interests. Therefore, it might be foolhardy to assume that the custodians of government are always impartial in the manner in which they interpret regulations and resolve conflicts. Indeed, Lewis A. Froman, Jr.[2] noted that: "Government is an authority established to settle conflicts, and parties to conflict [and those who feel intensely about a conflict] are likely to try to influence the decision to their favor." The most that is anticipated of any government, therefore, is to manage upheaval in the society and adopt policies that might mollify future clashes.

The Founding Fathers took cognizance of the perplexing issues of political governance and the modalities for assigning advantages and disadvantages to its citizens[3]. Indeed, James Madison wrote: "The regulation of these various and interfering interests forms the principal task of modern legislation and involves the spirit of party and faction in the necessary and ordinary operations of Government."[4] The realization of the existence of human diversity and their conflicting interests was not lost in the thinking of political philosophers and sages determined to establish a relatively stable society. But regardless of how well intended decision-makers are in formulating policies that might address the needs of the various contending groups in a society, lawmakers still have to contextualize their actions within the wider political environment in which they act. Put another way, the power and forces of the political culture in a political space could overshadow and even sabotage policies intended to resolve societal conflicts in attempts to unite the collectivities in a polity. For instance, if Italian Americans do not like African Americans and vice versa, benevolent laws are less likely to change their minds if such antagonisms toward each other are intense—that is to say that improvement in relations may occur with time and often incrementally. The politics of the South especially as it concerned the issues of race and de-segregation bear this thesis out. Nevertheless, as scholars of ethnic minority groups and politics would point out, the political struggle for access to power and the political benefits that flow from being in power are difficult for minority groups in most polities. The denial of opportunities can be painful.[5] But how might the political misfortunes of ethnic minority groups, such as African Americans, be remedied in a system in which they lack the numerical strength and economic clout to effect major changes in their favor? This question has always engaged the intellect of scholars interested in this issue. Generally, some observers have suggested that if only African Americans could be given the vote, they might be able to influence policy makers to enact regimes that would take their interest seriously. But a number of scholars wonder if that is all it would take.

In fact, Walton Jr. affirms:

> The study of black politics—i.e., of the attempts of one group of individuals in the American political system to implement their preferences as public policy—has suffered from a narrow conceptualization. Although politics encompasses the actions of legislative assemblies, political parties, election contest, and other formal trappings of a modern government, the beginning and end of studies on black politics have been primarily from the electoral angle. Heretofore, those students of the American political process (black and white) have begun their scholarly analyses with the elemental assumption that if blacks could not vote, they had little chance to have any meaningful effect on the political process. In fact the *vote* has come to be seen as the basis for all other political action. For although it is admitted that the vote is only one weapon among many that are available to groups, students of black politics tend to feel that the alternative devices (e.g., lobbying, pressure groups, demonstration, etc) derive much of their value and significance from the existence of the vote.[6]

The importance of the vote for Blacks was promoted by members of the informed public. These included journalists, civil rights leaders and organizations, and politicians. The vote would not only lead to economic enfranchisement of Blacks but also lead to their social and economic integration into the American society.

Indeed, a number of prominent Americans including Presidents Eisenhower, Kennedy, Johnson and attorneys-general held onto this view. Martin Luther King, Jr., stated emphatically that in democratic political system the giant step that Blacks can take is in the "direction of the voting booths."[7] Congress of Racial Equality (CORE), Student Coordination Committee (SNCC) and the Southern Christian Leadership were in the forefront in the socio-political struggle to enlarge the political space to include Blacks through the ballot and ballot box.[8]

Historically, studies have continually stressed the significance of voting for the Black as the "only" way to remedy the socio-political problems that African Americans are confronted with. While there might be some truth to the import of voting in opening up the political space, there are also reasons to examine other possible variables. The emphasis on voting behavior as the panacea for African Americans has led to a groundswell in the literature on the relationship between voting and social and political emancipation of blacks in American political system. Indeed, some scholars have argued that African Americans inability to vote affected Black's overall social and economic welfare.[9] This was a development that V. O. Key picked up in his impressive and groundbreaking study on Southern politics. He looked at black concentration in the so-called Black Belt regions of the South. The strategy was to observe the political behavior of Blacks and Whites in the area. His conclusion was that the Black Belt whites were determined to impede black political participation and progress in the society especially as it concerned the ability of African Americans to vote in the political system.

Other students of black politics have highlighted the obstacles and consequences of the Voter Education Project (VEP) intended to use the ballot to emancipate African Americans, and the direct effect or influence of the 1965 Voting Rights Act (VRA). Indeed, after thoroughly investigating

> the weaknesses and new trends of the black community, the absence of meaningful leadership, strong socio-economic strata, *et cetera*, the lingering racism and intransigence of the white community, and the changing economic and social bases of central southern cities, the book concludes that the sudden arrival of blacks in southern electoral politics will not produce sudden change in the things that gravely affect southern blacks—i.e., exclusion, prejudice, slums and rural poverty.[10]

Other studies have suggested that voting power has considerable restrictive conditions, and black voting even more so. Thus, the success of African Americans altering the political system in its favor through the ballot may be of necessity small in nature and effect.[11] The issue, then, is that analysts must be cautious in their explanations of a correlation between the vote and social change in the society. Indeed, the study of the black vote is in reality the study of the black electorate but the political behavior pattern of the black electorate is nearly always in flux. Thus, one could be doing injustice in studying the entire black political life within the context of Blacks and their votes. Walton, Jr. expressed misgivings at such a reductionist approach by positing that:

> One who attempts this approach is bound to leave out numerous essential items. For instance, in none of the hitherto mentioned studies is there a comprehensive analysis of black political parties, black political groups, black political machines, blacks and their participation in the major and minor political parties, black public officials and their public legislation or their relations to the black masses and community. A narrow and microscopic technique of trying to view all of black politics from the point of view of the black voter [through a single political prism] leaves out blacks in the cities, blacks in the metropolis, blacks in state and local governments, and blacks at national conventions. [12]

At the macro level, African American political activities flow from the "tribal" politics that are noticeable in the different settings in which Blacks find themselves. Put another way, the segregationist politics that exist in different environments and the nature and kind of segregationist attitudes manifest in these societies determine to some extent the character of black political activism.

Take for example, in some southern states Blacks were fully integrated in the political process during the period of Reconstruction, but the Compromise of 1876 and the concomitant disenfranchising actions of Blacks in numerous southern legislatures led to the retrogression of Blacks in American politics. [13] This problematic development for Blacks not only killed the vibrant black politics before 1876, but also froze it in time for almost a century. Despite the Fifteenth Amendment to the constitution of 1869-1870 which states that: "The right of citizens of the United States to vote shall not be denied or abridged by the United States or by any State on account of race, color, or previous condition of servitude," its implementation as it related to black political participation has been to say the least problematical.

In any case, one of the basic arguments made so far is that while the enfranchisement of blacks through the voting rights bills is significant for African Americans, it is only one important step in the political calculus in American political system. In other words, the importance of getting the vote does not always imply that the vote would be used to further the interest of the group that got the franchise. It is within this context that a brief case study to illustrate the foregoing political dilemma might suffice.

Case Study

In the summer of 1996, as a participant-observer, I had the privilege of serving as the campaign manager of an African American candidate, Poiette McGill, who ran for South Carolina House Seat 57, in Marion County. District 57 has a population of "15,200" out of which about 8,972 Blacks and Whites were registered to vote. She ran against two white candidates, Jim Battle and Susan Crotts for the seat. The demography as it concerned citizens in the district that registered to vote was as follows:

Table 2.1 Black Voter Registration Tally

Precinct	Black	Female				
	Total	Total	18-21	22-34	35-64	65-up
Britton's Neck	622	380	21	90	207	62
Friendship	158	96	3	27	52	14
Centenary	472	282	9	53	154	66
Rains	265	157	7	36	82	32
Marion No.1	591	385	22	97	175	91
Marion No. 2	123	81	5	22	43	11
Marion North	137	80	4	24	43	9
Marion South	1,546	1,032	55	273	484	220
Marion West	344	224	13	57	99	55
Sellers	284	161	10	46	77	28
Temperance	279	188	12	45	103	28
Zion	206	177	5	25	68	19
N.W. Mullins	852	518	41	124	239	114
S. W. Mullins	694	424	39	98	204	83
N. E. Mullins	810	517	39	128	258	92
S. E. Mullins	187	109	11	26	58	14
Nichols	268	167	10	40	76	41
	7,838*	4,918	306	1,211	2,422	979

Table 2.1 (continued)

Precinct	Black	Male			
	Total	18-21	22-34	35-64	65-up
Britton's Neck	242	8	55	141	38
Friendship	62	2	12	36	12
Centenary	190	8	70	88	24
Rains	108	3	26	63	16
Marion No. 1	206	10	66	91	39
Marion No. 2	42	4	12	23	3
Marion North	57	2	19	26	10
Marion South	514	31	134	260	89
Marion West	120	5	24	70	21
Sellers	123	11	40	56	16
Temperance	91	6	17	57	11
Zion	89	7	17	52	13
N. W. Mullins	334	28	89	164	53
S. W. Mullins	270	21	61	147	41
N. E. Mullins	293	27	78	147	41
S. E. Mullins	78	6	19	44	9
Nichols	101	9	29	50	13
	2,920	188	768	1,515	449

Source: South Carolina Election Commission (4/01/96): 177
*7,838 is the total registered black Female and male electorate

Table 2.2: White Voter Registration Tally

Precinct	White	Female				
	Total	Total	18-21	22-34	35-64	65-up
Britton's Neck	374	202	3	51	116	32
Friendship	60	33	1	3	23	6
Centenary	259	141	5	36	68	32
Rains	219	116	1	22	56	37
Marion No. 1	561	332	4	57	151	120
Marion No. 2	1,171	639	17	94	318	210
Marion North	363	202	9	52	104	37
Marion South	549	302	21	75	167	39
Marion West	487	253	8	59	137	49
Sellers	31	17	-	6	7	4
Temperance	175	105	6	27	58	14
Zion	122	67	4	13	39	11
N. W. Mullins	474	281	5	48	143	85
S. W. Mullins	484	253	8	52	145	48
N. E. Mullins	719	397	10	73	212	102
S. E. Mullins	902	505	18	91	273	123
Nichols	390	209	4	37	116	52
	7,340	4,054	124	796	2,133	1,001

Table 2.2 (continued)

Precinct	White	Male			
	Total	18-21	22-34	35-64	65-up
Britton's Neck	172	4	45	92	31
Friendship	27	2	1	20	4
Centenary	118	1	23	73	21
Rains	103	2	17	57	27
Marion No. 1	229	11	43	106	69
Marion No. 2	532	20	97	263	152
Marion North	161	4	42	88	27
Marion South	247	7	64	140	36
Marion West	234	8	55	127	44
Sellers	14	-	4	7	3
Temperance	70	-	11	47	12
Zion	55	1	14	33	7
N.W. Mullins	193	-	38	102	53
S.W. Mullins	231	7	51	132	41
N. E. Mullins	322	9	63	181	69
S. E. Mullins	397	13	74	216	94
Nichols	181	7	32	99	43
	3,286	96	674	1,783	733

Source: *South Carolina Election Commission* (4/01/96):178

The dossiers of the three candidates who vied for the S.C. House Seat District 57 are as follow:

Name: Jim Battle
Position sought: House District 57
Party Affiliation: Democrat
Age: 53
Address: P.O. Box 211, Nichols
Hometown: Nichols
Education: Mullins High School, Citadel, University of South Carolina
Military Service: Two Years in the U.S. Army
Employment: Vice president and treasurer of Battle L. P. Gas Co.
Family: Wife, Catherine, daughter, Bess
Community involvement: Marion County District chairman, member of Marion County Progress, Francis Marion University Board of Visitors, Coastal Carolina University Marine Wetlands Study chairman, American Legion, VFW, Clemson Board for Recreation and Tourism
Prior Offices: None
Why running: Lost faith with the political system and its distance from the people, give rural areas of Marion County a voice
General outline of platform: Education, jobs/economic development and quality of life are major issues.
Name: Susan Crotts
Position Sought: House District 57
Party Affiliation: Democrat
Age: 42
Address: Powhaton Drive
Hometown: Mullins
Education: Mullins High School, University of South Carolina
Military Service: None
Employment: Pharmacist and owner of Mullins Pharmacy, president of TLC Home Healthcare
Family: Husband, David; three boys
Community involvement: Teaches Sunday school at Macedonia Baptist Church, Cub Scout leader, Wildlife Action
Prior Offices: None
Why running: Want youth of area to have somewhere to return and want to spend their lives, concerned about health care
General outline of platform: Jobs/economic development, health care and education are major issues.

Name: Poiette McGill
Position sought: House District 57
Party Affiliation: Democrat
Age: 27
Address: Cooper Street, Marion
Hometown: Marion
Education: Marion High School, American Academy, McAllister Institute of Funeral Services, Francis Marion University, S.C. Municipal Association of Institute of Government, Mary Brewer School of Insurance
Military Service: None
Employment: Funeral director and embalmment at Jackson and McGill Funeral Service
Family: Ivan L. Williams; two daughters
Community Involvement: Mt. Pisgah Missionary Baptist Church, S.C. Municipal Association, National Funeral Directors and Morticians Association, Mu Sigma Alpha Funeral Service Honor Society, Epsilon Nu Delta Mortuary Society, 100 Black women of Funeral Service, third vice president of Marion County Democratic Party, Marion County Branch NAACP youth advisor, United Negro College Fund County Coordinator, National Speakers Bureau, Operation Common Sense Inc., Healthy Start Advisory Board, Fetal Infant Mortality Review Board
Prior Offices: Marion City Council, 1992-present (1996)
Why running: Can't complain unless you try to do something about it
General outline of platform: Education, jobs/economic development and childcare are major issues.

Source: "The Primary," *Florence Morning News*, Sunday June 9, 1996, p. 3-B

Tables 1 and 2 provide the breakdown of the Black and White populations in the precinct under consideration. It shows 7,838 for Blacks and 7,340 for Whites. Out of the total registered to vote, there were 4,918 for Blacks and that represented 63% of African Americans and 4,054 for Whites that represented 55% of white registered voters. The June 11, 1996 primary election was held only for the Democratic Party since the Republican Party is relatively weak in the area. The election for House District 57 was contested among three candidates—Jim Battle, Susan Crotts, and one African American candidate, Poiette McGill. And the results of the polling were as follow:

Table 2. 3 Polling Results

	Battle	Crotts	McGill
	(White)	(White)	(African American)
Britton's Neck	223	64	242
Friendship	44	12	57
Centenary	108	54	183
Rains	81	31	118
Marion No. 1	234	46	217
Marion No. 2	*	*	*
Marion North	116	19	53
Marion South	263	53	562
Marion West	*	*	*
Sellers	*	*	*
Temperance	*	*	*
Zion	49	42	72
N. West Mullins	208	135	186
S. West Mullins	171	134	178
N. East Mullins	251	168	172
S. East Mullins	370	164	49
Nichols	214	46	34
Curbside	10	2	12
Failsafe	11	13	21
Absentee	89	117	100
Grand total	2442	1100	2256

*Represent cities outside House District 57

Source: *Marion County Republican and Democratic Primaries-Final Results* (June 11, 1996), p. 2.

The primary election showed that Battle picked up 42% of the vote, Crotts 19% and McGill 39%. Thus, the two white candidates picked up 61% of the total vote and 39% for the African American candidate. Since no candidate received more than half of the votes cast as required by law, a run-off election was conducted between Battle and McGill. In that run-off election Battle won a majority of the vote cast in House District 57.

Interpretations

What are some of the interpretations of the outcome of this election—particularly with respect to the power of the vote for African Americans and some probable theoretical implications for this chapter? As noted earlier, I was a participant-observer in both the primary and run-off elections having served as the campaign manager of the African American candidate, Poiette McGill. My analyses and conjectures on the results of the elections will come later on. In any case, it will suffice to briefly examine the literature on voting behavior and to make attempts at extrapolating important opinions relating to how African

Americans voted with the view to explaining the character of this local election in House District 57.

Since the founding of America, the dominant political philosophy among members of the informed public has been grounded on the democratic theory. This theory suggests that citizens are interested in politics, are informed and knowledgeable about the process of government and consequently vote with a view to setting the values and principles of the society.[14] But as Neal Riemer and Douglas W. Simon[15] have noted, "studies in American voting behavior show that voters are not fully informed, keenly discriminating, totally rational, supremely dedicated to the public interest. Nether, on the other hand, are they vastly ignorant, utterly lacking in power of analysis, completely irrational, or unaware of how their **self-interest** relates to the common good [of the group to which they belong and their community]." Clearly what the foregoing assumptions suggest is that voter enthusiasm or apathy is contingent on a number of external factors that are often related to self- and group- interest.

In general, voting represents one of democracy's most basic functions. Thus, it is the medium through which the grassroots give their consent and power to legislators of different parties to run the local, state and national governments. Indeed, most modern democratic systems recognize the supremacy of the ballot box for providing the polity with the legitimacy that is needed in the process of governance. In a way, the ballot box tends to balance the perceived power between the rich and poor in that it is based on "one person one vote" regardless of one's station in life. Moreover, voting may further the political system's legitimacy because it permits the adult population and electorate to decide who should be governing the polity. Just because democratic theory implies the right of citizens to select their leaders by voting does not indicate that the principle is always adhered to in the governance of a society.

Arguably, the decision to vote is informed by socio-economic circumstances—these include, but are not limited to, education, race, gender and age.[16] Overall, nonvoters tend to be the poor and uneducated minorities. Education and race have become particularly important variables in the voting practices in the South, and are likely to remain that way for sometime to come.

Indeed, some scholars have contended that education is the most significant variable affecting the desire to vote and voter turnout itself. The more formal education one has the more likely one will vote.[17] The rationale for this hypothesis is clear: more formal education tends to lead to more awareness of social, political, economic issues that affects one's life and how the political system works to further or hinder one's individual interest. Put another way, the more education a person has the more likely he/she is going to be concerned about policies that affect his/her interests. This is particular the case if one were to accept the popular political colloquialism that government policies tend to "affect one's pocket book." Therefore, it is important to vote in order to participate in the decision making that could decide those who will become the custodians of the state and thus make those vital fiscal decisions that affect the purse.

Moreover, the more education one has the more likely that could lead to greater wealth. Improvement in education, in the sociological lingo, influences one's socio-economic status (SES). That is to say the more education the higher the SES. And, one's SES tends to determine where one lives, the civic, social, religious and political organizations one joins. In short, these factors affect one's political activities in various ways—in particular voting with respect to this study.

The most fundamental variable necessary for understanding the thrust of this chapter and volume itself is race and ethnicity that are highly sensitive issues in all societies. The impact of race and ethnicity in the voting pattern in the South is one that has been studied and re-studied. That the literature on this matter in particular, and southern politics in general, is inundating and intimidating is obvious and does not need to be rehashed here. But to truly understand the character of this study one must situate the study within the context of the racial and ethnic politics that has in the main defined the political and social relationships in southern politics—at the state, county and city levels.

In their illuminating study on "African Americans in South Carolina" Botsch and Botsch brought to the limelight the centrality of the character of politics as it affects African Americans in South Carolina and *a priori* other southern states. As a point of departure, they noted with clarity and emphasis that: "a first axiom of southern political history is that southern politics revolves around race."[18] They further supported their thesis by quoting an important phrase in the political lexicon of students of southern politics that is often attributable to V. O. Key. The expression stressed that "...whatever phase [or aspect] of the southern political process one seeks to understand, sooner or later, the trail of inquiry leads to the Negro."[19] Indeed, contended Botsch and Botsch Key saw South Carolina as an exaggeration of this fundamental fact and subtitled his chapter on South Carolina as "The Politics of Color."[20] There was little wonder, then, that after over 50 years of Key's groundbreaking volume, a prominent politician in the 2002 Republican Gubernatorial primary election appealed for vote from South Carolinians by playing the race card. He reminded voters that he was the only candidate in the primary who stood up as Attorney-General of the state to break the backbone of NAACP in South Carolina for agitating that the Confederate flag should be housed in the State Museum instead of in front of South Carolina Legislative Building. He made the appeal both on the televised debate conducted at Francis Marion University, Florence, South Carolina, on April 23, 2002, and also his political ads on television.

This sort of politics is neither new nor peculiar to South Carolina. In fact, many "see race as continuing to define and divide the state. They see the 1990s [and possibly the early 2000s] as a strange reflection of the 1890s, in which traditional white elites—this time some Republicans—exploit fears and build power around a white backlash to the Federally-imposed civil rights revolutions."[21]

In order to historicize the dilemma faced by African Americans in the political process one may have to situate the development within the context of the Fourteenth and Fifteenth Amendments to the Constitution. While the

Fourteenth Amendment of 1866-1868 declared that no state could deny a group of eligible citizens the right to vote slightly opened up the political space for Blacks, it was the Fifteenth Amendment that legitimized the vote for Blacks.[22] One of the issues that many students of politics sometimes find to be frustrating is that it is one thing to pass legislation and quite another to enforce the law. Interpretation and enforceability of policies often depended of the politics of a particular era, and how the major political actors driven by their party and self-interests compete in the politics. So, whereas the Fourteenth and Fifteenth Amendments could be interpreted to imply that states could not deny a citizen the right to vote on the basis of race or ethnicity alone, the guardians of the states were not prevented from using other criteria in deciding on a voter's eligibility. Thus, it was possible to keep Blacks out of the polling station by applying "legitimate" obstacles. One such barrier applied by the dominant group to impede African American participation was the literacy test since most Blacks as a legacy of slavery could not read and write. Moreover, states adopted a poll tax strategy to deny Blacks the right to vote since a majority of African Americans were poor and could not afford to pay it. To further dilute the votes of the few African Americans that could participate in the political system, the "grandfather clause" was evoked. This clause asserted that if one's grandfather voted before 1867, one were eligible to vote. This policy was enacted in order to allow poor Whites to bypass the poll tax.

The history of violence brought on Blacks that attempted to vote mitigated the interest of African Americans that sought to exercise their constitutional rights. Even after several court decisions to remedy the violation of the rights of Blacks to vote were implemented, the socio-psychological impacts has continued to inflict strong negativism on succeeding generations of African American electorates. The phobia to vote is felt among African Americans up to the college level in some southern states.

The right to vote in South Carolina has followed the same pattern elsewhere in the South. Indeed, during Reconstruction, African Americans males voted and some were elected to offices.[23] That notwithstanding some Whites employed violence, and related strategies, to marginalize Blacks and regain political control and power.[24] After taking control in 1876, Whites added legal impediments to lessen black participation. For instance, they got rid of some precincts in black areas and mandated separate ballot boxes for Federal and State elections, making the voting process more arduous. Delegates to the South Carolina Convention of 1895 were so determined to reduce and dilute African American political power that they had to consider the "lesser of two evils"—i.e. grant suffrage to women that owned property.[25] In any case, for some white males, the psychological "anguish" that they suffered as a result of attempts to elevate the political role of women in the society in which women were traditionally marginalized was too much to bear. Nevertheless, the delegates opted for such a device as "male property ownership and literacy to deny the vote to Blacks."[26] Since Blacks did not own as much property as Whites, it was clear that this strategy was a political maneuver intended to whittle down African American political influence.

After the 1895 constitution was passed, Blacks were literally marginalized politically as the group's influence dwindled significantly. Indeed, the political history of African Americans in South Carolina from the late 1890s to the 1990s was summed up thus:

> . . . by 1896, about 50,000 whites and only 5,500 blacks were registered. Although African Americans comprised about 60 percent of the population, they were relegated to under five percent of the registered voters. Electing African American politicians was impossible. No African American was elected to Congress from South Carolina after George Washington Murray's defeat in 1896 until the election of Jim Clyburn in 1992. After John Bolts left the state legislature in 1902, no African American was elected to that body until 1970.[27]

It is against the backdrop of this concise historical development that an analysis of black voter turnout in South Carolina might be visualized, and its intricacies better understood. It is a development that in many ways is similar to those in Georgia, Alabama, Mississippi and elsewhere.

Be that as it may, they provide the analytical tool with which to contextualize my analysis of the outcome of the elections in SC House District 57 of 1996 as it concerned the candidacy of Poiette McGill, an African American. Further, the analyses that follow will demonstrate the extent to which such variables as education, income, ethnicity, gender and age, for example, mattered in this election. Also, as an extension to the central focus of this book, it is hoped that the preceding brief history should help shed some light not only on the theoretical analysis in this chapter, but also the investigation of the politics of African Americans in rural America—particularly Florence County.

Given the political history of the South and the district in particular, the strategy of "the McGill for House District 57 seat" was based on race. At the strategic meetings that were held, we had written off the white votes, and had deliberately done so because of the limited funds we had and the assumption that we were not going to attract white votes regardless of how hard we campaigned in white neighborhoods. Indeed, in some of our meetings, it was suggested that while some Whites (for whatever reasons) might vote for McGill, it was not worth the straw to spend money and time in the white areas. The strategy was to spend our time politically courting the black vote. Our stance to court the black vote, to the "exclusion" of the white vote, was informed by two conflicting reasons. First, our candidate, McGill, was deeply committed to the empowerment of Blacks, particularly poor Blacks. Her strong attachment to Blacks and black activism was an outcome of her racial experience in the area. That is to say that it had its roots in the racial problems that she had experienced and encountered in the political environment of the region. One way that she dealt with the issue was to withdraw into the African American community that provided her with a sense of worth, protection and purpose. In short, she derived her strength from membership in this group. Second, and this flows from the first is that because of her strong sentiment and deep attachment to her African American community, she was not all that enthusiastic when it was suggested that it might be politically expedient for her team to consult with the Susan Crotts' group for support before the runoff election between her and Battle. She was determined and optimistic that she could win the election with support primarily from the black electorate. In this way, it was hoped that she would not be beholden to "white power brokers" in the community should she represent the district in the state capital, Columbia.

Given the plausibility of the hypothesis that suggests that the higher one's socio-economic status, the more likely one is going to vote, our campaign organization was determined to challenge this supposition in a practical way. Fundamentally, District 57 is rural and education above the high school level remains low. This situation is informed by the history of the area in which many poor Blacks had limited access to education. Moreover, unemployment is high among African American population. How, then, do we attract this group of electorate to the voting booth to support our candidate given their socio-economic problems?

Against this grim reality, our strategy was to say "forget all about socio-economic status (SES)" and other important political indicators and variables that tend to influence voter turnout. We mobilized members of the campaign team in strategic locations within the municipalities of the district. In Marion, Mullins, Centenary and elsewhere in the district, we targeted black neighborhoods, and trailer parks, where we pounded doors after doors appealing for black votes. Moreover, we paraded the candidate, McGill, throughout much of the black communities. Her understanding of the character of the local politics, having served on Marion City Council, helped tremendously in our bid to get out the black vote.

We also relied on the local black churches that have traditionally played what has become their positive role in promoting the candidacy of politicians that are likely to further the interest of the black community. We provided transportation and appealed to Blacks to go to the poll, and to cast their vote for our candidate. This was particularly the case in Marion-North where our candidate was popular and strong.

While we successfully rallied support from the black communities in the district, it was clear that the other candidates, Battle and Crotts were doing the same in the white communities. Put another way, our determination to get out the black votes energized the white electorates to the voting booth as a counter-punch to our vigorous campaign in the African-American neighborhoods. Although we got an overwhelming support from black voters in the first and second democratic primary elections, it was not sufficient to give us victory in the run-off election that pitted Battle and McGill.

Lesson Learned

But what is the lesson, if any, to be learned from this political anecdote? First, we learned that while such political determinants as education, income level, race and ethnicity, gender and age are important variables in inducing voter turnout that other variables are equally important. The sheer fact that we went from door to door appealing for votes from blacks with little education and income and that they came out to vote in large numbers suggested in this case that higher SES is important to the extent that candidates wish to campaign through the mass media (radio, TV, newspaper and internet). It also suggested that the old fashion campaign technique of going from door to door can be useful in rural politics especially in areas with low income and education and where powerful patron-client system exists—in this case church ministers.

Theoretically, black political activism tends to be generated in areas in which there exist a large number of Blacks, and when policies formulated by the custodians of power tend to marginalize African Americans. While the desire to use the vote to pursue group interests is often desirable especially in a democracy, it is possible that other methods for changing policies might work just as much as electing a member of one's racial group to office. In this regard, the earlier conjectures made by Walton Jr.[28] that demonstrations, sit-ins, boycotts and so on (short of violence) are also effect methods for altering "evil" and unjust policies are instructive. These dimensions are not illegal within the context of democratic theory as long as they are conducted within the rule of law. Thus, while the ballot remains an important device with which to "throw the rascals" out of office, it might be difficult for minority groups to use this strategy alone. This is especially the case since their minority status and ethnic voting pattern in the community suggests that it would be difficult, though not impossible, for Blacks to gain political power through the ballot box. The difficulty in African Americans rising to political power is made more complex by the fact that politics in part involves the clashing of competing interests. Whichever group accedes to power determines who gets, what, when and how. In the competition to control resources, politics tend to sharpen ethnic and racial differences. Indeed, as Alvin Rabushka and Kenneth A. Shepsle[29] have argued, the political equation becomes more confounding and discordant in democratic and pluralistic (and plural) societies. They have noted that a sense of communal solidarity tends to intensify ethnic preference, so much so, that, in the struggle for political power, to promise less for one's group in the name of harmony and accommodation was tantamount to betraying that group's interest. Politicians, in general, are less likely to alienate their base of support and are often determined if necessary, to "demonize" other competing groups in the competition to control power in order to satisfy their interests and those of their constituents. This sort of politics may, invariably, impede attempts at promoting peaceful coexistence, and render problematic the possibility of implementing some of the useful tenets of democratic theory.

Chapter 2: African American Politics: A Theoretical Analysis

1. Walton, *Black Politics: A Theoretical and Structural Analysis*, 1.
2. Froman, *People and Politics: An Analysis of the American Political System*, 3.
3. Walton, ibid, 1.
4. Wright, *The Federalist* (Hamilton, Madison, Jay): 131.
5. Glazer and Moynihan, *Ethnicity: Theory and Experience*, 1-26; Hall, *Ethnic Autonomy-Comparative Dynamics*, 3-5; Udogu , "The Issue of Ethnicity in Africa: Toward the Millennium" in *Journal of Black Studies*, Vol. 29, No. 6:790-808; Udogu, *The Issue of Ethnicity in Africa*, 13-34
6. Walton, ibid., 2.
7. Matthews and Prothro, *Negroes and the New Southern Politics*, 11
8. Walton, ibid., chapters 1 and 2.
9. Lewinson, *Race, Class and Party: A History of Negro Suffrage and White Politics in the South*, 197
10. Walton, ibid., 6; Walters and Cleghorn, *Climbing Jacob's Ladder: The Arrival of Negroes in Southern Politics*, 357).
11. Keech, *The Impact of Negro Voting: The Role of the Vote in the Quest for Equality*, 106-109.
12. Walton, ibid., 8.
13. Dye, *Politics in America: Basic Edition*, 97.
14. Pateman, *Participation and Democratic Theory*, 14.
15. Riemer and Simon, *The New World of Politics: An Introduction to Political Science*, 318.
16. Verba and Nye, *Participation in America: Political Democracy and Social Equality*, i.
17. Wolfinger, *Who Votes*, 20.
18. Botsch and Botsch, "African Americans in South Carolina Politics" in *SC Journal of Political Science*, Vol. 24, 63.
19. Key, *Southern Politics in State and Nation*, 5.
20. Ibid, 130-155.
21. Botsch and Botsch, ibid., 65; Black and Black, *Politics and Society in the South*, 167-70
22. Edwards, *The American Political Experience*, 647-648.
23. Underwood, *The Constitution of South Carolina, Volume IV: The Struggle for Political Equality*, 25.
24. Ibid., 28-29; Botsch and Botsch, ibid., 66.
25. Underwood, ibid., 81.
26. Ibid., 103; Botsch and Botsch, ibid., 66.
27. Ibid, 194; ibid., 66-67.
28. Walton, ibid.
29. Rabushka and Shepsle, *Politics in Plural Societies: A Theory in Democratic Instability*, 66.

Political Behavior, Attitudes
and Leadership

Relevant to this chapter is a broad analysis on political behavior, attitudes and leadership. In particular, this chapter is concerned with how these political dimensions influence an individual's desire to participate in a political system. Put another way, the focus is on how the overlapping factors of political behavior and attitude impact on an African American and his or her quest to participate politically as a candidate for political office, a voter or non-voter. To the extent that political behavior and political attitudes are important variables that might affect voter participation, their comprehension become useful in the study of the politics of African Americans in rural America—particularly in the South where most Blacks live and work.

Students of political behavior are quite adamant in stressing the importance of the individual as the empirical and major level of analysis in a political system. The literature on political behavior is replete with analyses of notable scholars who have attempted to explain the significance of the political role of the citizen in the society. For example, S. Sidney Ulmer [1] argued that: "The political behavior approach does, after all, focus on the behavior and the psychological and sociological variables which affect it." Another scholar, Lester Milbrath[2], contends that: "The major concern is to explain individual human behavior as it relates to the political system. Therefore, the human organism, rather than groups or the political system, usually is taken as the unit of analysis." Behavioral theory, contends David Apter and Charles Andrain, is "concerned with motivation and perception, learning and adaptation... Thus in behavioral research, analysis of both individuals and small groups has been central"[3] to understanding how individuals and groups conduct themselves in a political space.

Political Behavior

What, then, are some of the elements that influence an individual's political behavior? These include, but are not limited to, one's childhood experience, gender, occupation, religious affiliation, income, education, institutions, neighborhood, race, the values of one's primary and reference groups, the association to which one is a member.[4]

As agents of political behavior, some of these factors are worth brief exploration just for the purpose of illustrating their relationship to political participation. Sociologically, the impact of one's childhood refers to the environment in which a child is nurtured. If the environment is one that is characterized by political apathy, chances are that one might grow up adopting an apathetic attitude toward politics. Anecdotally, in order to demonstrate the political sociology of this assumption in an introduction to political science class in 1996 and 2000, I offered extra credit to students who went to vote for the presidential candidate of the party of their choice and to present me with a voter registration form or an insignia that read: "I voted," for extra credit. This emblem is generally given to the electorate after voting in the city of Florence to be worn like a badge on the chest. It is, among other things, intended to remind other electorates that had not voted to do so. On the two occasions, that were presidential election years, about one-half of the 45 students took advantage of the offer of extra-credit to go to the poll. Although a few students who did not vote said that they were unable to do so because of their status as foreign students, had to work, and could not vote because they were underage, one-fourth said that they just were not interested in the political process. A further probe into the rationale for their political apathy suggested that their parents were inactive politically. Besides, noted some of those who did not vote, it did not make any difference to them as to who was elected president since the policies of a democratic or republican leader were less likely to affect their lives and interests in a major way.

As to gender, some studies suggest that more males participated in the electoral process than females—although this trend appears to be changing with more females participating in recent elections than in the past. Historically, the political roles of women tended to be subservient to those of men in most societies. In such a male-centric world, women were restricted to the traditional role of being a homemaker. Indeed, as Stephen Bennett explained, individuals not employed outside the household acquired less politically relevant information, are less likely to develop the strategies for political activism, and are less likely to understand the consequences of political events. As a result of the preceding supposition, they tend to be less interested in politics and often vote less.[5] Further, women who work have even less time to keep up with politics, for they are overwhelmed with the responsibility of maintaining both home and business pressures. The low level of politicization of women is also explained within the context of the political socialization process. Generally, girls are socialized to view politics as more germane to boys. As girls, they had seen their fathers and brothers more actively involved in politics than they had seen their mothers and sisters.[6] Increasingly, too, politics have become, and continue to be visibly, conflictive and many women tend to regard with disgust the combative character of political contest in the struggle for power.

One of the reasons for the disparity in political participation between men and women is attributable to past laws restricting women from voting. After all, it was the Nineteenth Amendment (of 1919-1920) to the constitution that granted women their suffrage. Even after the ratification of this amendment women, overall, have come to see politics like a contact sport—the outcome of which could leave a weak candidate "crushed" both psychologically and economically as contended in the foregoing analysis. Thus, women stayed away from politics for awhile until recently when fundamental social and economic issues affecting women and the family in particular tend to galvanize them into action as they put themselves up as candidates in order to join the battle to tackle these problems. In other instances, also, they rally behind those male candidates whose political views and interests are congruent with theirs. In short as individuals or groups, they cast votes with a view to addressing their concerns and social needs.

One's occupation can affect an individual's political behavior. For instance, the impact or influence of labor union activities (AFLCIO, Teamsters Union, etc) in American politics is significant although it is gradually dwindling in recent years. They educate, inform and register members to vote in elections based on the group's interests. That notwithstanding, it is generally true that those individuals with white color jobs (and higher SES occupationally) tend to participate more actively than those with blue color jobs.

Religious affiliation is an important variable that affects the political behavior of the electorate. The significance of the role of Southern Baptist on both black and white congregations in pursuing their interests in the political system is one that must be reckoned with in contemporary politics. Their political activisms have swayed the political outcomes of local, state, and national elections one way or the other (i.e., Democratic or Republican candidates).

As to the church and black socio-political behavior, Yvette Alex-Assensoh and A. B. Assensoh in their illuminating and impressive study, titled "Inner-City Context, Church Attendance, and African-American Political Participation," raised two basic questions relating to African-American political behavior thus:

> First, do concentrated neighborhood poverty, never-married
> parent households, and perceived isolation from neighborhood
> role models affect church attendance, above and beyond the
> influence of individual factors? Second, do concentrated
> neighborhood poverty, never married parent households, and
> perceived isolation from neighborhood role models affect
> political engagement, organizational membership, and voting,
> which emanate in part from church involvement?[7]

Their research was constructed on the theories of politics that affirm that political behavior is socially contingent on significant environmental variables. Also, they argue within the context previous existing theories and assumptions that: "variations within black churches are important in determining the extent of racial identification, political engagement, organizational membership, and voting participation...and demonstrated that the inner-city context in which African Americans reside matter for overall political behavior."[8] The above contextual assumptions in "Inner City" politics are not different substantially from the politics of small cities and towns in the rural America. In other words, the church remains one of the most sophisticated milieus in which the political behavior patterns and attitudes of African Americans are molded in cities and towns throughout Florence County.

The purpose of this brief chapter is not to delve into the psychological complexities and intellectual debates regarding the factors that influence political behavior and attitudes of African Americans. It is aimed at providing the substructure from which to explain the politics of African Americans as they relate to this study.

Attitudes

The values of one's primary and reference groups influence political behavior and attitudes in various ways. Indeed, the studies of Angus Campbell, Philip E. Converse, Warren E. Miller, and Donald E. Stokes[9] on the foregoing factors are instructive. They explained three ways in which the political behavior and attitudes of an individual is defined by his or her membership in a particular group within the following hypotheses:

- First, as an individual's identification with a group increases, the probability that he or she will think and act in ways that distinguish the group from nonmembers will also increase.

- Second, as the proximity between a group and the political world increases, the political distinctiveness of the group will also increase.

- Third, as the perception of proximity between the group and the political world becomes clearer, a group member's susceptibility to group influence in political affairs will increase.

Thus, it has been contended that: "blacks who identify relevant political issues with race tend to have a greater awareness of their status as a deprived group and to be more active politically."[10] In a way, the consciousness of being an African American, among the racially conscious, produces behavior and attitudes that "define" and explain the participation of African Americans in politics.[11]

In addition to the dimensions that influence all political behavior in America, argued some scholars, black political attitudes are affected by other unique factors in the system. They vary somewhat from other groups in America in that [political attitude] is "inspired by and shaped by some features and currents that do not form the basis of all American political behavior because it is rooted in the black experience in America. And this experience is radically different from the experience of other immigrant groups."[12] In order to comprehend black political behavior, therefore, a researcher may have to historicize and contextualize his or her analysis by examining the source of the individual's political socialization. Thus, it has been suggested that:

> Black political behavior is a variety of political patterns, experiences, and activities. It is heterogeneous, at times and in some places more factionalized than unified, more conflictive than cooperative, and more discordant than harmonious. These differences arise from the numerous divisions in the black community, divisions in class, ideology, politics, and culture. Moreover, black political behavior is not monistic, static, or time-bound. It undergoes cycles of stagnation, deviation, and regeneration. The flux of social growth and decay affects the black political milieu as it does any sociopolitical milieu. In short, the current realities of black political patterns might not be the same tomorrow.[13]

Indeed, many students of African American politics do concur with the above opinions. They contend, and rightly so, that black attitudes are fundamentally heterogeneous and that scholars who assume that "if you see one black political actor, you have seen them all" may be doing so at their own intellectual peril. Indeed, Katherine Tate, among others, brought to the fore the dissimilarity in black political attitudes and behavior in her provocative research. Tate's work discovered that socio-economic factors differentiated black political attitudes, and found that "affluent Blacks were opposed to the principle of a minimum standard of living for every American as well as the expansion of most welfare programs, except Medicare...[therefore it appears that there exist] two types of middle class Blacks: those who remain racially identified and may even 'misidentify' with the working class and poor blacks and those who identify with the upper classes and, as a result, are less race-conscious, viewing their lives as fairly independent of the group."[14] What these observations generally do is open up another intellectual flank in the discourse as to whether class, rather than race, is a significant dimension in the life patterns and political attitude among African Americans. [15]

The preceding discussions only suggest that there are different ways of examining the political character of a group and that different approach could be used in defining African American political behavior at a given moment in time—for instance, the 1960s that saw the civil rights movements and regimes. Sometimes political behavior or attitude is explained within the historicity and specificity of the political culture and subculture of that society. Here political culture relates to the generally shared ideas about "who should govern, for what ends, and by what means...and subculture may arise from such diverse bases as religion, racial or ethnic identity, or political group membership including, but not limited to, one's socio-economic status."[16] But to further comprehend the political behavior and attitude of African Americans, like other groups, one may have to understand the leadership genre of the collectivity.

Leadership

Leadership, as an intangible variable or element of power, in any setting, is a very perplexing phenomenon.[17] In spite of that, however, an excellent leadership-followership matrix is a crucial attribute necessary for the successful governance of any group in a society.[18] According to John Cartwright[19] leadership is "a relationship between individuals, in which one person manages to get others to do what he [or she] wishes.... It involves voluntary compliance by those over whom it is exercised." Robert C. Tucker[20] explains leadership as "a process of human interaction in which some individuals exert, or attempt to exert, a determining influence upon others." James MacGregor Burns[21] identified the concept as "leaders inducing followers to act for certain goals that represent the values and motivations—the wants and needs, the aspirations and expectations—of both leaders and followers." But what is followership? After all, leadership does not take place in a vacuum. Politically and operationally, followership relates to citizens who, as a result of the quality of leadership issuing from an individual declare their allegiance to the (political) person and the (political) system or group that he or she leads. The late Dr. Martin Luther King Jr., is a superb case in point. Further, as James McGregor Burns maintained:

> Leadership is an aspect of power, but it is also a separate and vital process in itself ...leadership over human beings is exercised when persons with certain motives and purpose mobilize, in competition or conflict with others, institutional, political, psychological, and other resources so as to arouse, engage and satisfy the motives of followers. This is done to realize goals mutually held by both leaders and followers.[22]

The above brief explanation of the character of followership and leadership aside, it might be share self-delusion on the part of any serious scholar to assume a total comprehension of the character of leadership, let alone the complex leadership-followership matrix in the African American community. Little wonder, then, that it has been stated that: "leadership is a phenomenon that we think we can recognize, but which becomes elusive and changeable when we try to analyze it."[23] Charles E. Merriam[24] was clear in his analysis of political leadership when he noted that: "The precise nature of political leadership is one of the most difficult problems in the domain of politics, or indeed, in social action, yet it is one of the most real phenomenon [or event] in political and social behavior."

In a real sense, the foregoing analyses were intended to introduce the reader to the broader concern of this chapter that is based on political behavior, attitude and leadership. In particular the following concern is that of leadership within the African American community in general. And if there is one lesson to be learned, as students and scholars conducting research of this kind, it is neither to be too specific nor to over-generalize. Thus, the discussions that follow should be visualized as compasses with which to navigate through the intricate issues of the subject matter.

African-American Leadership:
A Theoretical Overview

It should be very interesting to political scientists and policy makers that some of the fundamental research undertakings done on African Americans in America have been studies conducted on leadership.[25] Whereas there is a tendency in the social science discipline to formulate theories for the purpose of explaining complex events in the discipline, it is sometimes true that theories alone do not always fully explain the political attitudes and behavior of a group in any polity. This is essentially the case when the political experience of those groups been studied are unique to the extent that their behavior patterns are sometimes conditioned by a dominant group (or dominant groups). Arguably, the experience of Africans with European colonialism, the experience of African Americans with slavery and the concomitant attitudes of the dominating group toward the groups being dominated inform black leadership genre. How the dominant group/s (for example, Europeans in Africa and the Americas) perceive and construct the lives of the weak groups in a society can distort and often complicate the generalization of theories in the explanation of the character of the weak group. In other words, theories that might be relevant to the analyses of a "predictive" dominant group might not be appropriate to the study of subjugated and not easy to predict groups. Thus, the usefulness of theories is basically relative to the political culture of the universe being studied—Western Europeans, for example. Any attempts to apply identical theories to the explication of the behavior patterns of non-Western societies might be futile given the historical and cultural differences between both groups (i.e., Western and non-Western societies).

Generally, empirical social science theory rests on three major assumptions. These are:

- It should serve as an aid to the inventory and codification of the existing knowledge or phenomena.

- It should serve as a guide to areas where further research is required, and

- It should contribute to the development of the capacity to invent explanations of phenomena in a series of interrelated verifiable propositions.[26]

The relevance of the preceding opinions in social science study cannot be over stressed. In a way, it informs the succeeding analyses to the extent that one is cognizant of the fact that they should be applied with caution and careful explanations given the historical and cultural specificities of the group being studied.

It is a given that the character of leadership among African Americans is quite complex. This is equally true with respect to other nationalities or ethnic communities, too. Perhaps, its fluidity and complexity rests with the character of the human being. A leader in a religious, educational and political sphere, for example, can only remain a leader to the extent that those under the individual's leadership perceive and accept him or her as the legitimate chief. And, the duration during which such a person could maintain his/her leadership genre over a group cannot be guaranteed. In fact, much would depend on the ability of the leader to sustain, mutually, the leader-follower relationship (through any or whatever means feasible).

Theoretically, it has become exceedingly obvious that in multi-ethnic, multi-racial and multi-lingual societies the quest to seek out an important spokesperson or leader to represent an ethnic or racial group, for instance, can be problematic. Moreover, the process of selecting a leader can be an issue within the majority, and as well as minority, group. But leadership tends to be more of a problem among marginalized ethnic or racial minority groups in many polities. Frankly, the perplexity of the matter tends to worsen or to appear more severe in a political system in which a dominant group may apply certain negative stereotypes on a minority group in attempts to diminish the social and political significance of the politically marginalized groups in a society. This supposition is relatively true for African Americans, Native-Americans and other similar groups in the polity.

Indeed, identifying African American leadership in American polity is often a problem when the question of leadership is put in historical context. After all, Blacks have since the days of slavery been subservient to their slave masters no matter how unpleasant the process was to most African Americans. Within the social construct of a master-servant relationship, the issue is: how can a people who have been historically socialized into thinking of themselves as economically and politically "inferior" to the dominant ethno-racial group develop a leadership skill—beyond members of their own kith and kin?

To be sure, Black America has had some men and women of timber among the group historically. For example, there were "Free Negroes in the pre-Civil War period; educators, artisans, and shopkeepers during the Reconstruction period; business persons and black college professors in the years of Jim Crow laws; prominent athletes, entertainers, and white collar personnel after World War II all serve as examples of black middle-class status prior to the passing of the Civil Rights Bill in 1964 and the Voting Rights in 1965."[27] But these exemplary African American actors were seldom considered leaders among the dominant group and to some extent within the black community itself. Thus, for some writers the difficulty in discerning individuals with leadership quality in such a social setting (i.e., African American community) is not without its problems. Any wonder, then, that many scholars did not bother to investigate, let alone develop a concept of Black leadership from the outset—indeed, the chief concern of scholars was how to define Black leadership.[28] Generally, the definitional issue of what leadership should entail has taxed the intellectual wits of scholars, especially among students interested in the study of African American politics. So, attempts are made here to explain the characteristics of leadership within the black community rather than defining the concept itself. This approach—that is of examining the characteristic of leadership—is taken first before attributing possible explanations to black leadership. For example, African American leaders are considered to be "persons able to make decisions affecting the choice of race objectives and/or the means utilized to attain them."[29] Generally, an African American leader can be described as one that is able at least for an era to be able to openly and strongly identify with, and work toward, black objectives to attain social goals considered crucial among African Americans. This philosophy is referred to as the "functional approach to leadership."[30] The emergence of leaders within the context of race in Southern politics is one that has clearly dominated the political landscape and analyses of many scholars—particularly black academics. This intellectual discourse and development has been the case on both sides of the racial divide. But since the political and social denigration of African Americans historically in America and the constant fight for equality, especially in the South, there have been numerous "functional leaders" in the black community. These leaders appear as individuals or groups in the political scene to fight against policies deemed to be insensitive toward the group's issues and interests. For instance, there was a major confrontation between opponents and proponents in South Carolina with respect to the confederate flag flying atop the State Houses in Columbia. Moreover, the concerns of African Americans relating to unequal pay for the same work,[31] discrimination at some restaurants in the state are few examples of what African Americans perceive to be the insensitivity of some members of the dominant group toward black social and political problems.

The outgrowth or appearance of black leadership in the politics of rural America with its limited resources to sustain the struggle for change tends to be *ad hoc*. The lack of sufficient resources in the black community and the existence of competing interests have, in many cases, helped define the character of leadership within this group. Further, the issue of leadership development in the black community is complicated by the theory of group interest and some might add the doctrine or ideology of racism.[32]

The theory of group interest suggests that groups, of whatever socio-ideological form, act to promote their group interests and that the methods through which they derive their collective interest/s (whether moral or immoral) are irrelevant. What is relevant, within the context of group theory, is that the group attained its objectives. In its "crudest" form, this view is analogous to the Machiavelli's philosophy of "the end justifies the ends." Often, the ability of a dominant group to pursue its interest in the polity may rest on its control of power—particularly economic and political power. It is with the political and economic influence that the dominant group wields the authority with which to determine the contours of relationship within the society. In addition, the powerful political cleavage in a polity dictates (sometimes legitimately and sometimes illegally) how the society is to be organized—the nature of laws to be formulated—and the character of leadership to govern the polity. Because of the large population, industriousness and wealth of Whites in America they have traditionally controlled political and economic power and have used the authority and influence that flow from these dimensions to control local, state and national politics in favor of the group's interest. Little wonder, then, that it has been contended that the white establishment use their power in many cases to determine the leadership of Blacks (and they do so within the context of the theory of group interest, or to further the interest of the powerful white group). Indeed, Walter and Smith summed up the dilemma this way:

> "This fact flows from the reality of the preponderant power Whites exercise over society in general and in particular, the control over specific social activities that shape Black community structure such as jobs, housing, finance, the production of consumer goods, the management of the processes of law and political leadership, and other activities."[33]

To be sure, there are exceptions to the proceeding political framework on the part of the dominant group to coronate a black leader of their choice. But the ability of African Americans to do so generally issues from the dogged determination of the black community to produce its own leadership, come hell or high water. An anecdote with respect to the 1996 senatorial election to the South Carolina House of Assemble in the Pee Dee region of the state will suffice. Senator Maggie Glover, an African American, represented parts of rural Florence and some of the surrounding counties in the State House. Her political activism in South Carolina politics, and strong advocacy and support of the interests of the black community in her constituency irritated some members of the white power establishment. The desire for her to be politically defeated was spearheaded by the power elite through the use of the media and some black political leaders. The plan was to suffocate her attempts for reelection to the Senate by demonizing her before the electorate, and to finally dislodge her quest by urging voters to elect her challenger at the polls. Her campaign (in which I participated in her Marion county constituency) was fierce. In the end, Maggie Glover was able to retain her seat in the Senate through the strong support of her campaign team and from the black community in general. Thus, there are moments in which African Americans have exhibited their quest to determine who their political leaders should be. Councilman Ed. Robinson in the case of Florence City Council in Chapter six is another case in point. But the ability to sustain such a force is not always guaranteed because of exogenous forces that are often brought to bear on the nature of the African American leadership by the dominant power in the society.

The desire to create confusion among African-American leadership by applying astute strategies such as playing one group against the other is one that has been used effectively by powerful interest groups within as well as without the black community. The result is that weak leaders are sometimes substituted for powerful ones.[34] Nevertheless, it is quite possible to groom altruistic individuals within the African American political leadership that can function effectively within the political landscape of the American nation-state. That is to say that black political leaders have to participate effectively within the larger system in order to do what politicians are expected to do by members of their constituencies—bring home the "pork." Since the politics of race is alive and well in America, particularly in the South, the question is how to pinpoint the issues to be addressed and the ability of key black actors to influence the outcome of their concerns in favor of the interest of those in their constituencies. Historically, some powerful African Americans have been influential in bringing to the fore issues that impact on Blacks. But how such political questions are brought to the forefront of decision makers are not always easy since such issues might impinge on white interests. Thus, the political discourse between the races based upon competing interests tend to be over,

> the nature of the agenda of importance to Blacks, and (2) who will exercise the leadership over that agenda and in what arena. The forceful demands made by black leaders on presidents in the process of "agenda setting"—for political inclusion and an end to segregation [were made by such leaders as] W. E. Du Bois to Woodrow Wilson, for jobs in the war industry, A. Philip Randolph … to Harry Truman for civil rights and social justice and that of the civil rights movement made on President Kennedy and Lyndon Johnson. [These demands] have raised the question of whether the demands would be resolved in favor of one or the other force.[35]

The same scenario of agenda setting is played out at the State Houses, County and City Halls where citizens reside. Whether State governors, County chairpersons and City mayors/managers act upon these agendas is another matter in the political system. What is important, however, is the continued determination on the part of African American leaders to press for the implementation of their agendas even when confronted by strong opposition from the custodians of power.

Politically, there should be no illusion that when there are clashes between the interest of the dominant group and the weak ones in most political systems the position of that of the dominant group generally prevails—the merits of the issues pursued by the weak and the appropriateness of their demands notwithstanding. What is particularly perplexing to close observers of conflictive politics in a society is that the decision that weighs against the interest of the black community is made with the connivance and blessings of some Blacks who have been carefully selected as community leaders by power brokers and are enthusiastic about pursuing their individual and parochial interests generally at the expense of the larger community. This genre of politics is often practiced in virtually all political systems. Probably, it was such a development within the black community that prompted the late Dr. Martin Luther King Jr. to assert that:

> The majority of Negro political leaders do not ascend to prominence on the shoulders of mass support. Although genuinely popular leaders are now emerging, most are still selected by white leadership, elevated to positions, supplied with resources and inevitably subjected to white control. The mass of Negroes nurtures a healthy suspicion toward this manufactured leader.[36]

In fact, Dr. King was philosophically consumed with the desire for the African Americans to nurture leaders who are not seekers after the limelight, but are imbued with self-sacrifice for the betterment and advancement of Blacks in America. These are "men whom the lust of office does not kill; men whom the spoils of office cannot buy; men who have honor, men who will not lie; tall men, sun crowned, who live above the fog in public duty, and private thinking."[37] How, then, are African Americans to come up with such vanguard elements and leaders? Martin Luther King, Jr. affirmed:

> There is a dire need for leaders who are calm and yet positive, leaders who avoid the extremes of "hot-headedness" and "Uncle Tomism." The urgency of the hour calls for leaders of wise judgment and sound integrity—leaders not in love with money, but in love with justice; leaders not in love with publicity, but in love with humanity; leaders who can subject their particular egos to the greatness of the cause.[38]

The centrality of the above call for selfless leaders could be visualized within the context of the "organic theory of the group" whereby the interest of the black community supersedes those of the leaders—as is the tradition or culture in much of Africa. Therefore, the leadership should come from within the group because members of the community and the leadership itself comprehend the social, economic, political, historical and cultural factors that help mold the group. African American leadership should not be imposed on the group from outside in the same manner as black Americans do not imposed leaders on other groups. But, of course, the above contention is theoretically sound, but does not always work out so neatly in real politics. In political contests, the competing groups nearly always attempt to seek out the weaknesses of their political opponents, and may strategically interfere in the politics of the opposing group and groups in order to attain political advantage. Put another way, political actors may intervene in the politics of their competitors not necessarily because they detest the rivals, but because they wish to win and to further their interests and those of the group to which they belong.

Looking Ahead

Regardless of how one visualizes the nature and character of contemporary American political attitudes and behavior one thing that is clear is that they are more complex than what scholars attempt to portray. The racial dimension of politics could be interpreted within the context of self- and group-interests. Put another way, the tendency to invent or construct one's race or ethnicity politically flows in part from the competition for the control of the instrument of power. In short, it is informed by the group's desire to use acquired authority to regulate how resources are distributed in the polity.[39] In this context, therefore, the system that is established for legitimizing the claim to authority becomes crucial. In America, as well as other democratic societies, it is competitive politics that politicians regardless of their ideological complexions employ to vie for their interests in the society. It is the attributes of politics and its accessories—such as political parties, interest groups and so on—that help shape the political behavior and attitudes of citizens in a political system. Politics may also determine the caliber of leadership that could emerge from such a system. This is why I collapsed or dealt holistically with the issues of political attitudes, behavior and leadership in this chapter. The impact of political parties and their ideologies in molding the political behavior, attitudes and leadership of its members in a nation-state can be immense. This is especially so since politics played out in its various forms are autochthonous or indigenous to virtually every community and represent the central activity of most groups in a society.

The question of the racial divide in American politics and life and how it is to be bridged is one that has taxed the scholarship of many students of American politics who care to investigate the issue. Indeed, in spite of the federal government's pledge of implementing the political rights of African Americans, in response to the civil rights marches of the 1960s, the political differences and competing interests between Blacks and Whites are yet to be fully resolved. Since politics entail the struggle for power; authoritative allocation of things of value; who gets what, when and how, it is obvious that it might take men and women of good will to reduce the discrepancies issuing from ethnic and racial politics. The game of politics in America, as elsewhere, is not an easy tussle. In fact, it has been contended that: "In the aftermath of the civil rights movement and the urban unrest of the 1960s through the period of growing political conservatism in the 1980s and into the 1990s, public opinion polls have shown that Blacks and Whites live in different worlds, separated politically almost as much as geographically."[40] The political reality is very obvious in the politics of rural America-particularly in Southern politics.

As suggested earlier in the chapter, the tools and ammunitions with which politics are played out in America are important in determining the political attitudes and behavior of an individual and group in this society. Political parties are one of the vital political sources through which political actors profess doctrines, ideologies and so on that are capable of attracting supporters. Take, for example, the voting behavior of Blacks and the Democratic Party Presidential elections from 1948 to 1996 in American politics.

Table 3.1: Black and White Support for the
Democratic Presidential Candidates, 1948-1996

1948	Black 81%	1972	Black 87%
	White 53%		White 32%
1952	Black 79%	1976	Black 83%
	White 43%		White 49%
1956	Black 61%	1980	Black 83%
	White 41%		White 36%
1960	Black 68%	1984	Black 87%
	White 49%		White 34%
1964	Black 94%	1988	Black 82%
	White 59%		White 41%
1968	Black 85%	1992	Black 82%
	White 38%		White 39%
		1996	Black 84%
			White 43%

Sources: Huey L. Perry and Wayne Parent (eds.), *Black and the American Political System* (Gainesville: University of Florida Press, 1995): 43; Neal Riemer and Douglas W. Simon, *The New World of Politics: and Introduction to Political Science* (San Diego, CA: Collegiate Press, 1997): 320.

What is the usefulness of the contents of table 3.1? It suggests that African Americans have consistently voted for the Democratic Presidential candidate from 1948 to 1996 than Whites. Such a voting pattern and behavior represent the interests of African Americans as crystallized by the Democratic Party and its Presidential candidates. Indeed, African Americans attachment to the Democratic Party is informed by the gains that Blacks made during President Franklin D. Roosevelt's New Deal, and President Lyndon B. Johnson's civil rights legislation and Great Society programs. Moreover, the Democratic Party supported Public Welfare benefits directed at black poor.[41] It must be noted, however, that these gains were not made on a platter of gold. Indeed, these were developments that occurred after the lost of lives of many Blacks and some Whites in the civil rights struggle. Clearly, the national government was more amenable to the demands, while the states and rural Americans that are more in tune with conservative values and resistant to change often worked against such policies. Indeed, conservatives tend to remain "antagonistic" to regimes intended to bridge the social and political gap between Blacks and Whites in the society—and for sometime resisted so vociferously any attempt to address the plight of Blacks even for the sake of peaceful co-existence. The politics of opposition to national government regimes favorable to minorities and the poor were played out effectively in rural America. And some conservative

Republicans see pro-poor and pro-black policies of the federal government as handing out too many goodies to Blacks and other poor Americans, who may not deserve such assistance. They believe, and perhaps rightly so, that welfare handouts to the poor are done at their own expense. Behaviorally, it appears that as long as the Democratic Party opens up the windows of opportunity to Blacks, African Americans are likely to continue with their overwhelming support for the party. This was a fact that may have not being lost with President Bush's 2000 presidential elections slogan of "compassionate conservatism." Arguably, the word compassionate was used as a campaign strategy for attracting minorities—particularly African Americans and Hispanic voters. It is not clear whether or not President Bush's philosophy of compassionate conservatism will attract African Americans to the Republican Party in droves. The President and Republican Party, however, cannot be faulted for trying. Indeed, the party has already started making inroads among African American electorates.

The character of leadership is as complicated in the African American community as it is in other communities. To be sure, African Americans have produced more outstanding leaders in the non-governmental areas such as religion, sports and the academy. In the area of politics, however, the one central issue has been how to address the race question so as to bring African Americans fully into the political mainstream of America. The difficulty is exacerbated in the face of opposition from those who believe that the success of such a political integration might threaten their power-base. The ability to produce leaders in the area of politics in African American community suffers from the very nature of politics itself. Leadership in politics carries prestige and perks. Therefore the struggle for leadership could sometimes be fraught with intra-community conflicts. Nevertheless, those actors involved in the "intramural" struggle for power within the black community have never failed to lose their sight on the prize—i.e. full political integration, in a manner of expression.

Be that as it may Cornell West in his bestseller, *Race Matters*,[42] identified three genres of political leadership within the black community. These are:

- race-effacing managerial leaders,
- race-identifying protest leaders, and
- race-transcending prophetic leaders.

Race-effacing leaders are those leaders who attempt to strike a balance in the nature of the interaction between their loyalty to the black community and their quest to connect with the dominant white population. This process of working toward equilibrium between the races is done in the belief that in order to further black interests in America, such a union especially between blacks and white liberals was imperative. Thomas Bradley and Wilson Goode represent this cadre of leadership. But, critics of such a leadership genre argue that in attempt to bargain and compromise, which are essential ingredients in a democratic system, they tend to give away "too" much to the dominant group that is already enjoying a greater level of the economic and political privileges in the political system. In any case, there are many who contend that in contemporary American politics, this is probably the major political route to follow.

Race-identifying protest leaders are leaders who "often view themselves in the tradition of Malcolm X, Martin Luther King, Jr., Ella Baker, and Fannie Lou Hamer (and to this list one could add Jesse Jackson).[43] These leaders emulate Booker T. Washington style of leadership by launching their political crusade from the pulpit of the black substructure while simultaneously and assiduously working toward reconciling the contradictions between black and white interests. The strategy of such leaders is to use protests to "shake up" the political establishment, particularly the decision-makers, by reminding them that not until justice and fairplay in the distribution of goods and services in the political system were addressed for the Blacks, they (the privileged) were less likely to enjoy the robust fruits of the system that they gathered in the polity.

Paradoxically, some of the black leaders in this genre of leadership in the post-Civil Rights period have become political apostates. This is the case because after the rationales for the agitation of these protest leaders were appeased or mollified by the guardians of power with plum positions, the reward expected from these black leaders is to reduce, if not eliminate, the anger of their political flock. One problem is that whereas these national leaders now enjoy the privileges that flow from their new recognition by the White and African American communities, leaders at the local and national levels, the masses of the Black that they represent are forgotten. Indeed, sometimes these poor African Americans are reminded and soothed with the theological appeal that they would find their prosperity and glory in heaven.

Race-transcending prophetic leaders are epitomized by Harold Washington and to some extent Jesse Jackson of 1988, contended Cornell West.[44] Indeed, to be an elected and prophetic leader "requires personal integrity and political savvy, moral vision and prudential judgment, courageous defiance and organizational patience."[45] This caliber of leadership in the African American community and, in fact, other communities as well is rear. This is generally the situation in part because the "politics of morality" has in many polities being replaced with the "politics of immorality." This genre of politics that allows the actors to manipulate and apply whatever means necessary to win in the game of politics has become endemic in all systems though condemned by many who utilize this method and strategy. The outcome of this sort of politics is the difficulty in nurturing race-transcending prophetic leaders and the consequent "disfiguration" of the political system in the eye of the informed public who care about politics.

In all, the leadership issue in the African American community, with a few exceptions, is problematized by the sad truth that influential leadership in the black community tends to come in sputters and to be *ad hoc.* Witness, for example, the election of Mayor Dinkins in New York City, the late Mayor Harold Washington in Chicago and Governor Douglas Wilder of Virginia to name a few. The election of these African American leaders to the position of power, and the anticipation that the political space has finally being enlarged to accommodate Blacks, whetted the political appetite and drive for further involvement in the game of politics. Unfortunately, the excitement was temporary, and the hope that this development could boost black political gains was, at least, momentarily slowed down. The election of Barack Obama from Illinois to the Senate could rekindle African American interest in politics.

Lessons Learned

What, then, are the lessons to be learned at the rural level of Black politics from the foregoing discussions and analyses? The late Democratic Speaker of the House Tip O'Neal was correct when he stated that: "all politics are local." This assertion is especially significant in rural America, where a majority of citizens are domiciled, and on whose turf politics are usually played out. The political behavior and attitudes of these electorates are important in the analyses of the character of politics and the leadership that any collectivity can produce for the successful governance of a polity. In discussing political behavior, attitudes and leadership in this chapter, my intention was to present these paradigms as guides that might help the reader to better understand the politics in Florence County and by extension other counties in rural America. More importantly, it could inform the electorates and leaders of their political niche and place in the scheme of politics in rural communities throughout America. In cases in which the political behavior, attitudes and leadership genre fall short of expectation, the need for a dialogue to discuss ways in which African Americans could improve their political position through the democratic process might be explored. In this way, Blacks are likely to be able to concretize their hopes and aspirations within the traditional American democratic political system. This is the central concern of this chapter.

Chapter Three: Political Behavior, Attitudes and Leadership

1. Ulmer, *Introductory Reading in Political Behavior*, 2-3.
2. Milbrath, *The Politics of Black America*, 3.
3. Apter and Andrain, *Contemporary Analytical Theory*, 14.
4. Walton, Invisible Politics: Black Political Behavior, 2.
5. Bennett. *Apathy in America*, 77.
6. Conway, *Political Participation in the United States*, 28.
7. Alex-Assensoh and Assensoh, "Inner-City Context, Church Attendance and African-American Political Participation" in *The Journal of Politics*, 887.
8. Ibid., 886, 888.
9. Campbell, Converse, Miller and Stokes, *The American Voter*, 298-311; Perry and Parent, *Blacks and the American Political System*, 44.
10. Verba and Nie, *Participation in America: Political Democracy and Social Equality*, 149-151; Perry and Parent, ibid, 44.
11. Perry and Parent, ibid, 45.
12. Walton, ibid, 8.
13. Ibid, 8.
14. Tate, *From Protest to Politics: The New Black Voters in the American Electorate*, 43-47.

[15] Wilson, *The Declining Significance of Race: Blacks and Changing American Institutions*; Perry and Parent, ibid, 46.

[16] Dye, *Politics in America*, 25.

[17] Seligman, "The Study of Leadership" in *American Political Science Review*, 914.

[18] Udogu, "Political Leadership and Governance in Democratic Nigeria" in *Africa Quarterly*, 114.

[19] Cartwright, *Political Leadership in Africa*, 21.

[20] Tucker, *Politics of Leadership*, 21.

[21] Burns, *Leadership*, 19.

[22] Ibid, 18.

[23] Cartwright, ibid.,19.

[24] Merriam, *Systematic Politics*, 107.

[25] Walters and Smith, *African American Leadership*, 5; Morris, *The Politics of Black America*, 9; Jones, "A Framework of Reference for Black Politics" in Henderson, *Black Political Life in the United States*, 9.

[26] Walters and Smith, ibid., 5.

[27] West, *Race Matters*, 54.

[28] Walter and Smith, ibid., 7.

[29] Ladd, *Negro Political Leadership*, 4.

[30] Walter and Smith, ibid., 7.

[31] Botsch and Botsch, "African American Politics in South Carolina Politics" in *SC Journal of Political Science*, 63-101.

[32] Walter and Smith, ibid., 102.

[33] Ibid, 102.

[34] Washington, *A Testament of Hope: The Essential Writings of Martin Luther King, Jr.*, 178.

[35] Walter and Smith, ibid., 102; Cobb and Elder, "The Politics of Agenda-Building: An Alternative Perspective for Modern Democratic Theory" in *Journal of Politics*, 893-915.

[36] Washington, ibid., 308.

[37] Gregory, *Frederick Douglas: The Orator*, 278.

[38] Washington, ibid., 143.

[39] Udogu, *The Issue of Political Ethnicity in Africa*, 13-34.

[40] Parent and Stekler, "Black Political Attitudes and Behavior in the 1990's" in Perry and Parent, *Blacks and the American Political System*, 41.

[41] Perry and Parent, ibid., 43.

[42] West, ibid., 59-61

[43] Ibid., 60.

[44] Ibid., 61.

[45] Ibid, 61.

Florence County:
The Creation and the Issue
of Black Politics

This chapter is a brief synthesis of the illuminating work on the history of Florence County, South Carolina, that was organized by J. Madison Rainwater. It was a work that brought together some of the area's intellectual and community heavyweights to write an impressive historic inventory of how Florence County was created. These members of the community's intelligentsia were as follows: Mitchell Reames, James R. Rogers, Jr., Joseph Taylor Stukes, Horace Rudisill, E. N. Zeigler, Jr., Hugh L. Wilcox and G. Wayne King as the scribe. Professor G. Wayne King is a native of Florence and professor of History at one of the region's finest colleges, Francis Marion University, Florence, South Carolina. The completed work is titled, *Rise Up So Early: A History of Florence County, South Carolina*. It was published in 1981.[1] This book provides an in-depth description and rich historical analyses of events as they developed in the area. Also, the work of Lane and Cunningham[2] that provides a very rich pictorial and descriptive contribution of major African American social and political actors to the growth and development of this rural area and Florence County in particular serves as another source from which this chapter is put together. Lane and Cunningham's work on the social and political character of the region is articulated from African American perspective.

The analyses of the political struggles for the formation of the county that follow are not peculiar to Florence County; indeed, the fight, resistance and political tug-of-war that often preceded the creation of counties, cities and other similar entities in which the citizens share a common desire for governing themselves is commonplace throughout America and other democratic societies, too. And, the proceeding discussions are drawn, among other sources, from these two important works by Wayne King and Lane and Cunningham.

Historically, the area to be later known as Florence County has always existed in the bosom of two major counties, viz. Marion and Darlington. The story that follows chronicles the historic saga of some of the activities of powerful local luminaries to create a new county to the chagrin of the movers and shakers of Marion and Darlington counties. And the struggle to establish a county in which Florence would become the county seat gathered momentum in the 1880s although Florence itself was established in 1853 as a railroad junction and incorporated in 1890. The need to create a new county was borne out of necessity, astute leadership, and determination on the part of the political actors. One of the supreme arguments made in favor of the creation of the county when two viable counties already existed issued from an edit promulgated about a century before the concerted efforts to create the county. This was the County Court Act of 1786 that established a number of counties out of the Cheraw District. Two local administrative divisions that were established as a result of the County Court Act were Darlington County and Liberty District, later to be named Marion County.

The desire to create a new county arose from many factors. First, the distance and voyage from Florence to the city of Marion that housed the County Court was at this time Odyssean. The Great Pee Dee River separated Florence from Marion such that the trip between both cities was considered difficult and hazardous. Second, the population of Florence was swelling fast because of the impact of the railroad system that transported a large population from station to station and city to city. In fact, like the impact of the industrial revolution of the middle of the 18th century in England, the fascination of the new transportation system was magnetic. It not only boosted the business climate, but also attracted many entrepreneurs from the northeast of the nation and elsewhere to settle in Florence—and tapping into the success of the newly constructed railway system—for the purpose of conducting their business in the region. The cosmopolitan characteristic of the city of Florence in the 21st century arguably has its roots in part from its past character and magnetism. By 1880, Florence could brag about its population that reached 1,914 and by 1890 topped the 4,000 mark. In fact, Florence outpaced the older surrounding towns in population growth.[3] Third, with the influx of people into the city and its excellent transportation system the social life attracted some of the neighboring elites—particularly lawyers—to the city who saw greater opportunities to practice law and to represent litigants.

The architect and father of the railroad system, that became the major springboard for the creation of Florence County, was General William Wallace Harllee of Marion. In honor of his service and contribution to the construction of the railway system in the area, the town was named after his senior daughter, Florence.[4]

But in order to put forth the case for a separate county required the construction and establishment of a Courthouse for Florence, one that would deal with the needs of citizens living in southeastern Darlington County, western Marion County and northern Williamsburg County. As the argument went, if the city of Florence was to be chosen to house the County Court there was need to guarantee the neighboring counties that they were less likely to suffer from a reduction in their influence in the area should Florence build such a Courthouse. Moreover, the 1880 census showed a population of 34,107 for Marion County, 34,485 for Darlington County, 24,110 for Williamsburg County and 22,000 for the proposed new county.[5] So, in terms of population, Florence County was not going to dwarf the neighboring counties. Further, in terms of political expediency, it was reasoned that an additional county in the area could increase the number of legislators from the region. These legislators could collaborate in Columbia, the capital of the state, to bring home sizable political patronage. Eager to move forward with plans to concretize arrangements for the new county, proponents insisted that they would finance the construction of a jailhouse and court as a way of eliminating a burden to citizens of the neighboring counties for making Florence the county seat. It was an honor that Florence richly deserved because it had become one of the economic hubs—if not the major economic hub—in the region, not to mention its sophisticated outlook as wealth flowed into the city. In a way, the socialites in Florence felt that their neighbors Darlington, Marion and Williamsburg counties were reactionary and less progressive and thought that Florence's further political, social and economic advancement might be held back if it continued to be hitched to the relatively "slow" and conservative counties.[6] But the process of establishing the county was not going to be easy, politically speaking.

The political discourse between opponents and proponents of the creation of Florence County was bitterly severe but not unexpected. Opinion makers in Darlington County were particularly vocal in their opposition to the creation of a new county that could possibly diminish its influence—and in retrospect they were probably right. Editorial comments in the newspapers scoffed at the attitude of the superiority complex displayed by the agitators who argued for the creation of Florence County and wondered if it was even necessary to have two county courts within a ten-mile radius. After all, opponents of the creation of Florence County envisioned that that might be the case should Florence leaders be allowed to pursue their "vaulted" ambition of building a Courthouse and in the process establish a rival county to Darlington. In short, if Florence political chiefs were to be permitted to go ahead with their plans of inaugurating a new county, such and endeavor was likely to lead to the establishment of a "rival reign within the reign" that could further reduce the influence of Darlington and Marion counties. To some members of Darlington County intelligentsia any development that could lead to the creation of Florence County was difficult to bear. In spite of the political elbowing from all sides of the discourse regarding the feasibility of creating the county of Florence, however, it was not until 1883 that the real battle for the creation of Florence County began.

Indeed, the struggle for the creation of Florence County, South Carolina, arguably, followed similar intricate patterns and attempts to create counties in other states in America—i.e., from Maine to Florida and from New York to California and all of the states in between. In a way, the similar complex political jockeying of opposing factions in the quest to create counties or boroughs makes the discussion in this chapter invaluable and the study illuminating. The existence of powerful interest groups both in favor and in opposition to the emergence of Florence County locked political horns locally and in Columbia, the capital of the State of South Carolina. But in the final analysis, proponents of the creation of the county won the day after many years of politicking. In this regard, such important political actors as R. G. Howard,

Zachary T. Kershaw, Belton O'Neall Townsend and Dr. James Evans to list a few were towering figures in the whole process. Supporting these men in their attempts to establish a viable County, was the powerful Committee of Fifty made up of men of social and political timber in the society.[7] These men provided wise counsel and other invaluable support that were instrumental in the final creation of the county.

An attempt to formally create Florence County was made on November 25, 1886 when a bill sponsored by Kershaw was introduced and passed in the House of Representative but defeated in the Senate. In retrospect, the failure in the Senate was probably useful for a number of reasons. First, it re-invigorated and galvanized into action the proponents of the legislation, who sought other strategies for attaining their objective of seeing that the bill was passed the next time around. Second, and flowing from the first, it made the eventual success of the efforts exhilarating and greatly appreciated. To this end, the earlier failure did not deter the proponents of the new county. Instead, the local leaders rallied their forces and solicited support from some of the political heavyweights in the neighboring counties to back up the move. Two of such men were Dr. James Evans and Senator Thomas C. Moody of Marion. It seems paradoxical, but not in the character of politics, that support should come from these men. After all, Marion County might be on the losing end should Florence succeed in the putsch to de-couple from Marion and Darlington Counties. Be that as it may, politics can sometimes make strange bed-fellows since the act of politics is generally based on self- and group-interest. And such an interest, and pursuit for it, could come in different ways.

It was the combined efforts of these men, Howard, Kershaw, Towsend and other supporters of the county project that led to its eventual success. It was on December 4, 1888, that a bill to incorporate Florence as a county was introduced to the Senate and registered as House Bill 248. It was approved and following the endorsement of Governor John Richardson Florence County became officially recognized on December 23, 1888.[8] The seat of the new county, many argued, ought to be unique; it needed to be a special city in every way in view of its growth, status as a trading post and vibrant transportation system. Florence area leaders worked hard to establish its special identity. So, on December 24, 1890, by an act of the General Assembly, Florence became a "new city" and heart of the county. The impressive growth of the community occasioned by the trade in cotton and tobacco and with an important transportation network and center of the county legislature to boot, Florence grew phenomenally in a short time. It was in light of its rapid growth that Florence assumed the nickname "Magic City"—a sobriquet that is uses synonymously with Florence in contemporary parlance.[9]

Political Development in Florence County: a brief overview

As was the case in the county and elsewhere in the state and country, election was a significant dimension of political life in Florence in the 1890s and beyond. In May 1893, 816 voters were officially registered. Florence was divided into four wards and each ward had one representative on the city council. In the same year, the number of ward representatives was increased to two. Council members were required to reside in the ward that they represented. The mayor of the city was elected in at large election and he presided over the council meetings. The first appointed mayor of Florence City was Jerome P. Chase, a transplanted Washingtonian from the District of Columbia. The first elected mayor, however, was D. W. Haines, who assumed office in January 1873. His council members were J. E Schouboe, R. A. McCorkle, Joshua Wilson, and N. D. Harper. Wilson and Harper were African Americans.[10] Indeed, such was the political character of the progressive city in the late 1800s.

The impressive number of black electorates in the city of Florence and the county dwindled precipitously after 1895 following a constitutional act that curtailed black votes. This drop in voter participation for African Americans was in line with developments in the region. In fact, it mimicked the political marginalization of African Americans[11] and the reduction of voting rights in the South in the late 1890s. With the curtailment of the number of Blacks who vote through legislative acts, white voters, overall, became less enthusiastic about the political process since Blacks no longer posed a threat to their political interests at the polling booth.

In South Carolina, the constitution of 1895 not only disenfranchised most black voters but also many lower class Whites, too. The politics in Florence reflected a similar development in the state. But how did the dwindling political participation of African Americans occur? Lander Jr. affirmed:

> When the Convention of 1895 assembled on Sep-tember 10, Senator-elect Ben Tillman was in complete control. His new plan for voting requirements received little opposition except from the six Negro delegates in the body. According to the new regulations, any male over twenty-one could vote if he had established residence, had registered and paid his taxes due, and could read and write the state constitution, provided he was not an idiot, a pauper, insane or confined to prison ... After the constitution of 1895 went into effect, the Republican [party that housed most African Americans] vote gradually dropped from a normal 15,000 to 20,000 ballots to less than 5000.[12]

Moreover, in order to further concretize the marginalization of African Americans in the political process in the state within the context of the 1895 constitution, King noted:

> ...When the state constitutional convention met in Columbia in the fall of 1895, it was a delegate from Florence County who proposed that women be allowed to vote. W. F. Clayton, the former confederate ...represented Florence County. On October 28, 1895, he moved in the Convention that the state's constitution be amended to "extend the franchise to women who owned $300 worth of taxable property."...After urging the delegates to "throw aside their prejudices and give women this right," he asserted that it was "the true solution to the Negro problem."[13]

The attempt to disenfranchise African Americans in South Carolina politics using the constitution did not emerge out of thing air. The plan was carefully thought out by its proponents. One example of a group that articulated and later hatched the strategy was referred to as the Tillman Movement. It is to a concise discussion of the activities of this movement that I will turn to for further discussion.

The Tillman Movement

Besides the 1895 South Carolina constitution that curtailed black political rights, one of the most important political events in the state during the 1890s was the Tillman Movement—the political savvy of this movement significantly altered the character of South Carolina politics and that of Florence. Led by Benjamin R. Tillman of Edgefield County, the primary goal of this movement was to replace the Bourbon faction that had dominated the state government since 1877 and replace it with populist-type farmers. In truth, the movement's aim was to destroy the progress made by African Americans during Reconstruction. Ironically, Tillman began his campaign and quest to capture the state house with an important speech he delivered in a nearby city of Bennettsville. Overall, the diverse and progressive city of Florence did not embrace the philosophy of Tillman and his movement with enthusiasm. There were numerous reasons why many Florentines opposed the Tillman Movement. Some disapproved of his sharp attack on the Bourbon leaders of South Carolina. Others were skeptical of his charges of government corruption. Some were apprehensive and concerned about offending the sensitivity and sensibilities of the large African American population in the area. One of the most important reasons for denouncing the Tillman political ideology for the state, however, was the fear that Republicans and African Americans in particular, might take advantage of a split in the political ranks of Whites (who were mainly Democrats) to further black interest to the chagrin of, and at the expense of, Whites.

The discourse and disapproval of Tillman's philosophy in Florence by some in Florence County came with the Constitutional Convention of 1895. Indeed, some of the most vocal and enlightened opposition to Tillman's drive for a new constitution in South Carolina came from the county's political leaders. For example, one such leader, W. F. Clayton, who attended the convention, spoke in support of the state's constitution of 1868. The general thrust of the 1868 constitution represented opposing views to those espoused by Tillman and his supporters.

The Constitutional Convention of 1868 met in Charleston, South Carolina, in January. Its delegates were made up of 76 Negroes and 48 Whites. This proportion was natural, for African American voters outnumbered the Whites. Among the African Americans were exceptionally capable men. Some of the most notable men were Francis L. Cardozo, Robert B. Elliott, Richard H. Cain and Jonathan J. Wright.[14] It was also noted that:

> The Constitution of 1868 was more democratic than any previous one in South Carolina history. It included universal male-suffrage and omitted all property qualifications for office holding. It likewise provided for popular election of many officials formerly appointed by the governor or legislature ... The new legislature met in July, 1868. In the Senate ten of the 31 members were Negroes; in the House, 78 of 124 were colored. The Negro legislators remained in the majority until 1874.[15]

In any case, there were those who sympathized with the views of the Tillman movement. One such community leader was John P. Coffin. He was a newspaper editor who expressed misgivings about the rights of Blacks. Commenting on an appeal made by a Sumter African American leader for the right of Blacks to vote, Coffin asserted: "We believe in giving him the right to vote and the privileges of citizenship that he is entitled to under the Constitution of the United States. We believe in giving [Blacks] a feeling that all he needs to do to gain the respect of the Whites is to conduct himself as a good citizen must [by not representing himself as a political agitator and troublemaker]."[16] The presumed paradox of this view was that Coffin himself was a relatively newcomer to Florence County and that he had hailed from Baltimore, Maryland. The conventional opinion relating to the actions of Coffin's political philosophy was that he ought to have been relatively "liberal" to black issues given the character of the politics in the state of Maryland that was less hostile to Blacks than South Carolina at that time. Nevertheless, one cannot rule out the impact of environmental determinism and self-interest in molding one's social and political behavior and attitude. Perhaps the cliché: "when in Rome behave like the Romans" might be applicable in this instance. But again, he probably relocated in the area because of his ideological affinity with those in the South at the time. The foregoing discussions were intended to provide a prologue to the central concern of this chapter that highlights the development and problems of African American political participation in rural counties in the South.

The Death of African American Political Participation

The closing years of the 19th century saw the climax in the movement to eliminate black people from the political process totally and the re-assertion of a policy of white supremacy in virtually every area of society. Indeed, it was, and is, a period that most African Americans—particularly historians and political scientists—may remember and recall in infamy, to paraphrase President Truman powerful assertion following the Japanese attack on Pearl Harbor that got America officially into WWII.

In South Carolina, the concerted attempt at the political limitation and eventual removal of African Americans from political activities began when Governor H. Chamberlain was voted out of office in 1877 and culminated in the Constitutional Convention of 1895. The indifferent attitude of the custodians of power at the federal government level to protect the political and "human rights" of African Americans during the Reconstruction Period was symptomatic of the problematic nature of politics at that time. It also symbolized the acceptance of the "separate but equal" policy enunciated in the United States Supreme Court decision of *Plessy v. Ferguson* in 1896.[17] Florence politics mirrored the political events of the state and republic. It should be noted, however, that before the constitutional convention of 1895, African Americans participated effectively in the electoral process. The platform and policies of the Republican Party (as the emancipation party) endeared African Americans to the party.

Suffice it to say that Blacks were not denied the franchise and ability to participate and to represent their constituencies in the State House or Congress overnight. The process was gradual, culminating with the last black congressman in 1901. In Florence, for instance, there were 569 registered black voters in the city in 1896. There were 482 white voters. Thus, black voters made up the majority of the electorate in Florence.[18] Even after the constitutional convention of 1895 when it was obvious that black political power was being reduced significantly some black political actors in the area continued to hope for the better by holding political conventions to cheer the group up.

Among the various strategies enacted to weaken and dislodge African Americans from exercising their political rights to vote was the White Primary System. When the matter of the White Primary System was brought into the discourse in Florence City in 1899, it generated an upheaval. Those who argued in favor of the white Democratic primary saw the move as a master stroke—a sort of reform measure that was long overdue. This was the belief especially among those who felt threaten by the political strength and possible political muscles of Blacks in the community.

In fact, the perceived political threat that Blacks and its population posed for some members of the white establishment—especially the reformers—was to be immunized with White Primary (perhaps within the context of separate but equal principle). The heated debate among members of the political class in journals and newspapers was lively—and at times sharp and combative. A summary of the character of the dispute that arose following the issue of the white democratic primary reform proclaimed in 1899 is worth reproducing in detail:

> Shall the White People Control Florence? According to the reformers, elections in Florence had been a disgrace with the participation of blacks. A "citizen" claimed, "For many years past, municipal elections of this city should bring a scarlet flame to every white cheek." This indignation was caused by the way some blacks vote... According to the *Citizens* [a newspaper] in the past elections, black voters had been goaded with meat and drink, watched over by citizens of high standing in church and state, and finally driven like cattle to the polls. Further, more to our shame, Negro voters have been openly bought on the streets and exploited."...Bribes under the transparent pretense of paying for the time of the voters as workers for candidates holding high office in the Church of God [was rampant]. Dangers were still present. [It] was noted that a black mayor [since there were more black registered voters than white voters] could be elected with the assistance of a few white votes. Although that grave possibility had been avoided in the past by bribery, the best way, the good old Democratic way, the *Citizens* [concluded], is to give us a free-for-all white man's primary.[19]

Although new voter registration measures intended to mitigate electoral abuses were enacted, politicians still used unscrupulous political tactics in pursuit of their interests. Generally, politicians being politicos are often concerned about their political success and may do anything in their power to curtail any threat from the opposition—in this case, black political power. This was the case in Florence since it was possible for a black mayor to be elected with the assistance of few liberal Whites. To some Whites such a political development was unthinkable and, indeed, repugnant. Editorials in some papers such as the *Daily Times* opined that "Florence would be better off if left in the control of white people. We are responsible for it and we should settle these matters between us."[20]

As is generally the case on serious matters like this one in all political systems, it is true that tempers can flare up and that only a clever sage knows how to calm the political tempest. In fact, a letter from one of the city's luminaries, John Purvis, stated: "Corrupt practices used to happen, but now the few Negroes who vote in the election here are thinking...that they are not to be bought. [They] have the interest of Florence at heart and are not after controlling the government or getting into office."[21] It is plausible that an individual, as well as group, interest and instinct for survival tend to hold sway over moral or ethical questions in politics. There was little wonder, then, that not too many Blacks were confounded when the Supreme Court upheld the white primary system until 1946 when it was struck down.

The reaction issuing from the political marginalization of African Americans in the region and system in part led to their Great Migration to the north and elsewhere. The exodus of Blacks out of the South started after the end of Reconstruction and did not abate until shortly before World War I. Black Florentines participated in that wave of migration. By 1881, a substantial number had left the Magic City.

Economic, Social and Political Despair

In Florence City, some of the Whites competed against black economic influence especially in the area of Federal jobs. The national Republican administration continued to appoint Blacks to federal patronage positions in hopes of further boosting black political support in the South following the Civil War of the 1860s. The most attractive and prestigious federal post in Florence was that of postmaster. During most of the 1890s, Joshua E. Wilson, a prominent local black Republican, entrepreneur and preacher held the position of postmaster in Florence. In 1890, a number of white citizens who wanted the position for themselves, or who as Democrats would have liked the position given to a fellow Democrat, begrudgingly supported Congressman George Dargan who endorsed Reverend Wilson for the position as Postmaster. The rationale for his acceptance by the Democrats flowed from the belief that the Reverend was the least displeasing of the black Republicans. Though a Republican, Wilson was a religious and conservative leader and he was also an industrious businessman—a quality admired by white conservative democrats.

By the end of the century, however, attitude toward Wilson's acceptance had changed. The new Democratic Congressman for the district, John Norton, worked against Wilson's re-nomination for postmaster in 1899. The complex character of politics was played out in the county especially as it related to group interest. Norton obtained assurances from President McKinley's postmaster-general "that the 'colored preacher' could not be re-confirmed by the United States Senate. Wilson's opponents supported Dr. John Bacot, who was considered not offensive politically. It was reported that Bacot's selection was urged by nearly all the leading citizens of Florence without regard to [political] party."[22]

The political limbo in which African Americans found themselves in Florence County after Reconstruction was socially and political discouraging— and it was the same for other Blacks in the South. The difficulties confronted by African Americans followed by the lack of confidence in the political system at this juncture resulted in an acquiescence to Booker T. Washington's dogma enunciated in the "Atlanta Compromise," that was first affirmed at a Southern

Cotton Exposition in 1895. The thrust of the idea was that Blacks somehow complied tacitly and passively with the removal of their political rights while simultaneously emphasizing the less confrontational social activities—such as vocational education and self-help project. Washington has, however, had some critics regarding his opinion on this matter.

Be that as it may, the political atmosphere of a black conference that was held at the Courthouse in Florence in 1898 illustrated these sentiments and dilemmas that African Americans were confronted with in Florence. The participants were approximately three hundred people, mostly farmers who listened attentively and with concern to the addresses delivered by local leaders on the political and social conditions of Blacks in the area. Among the distinguished speakers at this convocation were Joseph Giles, the Reverend W. T. Williams, F. E. McDonald, and the Reverend E. R. Roberts. One of the strongly stressed themes at this momentous meeting was that Blacks in light of their experience could not look to white Northerners for their political salvation—for the white Northerners had their interests to protect, too. Therefore, political realism dictated that African Americans must have to foster closer ties and good relations with white Southerners. Some agreed with Roberts that Southern Whites not only understood better black idiosyncrasies but also were more sympathetic to Blacks and his poverty because they do not get any more for their cotton than the Negro does. Reverend W. T. Williams, the pastor of the A. M. E. Church, further challenged the group to correct "some of the evils affecting the home life of the Negro." The central, and perhaps most powerful, message conveyed at the conference was that the chief responsibility of African Americans was to improve themselves—[and that such responsibility has to come from within the black community itself]. The Reverend Robert Carroll maintained, theologically, that the Negro "could never be other than despised until he paid more attention to morality." He concluded by urging his colleagues to return to their homes and to do their best to promote friendship with their white landlords. In a closing address, F. E. McDonald, pastor of the Cumberland Methodist Episcopal Church, shared his opinion with the group by noting that Blacks were living among their "best friends [white farmers]." Socio-economically, it was quite revealing that among the caliber of farmers who were in attendance seventeen were out of debt, thirty owned horses, and twenty-two owned their houses.[23]

The preceding discussions provide a sketchy history drawn mainly from King's illuminating epic story of the founding of Florence County. The history highlights some of the character, nature and genre of the area's politics that, in the 21st century, sociologically define and determine the forms of political and social relations in the society. From the late 1890s to the late 1960s, African American politics in the country, and the South in particular, were moribund. Thus, it is the political saga of African Americans in the political, social and economic developments of this county in the post-civil rights period that is the central concern in the following chapters. But the political character of any community has its roots in the past. Put another way, the politics of contemporary Florence County, as is true of other counties in the union, is informed in many ways by the politics of the past. In short, in more ways than one, this opinion is true in all political communities in America and other polities.

Summary

To summarize, the experience of black political activism during the Reconstruction era in Florence County and its eventual demise is arguably identical to that of black political activism all over the South. Historically, the gains made following the Emancipation Proclamation all but died in the later half of the 1890s. In fact, scholars have alluded to the US Supreme Court decision in *Plessy v. Ferguson* case of 1896 that sanctioned the "separate but equal" policy between the races as the measure that concretized the marginalization of African Americans in the political and social life of the American polity. The interpretation of this ruling effectively gave the vocal members of the dominant group the political muscle and ammunition with which to implement policies that deprived Blacks of the franchise that they gained following the end of the Civil War. In South Carolina, the political equation was relatively "complex" within the concept of democratic theory, for in the 1890s Blacks made up 60 percent of the population,[24] and if the principle of majority rule had been "objectively" enforced chances were that Blacks would have remained a powerful force to be reckoned with in the political system. But the fact remained then, as it does now, that any group (White, Black, Yellow, Brown, etc.) that controlled wealth also controlled the politics of the polity and Whites in this case controlled the purse. The custodians of power applied different schemes to reduce black votes in other to maintain and optimize their political authority. One such strategy was the application of the "Mississippi Plan" of intimidation and violence to effectively dilute black political effectiveness and power.

The determination to reduce black political influence in Florence County through stereotypes and innuendos is similar to the problems minority groups face in other parts of the World—Europe, Asia, Africa, the Middle East and Latin America. Be that as it may, the politics of polarization and marginalization of African Americans continued unabated in Florence County, as was the case in much of the South. It was as a result of the struggles for political liberalization in the 1960s that African Americans were legally readmitted into the political system. Dr. Martin Luther King, Jr., and other civil society organizations were in the forefront in the struggle to enlarge the political space and to bring African Americans into the national political tent.

The foregoing analyses were intended to provide the springboard from which to assail the issue of contemporary black politics in rural America with specific reference to three cities in Florence County. The rationale and purpose for this brief historical description was, and is, to provide context, and possibly meaning, to the contemporary political behavior and attitudes of African Americans in rural politics in general, and Florence County in particular. Indeed, as the sages would say, the present is the mirror of our past.

It is the period after 1965, which saw the proclamation of a series of civil rights legislation and created the enabling political climate for black participation in American political life that will inform the analyses in the proceeding chapters. The chapters that follow will rest on personal interviews and analyses of the views of elected African Americans in Florence County. Specifically, one elected city councilmember of Florence and Lake City were interviewed. A third, the mayor of Timmonsville, was also interviewed in the succeeding chapters. It is hoped that in this way, I might be able, in a special way, to bring to the fore some of the fundamental functions of the political actors themselves as they address the "real character" of politics at the grassroots in rural societies in general and America in particular.

Chapter Four: Florence County: The Creation and the Issue of Black Politics

1. King, *Rise Up So Early: A History of Florence County*, vii, chapters 7, 10, 15.
2. Lane and Cunningham, *Notable Blacks of the Pee Dee Section of South Carolina: Past and Present.*
3. King, ibid., 92.
4. Baker, *A Brief History of Florence*, 1-2.
5. King, ibid., 93.
6. Ibid., 93-94.
7. Ibid, 101.
8. Baker, ibid, 11; King, ibid., 101; King, *Some Folks Do: A Pictorial History of Florence County*, 10.
9. Baker, ibid., 9.
10. Ibid., 8.
11. Ibid., 9.
12. Lander, *A History of South Carolina*, 41-42.
13. King, ibid., 221.
14. Lander, ibid., 11.
15. Ibid., 12-13.
16. King, ibid., 162.
17. Dye, *Politics in America*, 556-559, 570-571.
18. King, ibid., 234.
19. Ibid., 235.
20. Ibid., 235.
21. Ibid., 235.
22. Ibid., 236.
23. Ibid., 237-238
24. Bostsch, and Botsch, "African Americas in South Carolina Politics" in *SC Journal of Political Science*, 66

Councilman Lovith Anderson, Jr. and the Politics in Lake City

Writing on political participation in America, some scholars invented political categories into which individuals might be classified in a community. These are gladiators, spectators and apathetic. Gladiators are defined as those who not only participate actively in the political system, but also present themselves as candidate for elective office. Spectators are those who are very active in the political system. They vote, serve as campaign officials, go from door to door distributing campaign literature, but will not run for political office. Apathetic citizens are those who could careless about politics. They seldom vote, discuss politics and are generally turned off by political activities.

Gladiators, spectators and apathetic citizens are found in all democratic political systems—in urban and rural, progressive and reactionary, societies. There are a number of reasons or agents of socialization responsible for the political character of an individual within the context of the preceding categories. One of these is the family. For example, if within a family pedigree, there were individuals who had been involved in politics of different forms, chances are that the children are likely to become politically active and engaged at different levels in the political system. In short, political socialization within a family increases the chances of members of that family becoming politically active in a polity.

Such was the case with Councilman Anderson, Jr. of Lake City. His father was both a gladiator and spectator. He not only participated in the political system in a nearby county (Georgetown County) but also was elected a mayor. In a way, Councilman Anderson, Jr. learned the act of politics from his father through observation and participation with him. When in later life, he decided to plunge, as it were, into the politics of Lake City it was in part because of his earlier initiation into political activities

The position of a council member in Lake City is part time, and in terms of financial remuneration, it is not an attractive job. The assumption, therefore, is that serving on the city council should be visualized as a sort of voluntary work intended to attract only those who have the interest of the community at heart— a special characteristic unique to rural politics with its limited resources. However, given his political background competing for, and eventually winning a seat on the city council came, one might say, naturally.

In Lake City politics candidates generally run as an independent in at-large political system. In this political scheme, candidates neither ran as a Republican nor a Democrat, for example. This non-partisan genre of political competition is rather interesting but not without its merit especially in a city that is made up of more African Americans than Whites and other minority groups (Asians and Latinos, for instance). Another rationale for stressing a non-partisan electoral process issues from the belief and assumption that non-partisan politics could ameliorate the chances of creating conflictive political factions within the city and City-Hall itself. This presumed strategy of ideological neutrality is important to the extent that political ideologies might taken too seriously at the rural level of politics where democratic theories are sometimes misunderstood and democratic regulations inadequately implemented by political actors. This confusion can be made more complex in a strong patron-client alliance and system that tend to flourish in rural politics. Moreover, it is not unusual for relatives, even siblings, to stop speaking to each other simply because they belong to different political parties or that their political ideologies and philosophies are at odds. In other words, partisan politics at the rural level could, figuratively, become a "dangerous contact sport" if it is not carefully managed. In such a milieu, any process that allows an individual to run for a political office on the basis of his or her popularity and personal reconnaissance in the community reduces political and personal antagonisms and frictions that might have arisen from partisan affiliation. It also ameliorates the admonition issued by friends and family members to each other not to devolve their political affiliation at their workplace lest their boss could "punish" them if they belonged to opposing parties. The possible retributions that could be dealt out to political antagonists may include, but not limited to, withholding promotions, denying pay raises, unwarranted intimidation and the like just to teach them a lesson for supporting the "other" party.

If partisan politics are irrelevant in the political competition for council seats in Lake City, how might a prospective candidate for political office go about canvassing for votes among the electorates? Anderson, Jr. opted for a grassroots politics whereby he connected, among other groups, with those who are socially and politically marginalized in the society. In particular, he went after those who might be referred to as "political and social outcasts or deviants" because of their anti-social habits—i.e. drug addicts, alcoholics and so on. Drawing upon a theological proverb "it is the sick that needs a physician and not the whole," Anderson, Jr. went from street to street and from community to community addressing not only the problems of drug addiction among the youth, but also recruiting them into his political team and camp. His grassroots approach paid off in part because he was able to connect with them. He was once a drug addict himself and therefore was able to relate to some of them and their problems. But his political support did not come from this group alone. It also came from a community that saw him as a caring candidate who was less concerned with the prestige that flowed from serving on the City Council. His platform included the provision of more and better housing, empowerment of the people through the electoral process to become stakeholders in the political system and dissemination of useful information on social programs available to them in the community, among others.

Background

Lake City Council is made up of six council members and a mayor. The Council has more males than females, as is the case in Timmonsville and Florence. In terms of racial balance or imbalance, there were six African Americans and one white council member at the time of this study.

A major concern within the Lake City Council is adequate political communication—an issue that is not unique to Lake City since it is peculiar to most political systems in part because of conflicting political interests. The issue is not poor communication among members of the Council per se. It is the way in which divergent political ideas and interests are transmitted to each other or to members of the Council in general. This is especially the case as political actors sometimes "stubbornly" insist that their position must prevail over those of other members. But this is often the character and stuff of which politics is made in any political community with diverse political actors and interests. In any case, why did poor communication arise, or present itself, as an issue?

In theory, members of the Lake City Council run for office on a non-partisan basis. The assumption, therefore, is that these candidates as council members are non-ideological. That is, they might neither be liberal nor conservative. Further, they might have not gone into office with some strong personal agendas. These suppositions, of course, are far from the truth. Members of the Council go into office with their pre-conceived interests and agendas (sometimes with, for example, religious values given the strong influence of the Church in the area and the South in general). Some members are generally influenced by their socio-economic backgrounds.

When these gentlemen (and ladies) seat in the Council chambers to discuss policy issues, they are actually expressing their opinions based in part on their ideologies and idiosyncrasies that might not always be in sync. So, when discrepancies within the council's deliberations are said to be due to lack of communication, what the differences of opinions really suggest are that there exist strong clashing views over policies and interests. Such is the politics at the State House and Congress, too. And, if council members are not sufficiently schooled in the act of bargaining and compromising on issues in which they have strong opinions, the outcome could be said to be poor or lack of efficacious communication. Moreover, when political debates are heated, as they often are, the egotistical wound sustained by a losing member (or faction) in the chamber could, (short of a duel), be taken outside the City Hall. And what is more? The rivalry and antipathy could endure for a long time as such a "victim" might plot for a revenge of a greater proportion on the Council member/s responsible for thwarting his/her interests at a previous meeting. Thus, the explanation regarding poor communication in the Council may be seen within the context of the foregoing contentions and extrapolations.

Council Composition

Indeed, the ratio of six African American lawmakers to one Caucasian would, ordinarily, have meant an easy passage of bills brought before the Council if the African American lawmakers always shared a common interest. This is seldom the case, contended Councilman Anderson, Jr. The question, then, is why the lack of consensus among the African American actors given the composition of the Council? Members of the Council came to meetings with "hidden" agendas often articulated by men and women of power in councilmember's social group or religious denomination. In other words, council members attend meetings frequently determined to promote the agendas that enhance their interest and those of their social groups with insufficient interest paid to the interest of the whole community. Put another way, the attitude of some members of the council is that Lake City as a political community is important only to the extent that their social groups are able to derive their parochial interest from it first and then the entire community later.

The paradox in the manner in which politics is conducted in the area is such that when African Americans were outside the political mainstream in Lake City politics, they worked together in concert to pursue issues that were beneficial to the African American community as a whole. Now that Blacks are in charge politically, not necessarily economically, they are inventing strategies (based on class, religion, etc.) to divide the society in order to lay claims to a larger portion of the pie that it has to offer. This style of politics is not special to Lake City; indeed, in a comparative context, it is a politics similar to that in Africa when the continent started decolonizing from the European powers. Nevertheless, political disunity has its destructive tendencies in that it often divides the African American community. Such a division could lead to an uneven development within the black community.

A major assumption that could be discerned from intra-group contestation generally for scarce resources is that race in and of itself seldom impact on the character of politics. In the struggle for individual and group interests, intra-race competition could be fierce and sometimes virulent. This is true for the Caucasians as it is of African Americans. So, simply put, just because African Americans control the City Hall does not imply that groups within the race don't have conflicting interests that could come to the fore on the theater of politics—in this case Lake City Council Hall.

Councilman Anderson, Jr. was perplexed at the assumption—some might say reality—that many of the Council members went into politics without fully comprehending the intricacies of politics. But, one would have been pleasantly surprised if these political actors fully understood the complexities of politics. In any case, many politicians in all political systems go into politics to augment their business connections and to boost the presumed prestige that sometimes flow from political power. Be that as it may, Councilman Anderson, Jr. contended theologically that, if only representatives of the Council could be God-fearing—perhaps, and just perhaps, they might be able to put the interest of the people ahead of their parochial interests. This opinion probably might be feasible since they would not only practice "political morality" but also put forward enlightened, moral and people-oriented agendas and legislation before the City Council. In any case, it is clear that politics and religion, with a few exceptions, seldom mix. The process through which some political actors accede to power sometimes represents the very opposite of the teachings of most religions. This may be the case because the political platforms on which candidates run for office is often fraught with exaggerated promises intended to make the electorates feel good, if only, during the electioneering period or cycle. Moreover, negative advertising or politics of negativism and demonization of opponents in recent political contestations have little place in the philosophy of religion. Yet, even politicians who claim to be very religious sometimes cast away the moralistic religious teachings and indulge in the political demonization of their opponents for the sake of political expediency. Any wonder, then, that the constitution and other legal decisions made in this country attempt to assert, and in some cases reassert, the need for the separation of Church and State. The constitution and legal briefings intended to reduce conflicts that could emanate in a political system should the "marriage" between the State and Church on political issues erupt have often been treated lightly and sometimes ignored altogether. Thus, no matter the attempts and legal arguments made to separate these two powerful forces, Church and State, it is clear that their separation in a practical way is difficult—thus highlighting one of the contradictions between theoretical idealism and political realism in most political systems. Besides, that some applications of religious doctrines in the political life of a society can do politics some good is hardly disputed—especially those doctrines aimed at addressing the needs of the poor in a society.

Decision Making

One of the central activities of virtually every community is politics and politics by its very attributes tend to generate conflict. This is so because it often involves the struggle for power and the allocation of goods and services to the general population by those who control the seat of authority. The formula applied in the distribution of resources to the various groups and agencies in society may produce upheaval as each constituency, interest group and others vie for their share of the budget and allocation of services in the community.

In order to reduce conflict in the decision making process, it might be necessary, as suggested by Councilman Anderson, Jr. to hold a monthly or quarterly workshops. During such workshops, an expert or experts on an aspect of law-making may be invited to share with members of the Council his or her expertise on the subject matter. Such an experience could help council members in their deliberations and debate on major issues confronting the city. Council members may also use the knowledge gained from such a conference to sharpen the content of Council policies. Moreover, such a workshop could focus on defining how the city government should organize itself so that it could become more efficient and thereby produce more efficacious policies. Other important issues that might also be addressed at such a workshop are methods for adequately collecting revenues that are essential for the day to day running and operation of the city. Collecting revenues from the community is one thing, and distributing it to the various segments of society proportionately is another. Thus, council members could use these monthly or quarterly workshops to discuss how to effectively budget the limited city funds. Other areas to examine are the city's hiring practices that include the Fire Department, Police Department and Public Works Department. Seminars of this sort should provide council members with an opportunity to initiate new ideas, solve problems, and in general help council members to reevaluate those city projects that seldom yield the desired results with the view to rectifying or eliminating the inadequate ones. A collective effort on the part of council members to address the above areas is likely to further the legitimacy of such decisions by the entire community.

There is little, if any, racial tension in the city government. City Council has just 1 White member and 6 African Americans. Politically, as a minority, the white member of the Council is probably aware that there isn't much he could do if he chooses to be confrontational. But, as a "check" on political disagreements that sometimes exist among the African American council members, however, he generally presented "impartial" opinions that often motivated other members to re-examine and re-evaluate their position on major issues in the City Council. The African American legislators also take into account the sensibilities and sensitivities of the lone Caucasian on the Council when making decisions in order to appear fair and non-racist in their decision making process.

One of the strengths of the Council, and how it sometimes arrives at its decisions, flows from the fact that council members do not overtly assert their political ideologies. This is sometimes reflected in the voting patterns in that, overall, members tended to cast their votes on a policy based on what they presumed to be in the best interest of the community. This is often the case notwithstanding their strong individual and parochial interests to satisfy the demands of the "constituency" or interest group/s that elected them to the Council.

Community Concerns

Lake City has an at large electoral system. This implies that a council member has a city-wide constituency. In this way, the pressure to satisfy the needs of the ward or an area that elected a candidate, for example, may not be daunting to the council member. In this case, the concerns of Councilman Anderson, Jr. were similar to those of the other members—except, of course, that they may place different emphasis and allocate different sums of money for each community project. The areas that have been of general concern to the community include, but are not limited to:

- Communications/Cellular Towers
- Infrastructure, i.e. water and sewage system
- Fire Coverage and Training Center
- Affordable Housing and General Maintenance
- Education
- City Vehicles and Police Department
- Trash or Garbage Disposable
- Recreation
- Industry
- Health (especially Black males)
- Single Parent Families.

Communications

In order to move Lake City forward into the 21st century, and to compete with other cities in the area for development projects, the need to improve information communications technology (ICT) is imperative. The Council places great emphasis on technological development in the city. That means that Council has to attract companies that provide such amenities. The linkage between the above listed concerns to the city's policies is obvious in many ways if the city is to pursue economic development as a major objective.

Infrastructure

Infrastructure, which includes good roads, water supply, schools and health care facilities, among others, is important not only for the quality of life for all citizens in Lake City but also for attracting industries and manpower necessary for operating the industries.

Fire Coverage

Providing adequate fire coverage in the city is important in case of outbreak of fire and for the protection of private and industrial property. Providing training centers that could prepare those who would undertake this dangerous task of protecting the city from fire hazard is also significant. Without qualified individuals to run the fire equipment the purpose for purchasing such delicate machines could be meaningless.

Housing

Another area that concerns city lawmakers is affordable housing and their maintenance. Well-being is one of human's basic needs and it includes job, shelter, food, clothes, etc. The provision of housing especially for the poor remains a major concern for most city governments and administrators in rural America, and Lake City is not an exception to this pressure and demand. Funds for such projects are often scarce and that impact on the ability to maintain housing projects. The negative stigma attached to living in one of the subsidized homes does not help matters either. The high joblessness that often prevails in low-income housing projects increases the problems that cities must confront. Frustrations that issue from the condition of despair lead invariably to drugs, alcoholism and other destructive vices as forms of temporarily escaping from personal problems especially among the youth. The rippling effect of such damaging behavior is a rise in High school drop-out rate, crime rate and the saturation of the prison system with the youth, particularly African Americans.

Education

Education plays a great part within the policy formulation of the city. But the extent to which the school system should be improved may depend on growth in funding and how determined the citizens are to support the school plan. The major concern for the council members as to how to craft legislation to deal with the issues of quality education and funding can be frustrating. In order to hire highly qualified educators, council members have to be prepared to pay top dollars to attract superb teachers. But when there are insufficient funds to operate city projects, school districts may have to cut services or raise taxes. Both options are usually unpopular and this means that the problem will have to persist until an adequate formula and consensus is arrived at to tackle the problem of providing a high quality education system.

City Vehicles

The question of the use of city vehicles might appear trivial in the politics of a city. But when the permission granted by the administration to city officials to use government vehicles are abused by some government employees, it becomes a major issue especially as the budget of city governments in rural America are often limited. This matter of illegal use of city vehicles is quite problematic when the city must pay for the fuel with which to run the vehicles and also defray the bills for vehicle maintenance.

Police

The need for adequate policing in order to improve the quality of life of citizens is not debatable. It means the provision of security for individuals and property, particularly small businesses that provide jobs and serve as the backbone of the city's economy.

Garbage Disposal

Provision of garbage disposal facilities addresses the issues of health, environmental degradation, and other quality of life issues. Whereas it is very inexpensive to produce waste, it is not cheap to dispose of them. The city is not only saddle with the onerous task of disposing the city's refuse, but also concerned with making sure that funds with which to carry out the task are available.

Recreation

Recreational facilities are almost indispensable for the promotion of the wellbeing of citizens in the city. They provide means for children and adults to engage in meaningful physical activities other than school and work. In a real sense, the provision of recreational facilities in a community makes the adage "all work and no play make Jack a dull boy" come to life. Thus, children spend time at a little league baseball, soccer and softball fields where they make friends and bring families together. Recreational facilities also provide parents with a peace of mind knowing that their children are actively engaged in productive activities rather than causing trouble at the public Malls and elsewhere. For parents, they could spend quality time with the family at community parks. These leisure activities are also important in that they promote good health and general well-being of citizens and society.

Industry Attraction

The city has to attract industries in order to provide high paying jobs—for without jobs the city could die a slow death—because of the mass exodus of qualified citizens to other cities in which there are job opportunities. In general, it is the energetic and high achieving youth that are more likely to flee from Lake City to urban areas in the state and country. Therefore the need to attract industries with excellent incentives to locate in the city is a concern for city council members. The strategy to attract high quality industries must be carefully thought out since the competition for lucrative industries with other cities is always fierce.

Healthcare

Personal healthcare issues and the problem of single parent family in the community are extremely important matters. These basic community problems are peripheral legislatively speaking because they relate to personal issues. But they are nevertheless taxing to the city council members because of the economic and social implications of healthcare problems in single family homes. It is generally difficult to pass laws on moral issues that can be dealt with at home by the family. Thus, legislators are very cautious about intruding into such issues. But, City Council may be able to provide citizens with incentives that are likely to mitigate the lifestyle that could lead to poor healthcare habits; Council can also encourage sexual abstinence through education. In other words, City Council could appropriate funds for educating the public through public service advertisements and adult education program on how to improve good health and avoid out of wedlock pregnancies. The Council could also encourage non-governmental groups such as civic organizations to collaborate with the city in the war against these problems.

The significance of the concise discussion of the above community improvement strategies is that they constitute the fundamental issues that city governments are created to tackle. In short, they represent the very stuff that politics is all about—how to provide the citizens of a city with sufficient help and guidance for their daily survival. This means the provision of jobs, security, clean water, healthy environment and adequate housing. Indeed, the political survival—i.e., the reelection of council members to the Lake City council may rest on their ability to address these fundamental human needs.

Discussion

In order to comprehend African American politics in rural America one might have to do so believing that for the most part Blacks tend to react to issues, contended Councilman Anderson, Jr. That is to say, that too often African Americans don't have long range plans for tackling political issues. Thus, they tend to react to political problems as they are confronted with them. This approach does not always lend itself to a carefully thought out response.

A number of reasons account for why African Americans tend to react to political issues in the politics of rural America the way they do. With a few exceptions, African Americans are, overall, closer to the bottom of the economic ladder in American society than other groups. At the rural level, African American poverty is even sharper and more pronounced. When an individual is poor (and this is true of other nationalities) matters relating to his or her daily survival are more important to the family than politics or who the next city council member, mayor, governor and president is likely to be. Also, because of the relatively low literacy rate in the area, Black analyses of, and consumption of, information needed for the group's socio-economic empowerment is comparatively low. Hence, the reactions to political issues that might affect the lives of African Americans are not always assailed with enthusiasm by the masses. Their reactions to political issues tend to be *ad hoc*—since the perception is that political issues and even participation in the political process mean very little to a majority of African Americans. Indeed, politics don't pay bills, put food on the table and pay house rent—at least not directly as a result of their active participation in the political process.

Little wonder, then, that in Lake City, council members tend to be less proactive on issues, especially if they are likely to be acrimonious. This is arguably the case because a council member hates to be on the wrong side of a truly contentious issue that could generate antagonism between council members.

In order to encourage a proactive approach to city problems, contended Anderson, Jr. it is important to be well educated or informed on issues through constant dissemination of information. The more information the council member gathers on political issues affecting the community, the more likely he or she might make an informed judgment on that issue. More importantly, the more likely he or she might anticipate political challenges ahead and prepare to tackle the problem for the good of the whole community before it "erupts" at Council meetings.

Information collection and sharing should not only be limited to decision-makers. In a democracy, the citizens should also be well informed about political developments in the society in order for them to have meaningful input on decisions that could have lasting effects on their lives. Because of the closeness of the citizens in rural societies churches—and in particularly church leaders and other civic organizations, could be helpful in devising and advancing ways to share appropriate information with parents who are often too tired after a hard day's work to be bordered by political news items in the local newspapers and on television.

Comparison

Politically, the character of Lake City is somewhat similar to that of the city of Timmonsville. In both cases, the mayors are African Americans. They have more African Americans council members than Whites in the City Hall. So, African Americans technically control political power.

Economically, however, the character of the city is some-what different. In Lake City, the White population exercises economic control. Thus, a sort of equilibrium is created in that while African Americans control Lake City's politics, Whites control the economy. The question as to whether political power or economic power is more significant in the day to day operation of the city is left to the judgment of the observer.

It is suggested that approximately 70 percent of the population in Lake City are blue-collar workers, while 30 percent are white-collar workers. Also, about 90 percent of African Americans are blue-collar workers and 10 percent are white-collar. Among the white population the split between white and blue-collar workers is even. That is to say approximately 50 percent are white-collar workers and 50 percent are blue-collar.

One of the contentious areas of debate between the races, both nationally and in rural America is the question of the implementation of affirmative action programs intended to address the marginalization of minorities (including women, the disabled, etc.) in employment and other services. In recent discourses on this matter some opponents and detractors of this plan have referred to affirmative action program as a quota system intended to discriminate against white males.

Councilman Anderson, Jr. remains critical of the program probably because of the numerous negative implications attributed to the procedure. For example, the behavior of some members of the majority group that many minorities (Blacks and women) are often given jobs for which they are not qualified is unacceptable and insulting to many minority groups. This is particularly true of successful African Americans in Higher Education, Corporate America and other prestigious professions. What is called for, among other things, is a way of addressing the "negative" imputations and perceptions toward minorities who occupy important positions in society because many if not most earned them through the old fashion hard work. One way of addressing the issue in a polity that had historically marginalized African Americans, women and other minority groups is by providing a "level playing field" for everyone as is the case, for instance, on the baseball and football fields, and tennis and basketball courts.

History

The historic struggle for the "Second Emancipation" in the 1960s following the first in the 1860s was tough and at times bloody. The further marginalization of African Americans after the period of Reconstruction did not help matters either. In fact, during post-Reconstruction era political activities for Blacks were comatose. The vocal discourses, among members of the informed public, as to whether African Americans really belonged to this country in spite of the group's contribution to the economic growth of the republic reached its crescendo in the 1960s. If as the argument goes Blacks played a key part in the development of this country, then as in the Reggae lyric Blacks want "a piece of the pie right here and right now." The civil rights marches of the 1960s that was led by Dr. Martin Luther King Jr., his cohorts and representatives of religious and labor unions across this great nation culminated in President Lyndon B. Johnson's signing of a series of civil rights legislation. The civil rights legislation legally "reinstated" the political and social rights denied African Americans since the emancipation proclamation. The civil rights legislation granted African American their "human rights" and ushered in a new phase in American democracy that for African Americans in the South may be referred to as the "Second Emancipation."

A major question that confronted African Americans following the post-civil rights era was: "now that they had found freedom (through sweat and blood) what were they going to do with it?" Indeed, even after over four decades, the debate as to the place of African Americans in the political and economic development of this great and most affluent country in the world is still unclear. It is painfully true that in virtually all walks of life in Urban and rural America, Blacks are still struggling to find a political and economic niche for themselves. To be sure, a few African Americans have been phenomenally successful. The question is: what about the massive poor, within the African American collectivity especially in rural America? The economic gap between Blacks and Whites continues to persist although attempts are being made to address it through diversity programs.

It is against this backdrop of the preceding conjectures and the developments within the broader society that one could visualize the political and economic issues in post-civil rights Lake City. Despite the fact that the "Second Emancipation" occurred in the 1960s, full political participation for Blacks did not materialize until much later in the South. There is little wonder, then, that Lake City had an all-White city council until the 1990s. Historically, as noted in Chapter three, African Americans were intimidated and scared to vote during much of the late 1890s and much of the 20th century. To participate in the political system could result in disastrous consequences for the participants. With time and political education, however, African American political attitudes have changed incrementally as Blacks came to realize that with the vote they could make significant changes in society—particularly the political character of Lake City. Indeed, as political power shifted to the majority Blacks in the city so did some of the affluent and former custodians of power gradually relocated outside the city-limit. One paradox concerning this development, ironically, is that the white "economic flood" flowing out of Lake City swept with it a few wealthy African Americans, too. Thus, in the post-civil rights era, African Americans have been able to control political power but not economic power in the city.

Now that Lake City Council is dominated by African Americans, it suffers from some of those vices that are sometimes typical of legislatures that are dominated by one political party, ethnic group or race—the lack of adequate checks and balance. Indeed, the popular cliché that Americans tend to love divided government (for example, Democrats controlling the Legislature and Republicans the Executive) is lost when one group or party controls all institutions of government.

There is no doubting the fact that power tends to corrupt those who are entrusted with it. And, when there are no effective means of checking on the malfeasance of political actors and leaders, accountability and transparency suffer and so does the legitimacy of the government. The need for accountability and transparency are relevant in the politics of rural America in which some local heavyweights are able with their wealth and clout to establish their private political fiefdoms by pushing the politically illiterate constituents around. They often flex their political muscles with their established patron-client political machine.

Lessons Learned

The lessons learned, and rewards derived from the civil rights movement, should be sufficient to enlighten African Americans to insist on promoting leaders in the community that have moral principles and temperance. Black politics in rural America and how it is played out in the society could be given a boost if successful African American entrepreneurs, civil and religious leaders continued to invest in their communities. Not until successful African Americans invest their talents and resources in the black community, politics as usual whereby those whom Councilman Anderson, Jr. refers to as having the "old money" might continue to dominate and shape the character of small city politics to the chagrin of the majority of the population.

In all what Lake City needs, and the same is true in other cities in rural America, concluded Councilman Anderson, Jr. is improved education system that, among other things, relates what is studied to the promotion of good citizenship and good governance. Good citizenship implies racial tolerance, belief in diversity, community spirit and fair play. It should provide affordable housing schemes in a healthy environment that is conducive to the nurturing of children and the youth. It should provide social programs for the youth necessary to divert their attention from activities likely to lead them to criminality. Employment and provision of job training and development are also important in order to improve the social and political life of the community. Youths that are hungry and lack self-esteem are less likely to participate in civic and political development of the society. Indeed, they are more likely to be alienated from society and to turn to deviant behaviors as a way of escaping their misery. Politically, rural communities should seek out moral leaders who not only understand the "nature of politics" but also believe in transparency and accountability as strategies for furthering the legitimacy of their leadership. Occasional or periodical workshops intended to bring council members up to speed in modern democratic processes should be helpful. It is hoped that a holistic and unselfish approach to the "construction" of a good governance system could promote a unique genre of African American politics in rural America.

Councilman Edward Robinson
and Florence City Politics

Generally, political sociologists tend to suggest that family, peer group, school, among other factors, influence and affect an individual's behavior and whether one participates in a political system both as an electorate and an actor seeking a political office. The hypotheses that might flow from the preceding variables are that one raised and nurtured in a family of politicians is likely to be active in politics and also that one who lives in a neighborhood in which political activity plays a vital role in the organization of the community is probably going to be active in politics when he or she became an adult.

Councilman Robinson's political activism has its origin in the character of the environment in which he was raised and in particular his interest in grassroots politics. The 2nd district is his constituency and a majority of the population is African American. It has always been this way even as long ago as during the Reconstruction when the area was represented by black councilmen until it was altered following the South Carolina constitution of 1895. His political zeal is informed by his desire to address issues that affected African Americans in Florence and his district in particularly. Moreover, the nature of his vocations, particularly as owner and teacher of a driver education school, brought him real close to many of the youth and their needs. Furthermore, he was able to identify with his constituents not only by living amongst them, but also by sharing a lifestyle that was similar to those of his constituents. In truth, if one were to take the basic sociological classification (i.e., lower, middle and upper-class categories) seriously, the ward is probably populated mostly by the lower class—sprinkled with a few black middle and upper-middle class citizens.

In the city of Florence, the "politics of racial identification" is commonplace in the same way as it is in much of the region. By this, I am implying that African Americans tend to identify more with the Democratic Party than with the Republican. His ward is made up of approximately 65 percent African Americans and their voting pattern is such that they tend to support the Democratic Party. Put another way, a Republican candidate has a little chance of capturing the seat in an electoral competition—at least for sometime to come. It is, therefore, by virtue of the political character of his ward, Councilman Robinson's constant communications with the voters, and his sensitivity and sensibility toward their concerns that has led to his support and representation of the 2nd district ward for over a decade.

Background

The city of Florence houses the County seat. The County is made up of the following major towns and cities: Florence, Timmonsville, Olanta, Lake City, Scranton, Coward, Pamplico, Johnsonville and Quimby. The politics of Florence city, because of its sheer size and commercial clout, can hardly ever be separated from that of the County itself. Be that is it may, the central concern of this chapter is the City Council. The Council is made up of 6 councilmen (no women at the time of writing) and a mayor. The population is approximately 60 percent White and 40 percent Black. Racially, two city councilmen are African Americans and five are White (including the mayor). In 2004, the two African American representatives were Ed. Robinson (2nd district) and Billy D. Williams (1st district). It is arguable that due to the politics of race, composition of the population, distribution of wealth in the city, it might be difficult to elect an African American mayor—although not impossible. The difficulty in electing an African American mayor to some extent has an historic antecedent as noted in chapter four. But the politics of the 1890s in which some of the leading politicians in the area and a number of editorialists in their commentaries frowned upon the possibility of electing a black mayor (at a time when there were more African Americans than Whites) is, of course, anachronistic in the 21st century. In any case, what the above analysis suggests is that the electorates still tended to vote largely on the basis of race—Whites for white candidates and Blacks for black candidates (even when they are of the same political party). This voting pattern is not likely to change any time soon. Moreover, African Americans tended to vote less than their white counterparts. In "ideal" politics, the issue should not be race; it should be whether the political actor represents the community with a sense of fairness and equity—a pledge that has become a rarity in politics because of constant claims and demands that powerful individuals and interest groups exert on political actors.

To be sure, an African American, Reverend Terry Alexander has served as chair of the County Council. His appointment to chair the County Council was made by County Council members. In other words, he was not elected in at-large electoral process to chair the Council. But what point am I attempting to make here? It is that given the voting behavior in the county and city, it might be difficult for an African American in at-large election to be elected mayor (or county chairperson). The Florence City 2000 census figures (as illustrated in the appendices) show that the White population in the city is 16, 020, Black 13,541, Asian 352 and American Indian and Alaska Native 54.

Playing by the Rules of the Game

Nevertheless, the politics of Florence City Council, and the role of Councilman Robinson, is the concern of this chapter. The functions of a city government, like those of the state and national governments are, among other things, the apportionment of goods and services to the various competing constituencies in the polity. The size of the "pie" that is allocated to any group laying claims on the government depends to a large extent on serious politics and politicking with the custodians of power regardless of existing formulae and arrangements designed for such a purpose. In other words, the manner and strategy in which a politico pursues his or her objectives in political discourses could influence the outcome of the proportion of the budget going to his/her constituency. In short, a political actor's aptitude at bargaining and compromising could determine who gets what, when and how in a political system.

The political, social and economic clout that a community wields, within the larger polity, could impact on how a constituency is viewed by other constituencies. Tremendous political power tends to flow from districts that are inhabited by the wealthy and those whom Alexander Hamilton termed the "well-born." Major resources for city improvement tend to be allocated first to the wealthy neighborhoods in part because the upper class in society are generally responsible for appointing those who became major political leaders in a city government. In return, these men and women of political weight influence major policies affecting the community and also expect obedience—particularly political obedience—from their anointed political leaders. This sort of politics is referred to as "the iron law of oligarchy" by some political scientists. Moreover, the "reciprocal arrangement" between the wealthy elite and political elite is furthered and lubricated by common membership in a civic or religious organization.

In communities with inadequate social and economic power, resources tend to trickle down, if at all, to the constituents. Their representatives are often marginalized, sometimes treated with contempt since they are accused of taking in more resources in community tax revenues, and the like, from the rich who are often burden with taxes. Moreover, the assumption is that poor constituencies give little or nothing back to the larger community. Indeed, if there is anything that the lower class communities gave to the broader community, the powerful in society often contend, it is crime, drugs and trouble. Such is the perception—and sometimes an exaggeration of what some critics of support for the poor liken to a "Robin Hood syndrome."

As a representative of a ward that generally considered a social and economic "liability" to the larger community, it was difficult for Councilman Robinson to influence the judgment of a majority of council members on policies aimed at improving the condition of citizens of his constituency. To paraphrase the late American comedian, Rodney Dangerfield, it was difficult to "command respect" from his fellow councilmen—particularly from some of the white council members. He was considered brash and as one who did not truly understand the rules of the political game. But the issue was not that he did not want to play by the rules of the game; it was that in order to pursue his objectives of improving the general standard of living of his African American constituency, he had to proceed politically in a way that brought up his concerns about poor Blacks to the entire community. The situation was such that the "existing rules of the game" did not work for him and his desire to satisfy the needs of his constituents. Put another way, the rules of the political game are generally written in black and white. But, it is obvious that in virtually every political system politicians don't always follow the rules. In truth, they sometimes cleverly apply "certain unwritten rules" of the game if doing that could lead to their electoral victory and control of political power and policies.

It must be said that during the early days of Councilman Robinson's political **brinkmanship,** he played by the "unwritten rules of the game" by often drawing the attention of the Council and community to his demands through public demonstrations that sometimes landed him jail. His strong belief that because he was elected to his seat on the Council, just as other members were, suggested that he was to be "treated as equal" to the other members of the Council. But this was hardly ever the case during his inchoate years in the Council that were continuously confrontational. Naturally, he was bitter for being politically ostracized and, indeed, legislatively frustrated because he was having a tough time getting the Council to pass his bills intended to address the needs of his African American constituency. The issue, then, was why was he having so much problem persuading members of the Council to pass his bills?

Robinson represented a constituency that can claim of having the largest number of "lower class" citizens in the city. But, of course, there are a few middle-class African Americans in the district as noted earlier. Real pressure for better housing projects to accommodate members of this ward was always high on his agenda. Besides Billy D. Williams (the other African American on the City Council), the issue of public housing was seriously not on the agenda of the white council members. The white members on the Council generally represented the constituencies of those who owned their own homes (Whites and Blacks, but generally more Whites) and those who belong to one high professional class or the other. The perception still persists, wrongly or correctly, that citizens in the rich wards are over-taxed in order to subsidize the poor. This image generates frustrations in the broader society—as the well-off of all races and ethnicities tends to be angry, if not indignant, for being over burden with tax. The poor, on the other hand, wonder if the rich really care at all about their condition of poverty and argue that the wealthy in society are "selfish" and unsympathetic to their plight.

In any case, the correlation between poverty and school dropout rate in Robinson's ward is quite high in comparison to the other wards. Due to inadequate education, many lack the job skills needed to compete adequately in society. And, without job there will be no income. As a consequence, a large number of the youth resort to unconventional ways for making a living often with disastrous consequences for the individual and society at large. When bills that could help address such malfeasance especially by some of the youth in the community are brought before the City Council, white members of the Council tend to be lukewarm and reluctant in tackling such issues. Robinson's frustrated outburst with the politics of Florence City Council was informed by what he felt was the insensitivity of council members to the dearth of poverty in his constituency. He sometimes blamed the "aloofness" of council members to issues of poverty, joblessness and crime in the African American community on racism. But the constant badgering of council members for more resources directed toward his ward not only irks council members, but has also led to political agitation toward him for his political methods of drawing their attention and those of the public to these issues. Let it suffice to say that political demonstration was occasionally applied by Councilman Robinson in attempts to get Council and, indeed, those in a position of authority to act on major issues. The act of demonstration is especially a useful method for minority groups—to get those in authority to give an ear, or pay attention, to the stated concerns of such groups, and there are many examples worldwide including the civil rights marches of the 1960s to bear this thesis out.

Politics of Agitation

Having resolved that playing politics the way it should be played by submitting bills through the normal process within the City Council in hopes that members would react favorably to them did not work out Robinson turned to the politics of agitation. He launched public demonstrations against the administration for not only marginalizing him, but also his constituency. He believed that the condescending attitude of some members of the Council toward him might have arisen from the character of his district that he represented—the least powerful economically and politically in the city. In order to bring the issues that affected his constituency to the fore, he had to challenge the Council's genre of politics—particularly the council members' use of their numerical strength and power to crush his bills and by extension the interests of those he represented. If a dialogue with council members regarding the issues that affected his ward was not going anywhere, it was necessary to adopt other effective methods. Indeed, drawing from the lessons learned from the era of the civil rights movement, Robinson decided to rally his supporters in protest against the city and the attitude of its decision makers for not taking the concerns and interests of minorities in his ward in particularly, and those of African Americans in the city, seriously.

By bringing black issues to the public domain through demonstrations and civil disobedience, policy makers were moved to act upon problems relating to minorities brought before the City Council. The reaction to African American concerns following public commotions that were often covered by the media were swift not necessarily out of enthusiasm to see such policies passed but, arguably, because of the negative publicity that such public unrests might elicit for the vibrant city. Indeed, incessant agitations might tarnish the political reputation of the growing city that was historically very popular for its diversity and racial tolerance.

It would be wrong, and might even be politically foolish, to assume that Robinson always received support from members of his African American constituency and community on all issues affecting his ward and the black community. Part of his opposition in the politics of Florence comes from those who were uncomfortable—and often uneasy about his confrontational style of politics. Some of the older generations of African Americans did not see eye to eye with his approach to politics—particularly his demonstrations. Thus, they distanced themselves from him. They preferred, instead, a quiet and diplomatic approach to his confrontational politics. The youth, on the other hand, were more impatient. They represented those without jobs that blamed the system for all of their woes; they insist, moreover, that radical change in policies was necessary to address their immediate needs of jobs and the provision of better housing schemes.

But there is a paradox issuing from the 2nd district in that a substantial number of members of the youth are politically inactive. In other words, they seldom use the power of the vote and yet desire and demand help from the system. Many in this group also see the competition in politics as being too conflictive and do not wish to be part of it. Indeed, Robinson, like many other political activists before him, has been locked up as result of some public demonstrations. Still others fear losing their job especially if they backed the wrong political candidate. And, this is not to mention those who cannot participate in the political system because they had been convicted and thus have criminal records that prevent them from voting. In all, poor education, joblessness, law enforcement problems and alienation among some of the youth tend to be high in this community. The complex and daunting problems in the 2nd district make Robinson's job rather arduous. Indeed, the issues and politics confronting this community are particularly challenging to anyone who might represent it and its political interest/s. Robinson's political stance in the Council, arguably, should be seen against the backdrop of the preceding complexities in the politics of rural America.

Political Brinkmanship

Politics in a democracy often involves bargaining and compromising in attempts to achieve individual as well as group objectives. There are also moments when the application of political brinkmanship might be necessary against those in power because of their "obstructionist" tendencies aimed at protecting their parochial interests. The struggle to represent a complex community—particularly a relatively poor one like the Bronx in New York, the Mississippi Delta in Mississippi, for example, is not an easy task. Persistent struggles and well crafted bills aimed at persuading the leadership of the Council to address constituency needs sometimes pays a high dividend if the demand is seen to be just and fair by the larger community. Such was the case with Robinson who after many years of fighting City Hall politically can say with relish in later years that the struggles have been fruitful and worth it at least in the beginning of the 21st century. His political activism has started to yield positive results in terms of improved housing schemes, jobs and investments in his political Ward. One lesson to be learned in political struggles, argued Robinson, is that African Americans in rural America need convincing that they must be continuously involved in the political system if they wish to derive their objectives from the political system. After all, as the adage goes, Rome was not built in a day. Therefore, their fundamental needs are unlikely to be met in one fell swoop. Consistency in pressing for humane legislation and patience to see these laws passed should remain the guiding principles for African American political actors.

Members of the Council both Blacks and Whites work convivially today for the betterment of society. The collaborative spirit came about after a mutual understanding about the nature and working of politics and the need to move the thriving city forward in the new millennium. With time, members of the Council came to realize that Robinson meant no harm in his confrontational politics; he only had the interest of his constituency at heart to fulfill. He also realized, too, that the other council members had the interests of their constituencies to pursue within the overarching needs of the larger community—the city of Florence. By balancing their mutual interests they were able to get along very well. Moreover, the two men (Billy D. Williams and Ed. Robinson) who were members of the African American community on the Council got along superbly. Their political issues were similar and therefore they worked together to complement their interests on the Council. The four white members of the Council have remained cordial to the two black members. They articulated their bills and presented them to the Council just as the African American members of the Council did without mutual political suspicions. They discussed all issues bearing in mind the overall interest of the city. In cases that Council disagreed on policies, and there are many instances in which they did, Council simply debated and debated until members were able to thrash out their differences. It could be honestly said, and with confidence too, that the Council had started working together like a team, Councilman Robinson noted with relief.

Politics of Pragmatism

The politics of pragmatism that has become the character of Florence City Council took some time to evolve. In spite of this development, however, there still exists a general perception on the side of the African American council members that the white members on the council remain relatively insensitive to the social and economic needs of Blacks in the community. A number of reasons account for this sentiment and attitude. To begin with, it is clear that white members on the Council fight intensely to protect their interests as is to be expected. Moreover, white council members and their constituents in Florence posses more economic clout than the African American members on the Council and their supporters. Further, white councilmen are constantly in contact with the political and economic movers and shakers in the community who are also able to influence city politics and its policies.

For instance, when white council members argue for a better school system and tax reduction on homes or property such policies are less often favorable to Blacks who own fewer homes and property than Whites. Furthermore, there is resentment on the part of many Whites that their tax dollars are spent taking care of poor Blacks and their numerous needs—burden that many believe are too much for them to bear.

To the African American observer, the insensitivity to black social and economic issues and interests could be seen in the very structure of the city. For instance, there exist residential segregation in terms of race and class. The white members of the Council do not fully understand the needs and concerns of those who live in Low income housing areas because they don't live in these projects and consequently, they are unfamiliar with the cultural and social problems in these poor African American neighborhoods. Perhaps if the white lawmakers, as part of a workshop, are encouraged to live in these areas for a week or so, they might be able to adjust their positions toward issues affecting the poor in these areas at council meetings. In any case, the lack of understanding of matters concerning the lower class in the community and how to tackle them have been known to politically pit Robinson against the dominant members of the Council. This author, himself, observed some of the heated democratic debates on TV and the City Hall.

Admittedly, there were moments in the political activities of Florence City Council that Robinson was considered a political troublemaker by some members of the black, as well as the white, communities because he was adamant in pursuing his Ward's interests both at the Council and on the streets. To be sure, Robinson's liberal political ideologies were sometimes considered to be too extreme, offensive and controversial for the city.

It was, and is, sometimes the case that voting at council meetings on policies are done along racial lines—i.e., Billy D. Williams and Ed. Robinson, the black councilmen, would vote in support of a drafted policy and the white members would vote against it "regardless of its merit." Such voting patterns are not unique to Florence since council members take into account the interests of their constituency before casting their vote on a bill. But when major decisions affecting the entire city are made in private by men (and sometimes women) of power without the input of a segment of the community, the outcome of such policies might be problematic especially for those who might be in the loop when policies are privately formulated. Such decisions could become law because a majority voted to support the policies, but they could also be unenforceable in the areas that did not support such laws because of the lack of participation of lawmakers from these wards in crafting such regimes. In fact, the African American members on the Council tended to become alienated from such practices in which major decisions affecting the polity are secretly made in private clubs, for example.

Discussion

It is important for a council member to formulate policies after consulting with a cross-section of his or her community at regular meetings and intervals. It is true that such consultative conferences might attract a relatively few members of the informed public to such an assembly, except, of course, if the meeting was specific to issues that affected the entire group. In order to articulate community-based interest, Robinson summons community meetings from time to time. Additionally, information is gathered during informal day-to-day interactions with constituents. In the end, he generally called for a conference so that the community could exchange ideas, debate community-related concerns and arrive at a decision on a course of action to be taken to solve a problem.

The above outlined process represents a rational way of approaching policy making at the local level. What Robinson finds difficult, however, was his ability to educate his constituents on their rights and responsibilities as both citizens and important members of the community who needed to organize in order to promote their common interest. This problem could be attributable to the life experience of African Americans with respect to how the government functions—particularly one of its agencies—the law enforcement division and its criminal justice system. The contacts that so many poor African Americans have had with the law enforcement agency, especially in regard to the incarceration of Blacks for major and minor offenses create a negative perception and attitude toward this apparatus of government.

Race Relations

The issue of race relations is a sensitive matter in most multiethnic and multi-racial communities, and Florence is not an exception to this fact. Florence city council members are aware of the centrifugal tendencies of racial/ethnic politics but have had problems fully addressing the question. Because of the delicacy of the subject matter, the general attitude of the Council is not to discuss it in hopes that the issue would quietly go away. The result was that when racial problems came to the fore at council meetings, the strategy was either to avoid the issue or provide a temporary solution. As a consequence of such an *ad hoc* decision making approach racial problems continue to persist, fester and simmer underneath the superstructure of the politics of the area until it would again resurface. The creation of a race-relations committee is important only to the extent that it could be empowered to tackle race-relations problems head on before they lead to political implosion in the society. Such was the case when a senior member of the Council, Billy D. Williams, an African American, was politically "snubbed" by being denied the position of Mayor pro-tem by the Council at a time when the city sought a national recognition as a model city. The insensitivity of the Council to the African American community on this matter, among other factors, led to the denial of the city of this important recognition. It therefore might be important for members of the Council to attend a number of workshops to sensitize them on matters that are sensitive to all racial and ethnic groups in order to further political stability and peaceful coexistence.

Budget

The city's budget is transparent and council members always worked toward economic solvency. Overall, there are no confrontations or discrepancies issuing from budget allocation formulas. The ability of the City Council to work out the framework for tackling the city's financial matters is commendable. There is transparency and accountability on financial matters. Indeed, the Council has done very well in managing the city's budget especially since budget allocation issues could be contentious if adequate bargaining and compromising failed to develop among policy makers.

Opportunities

There is no doubting the fact that African Americans made social, economic, and political progress as a result of the civil rights movement of the 1960s. After "freedom" to participate in the political process was won through sweat, tears and blood black young adults appear to be taking the success for granted. It is true that the children of those who fought the battle for the enlargement of the political space are less connected and possibly less appreciative of the struggle. Sociologically, though, this political apathy is understandable. The issue today, however, is how to use the new opportunities created by the voting rights legislation to further the interest/s of African Americans in a society in which opportunities are abundant. To be sure, some Blacks through their hard work have already seen the social and economic "promised land." But, there is a long way to go for many to come close to living out the American dream of relative economic success.

In the politics of African Americans in rural America, as is the case in national and the international community, the practice of politics is still top-down. The argument is that those cities and political systems that wish to empower citizens to be participants should encourage grassroots participation. But, of course, this view is easier enunciated than practiced. Generally, the lack of interest in the political process in rural America has many dimensions foremost is that individuals, in the family, are often uninformed about political issues and how decisions made by politicians affect their daily lives. Also, citizens have too many family concerns—such as paying bills, taking care of children and the elderly to be bordered by complex and conflictive political issues. These facts of life are real and tend to promote the top-down system whereby decisions in politics are made by the political elite who are often well-informed and are concerned about how public policies affect their fundamental interests.

Moreover, it is clear from the political developments of the 1890s and beyond that the strategies applied in the 1960s to emancipate African Americans must be refined to suit the struggle in the 21st century. This approach is important since the needs of the 60s are markedly different from those of the new millennium. The idea today is not to organize a march for social and political empowerment in a polity just for the sake of marching. Reactions to public issues affecting African Americans in rural America require careful planning around the fundamental issues that a group is confronted with. In order to pursue successfully positive strategies, the black community will have to rally around some of the strong leaders in the community—especially those drawn from the local churches.

Many reasons account for why Blacks should look up to the church, but two will suffice for the purpose of illustration. The first reason is historical. Black churches in rural America have in the past and still continue to provide leadership in the African American community. Second, as church leaders, and relatively successful entrepreneurs, they are not beholden to external powers or political bigwigs; thus, members of the clergy are generally consulted for their wise counsel and support by politicos.

If politics are "played right" by the actors, reelections are almost assured. If politicians fail to connect with their constituents regularly, they might have problems seeking reelection. The need to create a balance between one's personal work and that of the constituency is important. Robinson made sure that he struck a balance between both. He planned community activities at the public park during which time he distributed voter registration cards to qualified African Americans so that they could register and vote. This process also provided him with the opportunity to educate the youth about the indispensability of politics especially how the activities around politics affected their lives even though the wheels of politics, in terms of rewards, tended to grind slowly.

Conclusion

What is important at the end of the day in politics is whether one was and is able to reach out through politics to touch people's lives positively. In order to further this objective, it was not uncommon for Robinson to attend functions specifically designed to entertain Blacks at the public park, contact constituents with problems particularly in the difficult area of the law enforcement agency.

Paradoxically, Robinson's political positions in the politics of Florence tended to receive more "respect" for his political positions from white members of the community than from African Americans. This was probably the case because of intra-ethnic rivalry for political leadership within the black community. This political development is informed by the unfortunate antagonism that competitive politics tend to create between contestants. But again it could be that the white community understood the conflictive character of politics and how to inoculate it better than the black community having participated in the game much longer than African Americans. In order to be an effective legislator, it is important to plan, implement projects and reevaluate policies in light of previous ones in order to ameliorate and eventually avoid previous mistakes. In this way, Robinson was able to address some of the fundamental issues confronting his constituency. These strategies were relatively successful because he placed the interest of those he represented first.

Mayor Henry Peoples
and the Politics in Timmonsville

The city of Timmonsville and its mayor, Reverend Henry Peoples, is unique. Its demography and characteristics are in many ways similar to those of small cities found in Alabama, Mississippi, Louisiana and elsewhere in the South and country. The community that is made up of about 2,500 to 3000 has an African American population of about 80 percent. Whereas 70 percent of the adult population in the city is registered to vote, only 25-30 percent of them actually go to the polls. This low voting record is not peculiar to Timmonsville; it is an issue nation-wide.

It is true that historically, African Americans were legally prevented from exercising their franchise and sometimes intimidated not to vote by forces that worked against their legal rights to vote. That notwithstanding, many reasons account for why African Americans are reluctant or better yet not eager about voting in the politics of rural America. Some are unenthusiastic about voting because they do not see any tangible reward for performing this civic function. Moreover, politicians often turn off voters by their political equivocation by promising the electorate what they can seldom deliver, and doing very little to improve the social condition of their constituents when in office. And then two or four years later politicians would return to their political base to give constituents political sermons and excuses as to why they were unable to fulfill their earlier pledges and to asked to be returned to office so that they could put finishing touches to their earlier promises. In general, the "double talk" and "political propaganda" of many politicians tend to alienate the electorates and prevent many from engaging in political activities.

Timmonsville's City Hall, unlike Florence City Hall, is very modest and unique in a very special way. It symbolizes a very close knit society that is typical of most rural communities all over America. In addition, Timmonsville's family-like character presents itself very much like a polity in which the citizens are at peace with each other, and a society more interested in providing for its subjects the basic needs to sustain the whole community rather than a few.

The job of the mayor is a part time position with a modest stipend. The political competition for the position of mayor, unlike San Francisco or Miami, is not driven by pecuniary need; it is therefore likely to be attractive to men (and possibly women) who are dedicated to serving the community. In any case given the nature of the position, particularly the familiarity of the citizens of the community with each other, the mayor at the time of this study has held the position for ten years. Before becoming mayor, Reverend Peoples had served for eight years on the City Council as a council member. Thus, is safe to suggest that in order to become mayor of the city, it might be useful, but not necessary, to serve as a political "apprentice" within the City Council itself. In this way, membership in the City Council does serve as an incubator for prospective mayors. In short, this experience allows for a relatively smooth transition from being a council member to mayor. It might also ensure continuity in the implementation of existing regimes.

The first African American mayor of Timmonsville was elected in 1984 and Reverend Peoples is the second African American to occupy this position. Arguably, his religious background helped to nourish and further his political legitimacy across racial lines since religion plays a central role in the lives of the citizens in the area. Nevertheless, when it came to politics and conflictive issues facing the city debates are often lively and educational. In fact, because of his professional background and comprehension of the nature of politics in the area, Reverend Peoples did not identify with any major political party (Democrat or Republican). He often contested elections as a non-partisan candidate.

The reason for his success as a politician who had won reelection several times is attributable to his platform that stuck to the issues that truly concerned the entire community. Despite that, however, he did not always receive 100 percent support from the Council and citizens. In fact, it would be difficult for any politicians to attract that kind of support except perhaps in an authoritarian system which the politics of Timmonsville was not. His strategy was to work on those concerns that were immediate to the welfare of the community.

Council Composition

The City Hall is made up of six council members and a mayor. There are five African American council members, one of which is the mayor. The ratio of Black to White members on the Council changes from election to election but at the time of this study there were two Caucasians. Interest shown in an election generally depended on the excitement generated both by the candidate and electorate on issues confronting the society at a given election cycle.

Community Issues

Housing

A major social problem in Timmonsville is inadequate housing. This is an issue that affects the poor who are often disproportionately African Americans. A popular American dream is to own one's home and therefore avoid the possibility of living in one of the federally subsidized housing schemes. At issue with many of the African Americans when it came to owning their own home is unemployment—especially among young black males.

Employment

Because of the high unemployment among poor black youth, their self-esteem could be deflated. Thus, as a result of the lack of jobs, they tend to seek other outlets to escape from this reality. Often the extended family support system that is an important social unit among African Americans is overburdened and consequently leads to problems in the society. In general, this is a problem that afflicts all poor people regardless of race or ethnicity except that it is rather serious in the African American community. So, the problem of inadequate housing for the poor is much more than a place to live. The lack of a place to rest after a hard day's work produces "collateral damages" to those who cannot afford a home, for example, work ethic. For those who already have steady jobs and accumulated some wealth, the issue of housing is often taken for granted. They eat well, have medical insurance and can afford family vacations. These life sustaining factors may set the poor and rich apart.

Recreation

The provision of recreational facilities is yet another major issue confronting the mayor. Perhaps the problem that Timmonsville is confronted with on this issue stems from the proximity of Timmonsville to the city of Florence that is approximately 5 miles. The budget of Florence city is very robust when compared to that of Timmonsville. Therefore, Florence is able to provide first class recreational facilities such as Freedom Park and Timrod Park to cite two examples. These parks are opened to virtually anyone who wants to use them—and that applies to citizens of Timmonsville. Be that as it may, the development of modest recreational parks in the city should add to the quality of life of the local citizens—especially those without transportation.

Police

Police protection remains a thorny issue in Timmonsville. Generally, the city's revenues from taxes, and other supplemental sources, determine the extent to which city law makers set aside funds to hire more cops to monitor activities on city streets and to fight crimes in the small municipality. The fact that the median income in the city is relatively low mitigates attempts to beef up the city police force and the community suffers as a result.

African American Participation

Given the City's many social issues with limited funds to tackle then, the way that the mayor has had to handle the problems is to prioritize them on the basis of immediate needs. Additionally, he has to address strategies for apportioning the city's resources to the various constituencies and interest groups. He has had to wrestle with many issues some of which are, should a larger portion of the budget be set aside for the African American community given its population? What about the budget to be allocated for the white minority constituencies? Reverend Peoples dealt with these issues politically and to some extent theologically by insisting on the need for fairness in the apportionment of resources to all areas in the city.

Historically, African Americans did not develop politically and economically on a par with their white neighbors—particularly in the South. One reason for the inequality in their development patterns is that African Americans had traditionally not been in a position of economic and political power in the city. But now that African Americans are politically in charge of the City Hall, should Blacks, as represented by an African American mayor, use their political power to marginalize the white minorities in the city? The Mayor suggested that he was not going to pursue a policy of reprisal—insisting instead that he would implement city policies within the framework and principle of fair play toward all groups in Timmonsville.

In the city, there are more blue-collar African Americans than white-collar Blacks. The preponderance of Blacks in this group has an historic antecedent. Indeed, the area was, and is, still famous for its agricultural base. Tobacco and cotton were grown in the South and Timmonsville cultivated its fair share of these crops. Education for Blacks was limited. Therefore, African Americans pursued vocations that they were most familiar with and at that time it was farming. Today, the farming tradition continues even though industries are replacing the farmlands in terms of economic rewards. One such example is the Honda Plant. Without adequate education, African Americans could not be placed in high paying jobs—a situation that might persist in the 21st century.

Some research findings suggest that, overall, blue-collar workers tend to be uninformed, have little opinion about the world outside their own, unlikely to be interested in politics, live below the poverty level, and so on. In spite of these dimensions, however, council members are able to come together around issues that affected the poor in particular and society in general. The council members are generally successful if the problem is well articulated by those concerned with the problems of blue-collar workers.

In fact, when it became important to the African American community that they should get involved in the politics of the city, they did so in order to control the City Hall. They voted for African American candidates for council seats so much so that at the time of writing the composition of members of the Timmonsville City Council was 5 African Americans to 2 Whites. One consequence of the ethnic voting pattern was the flight of upper class Whites with their substantial tax base—as if saying "no taxation on us without representation."

Whereas the increased political participation of African Americans has meant the political empowerment of those voted into power and by extension the black community certain problems still persist. While voting is important, it is useful for African Americans to study the political issues, understand them and cast their votes rationally. Before such an objective can be accomplished, it might be necessary for Blacks to understand how the political system works. The lack of comprehension of how the political system operates is not a special problem to African Americans alone—in fact, it cuts across race, ethnicity and class. The problem for most African Americans, though, is that the lack of understanding of how the political system works tends to be more critical since, as a group, they came into the political game rather late and need to use politics (as defined as the authoritative allocation of things of value) to improve their social condition. Political consciousness among African Americans in rural America will have to be awakened if they are to become useful political actors in the society. This is a tall order; indeed, given the overall negative perceptions that many in society have of politicians, and politics in general, a lot of work has to be done.

When the first African American elected mayor of Timmonsville resigned after two years in the position, it was due in part to the inordinate pressure that was brought to bear on him by the excessive demands of the office that was made more severe by his personal job. Also, the belief on the part of the African Americans who voted Reverend Peoples into power, was that with him in charge as a black mayor the proverbial lamb (i.e., the City Hall with its largess) had been slaughtered, therefore it was now time to figuratively share the meat among his supporters. In other words, they not only wanted jobs for themselves, but also for members of their extended family system; they wanted their streets paved or re-paved; and they demanded, sometimes in private conversations, that new housing construction should begin with immediate effect. Such were the pressing demands made on the leadership—generally without concern about where the funds for these programs and projects might come from. Thus, the lack of understanding of the intricacies of politics often led to poor communications and confrontation with policy makers in City Hall. And, when the electorates don't have their way, it is not uncommon for some to murmur begrudgingly, usually in an undertone, "it sure wasn't like this the last time we had a white mayor." The bottom line is that African Americans, particularly in rural America, need to be sufficiently educated on the basics of how the political system works so that they could be less frustrated when the system, on occasion, does not deliver their anticipated objective. But more importantly, political education should help them understand the complex processes of arriving at political decisions.

Mayor's Duties

In spite of the administrative issues that came with constant citizen's demands for services and his inability to fulfill most, the mayor derives some pleasure on the job. In general, it is soothing to be able to solve one or two community problems and to see those affected by his efforts express appreciation—for example, completing work on a poor drainage system and providing more signs on the road for children's safety, and so on. Other areas in which improvements were made to the city are the creation of jobs, improving the law enforcement system and race relations.

There are also many displeasing aspects of the job of being mayor. It was, and is, frustrating to observe the lack of knowledge of how the municipal government operates. The assumption that all of the city's problems could be solved in one fell swoop is, to say the least, misleading. Moreover, it is difficult to convince the electorate that policies, especially good policies, don't become law overnight. Any attempt to explain the complex processes in passing laws is not only met with skepticism, but also recriminations and sharp criticism at times. Indeed, it would be normal for citizens to disagree on political issues. Unfortunately, aggrieved citizens in the community do not hesitate to discredit the leadership and City Hall itself for not meeting their needs often because they had not done their research on the complex nature of the issues before the Council.

Disagreements with members of the City Council on a bill brought before the Council can be very heated. The discrepancies often border on priorities to be given to certain policies. Debates on budget allocations tend to be acrimonious. One white council member has a proclivity for being politically confrontational. Perhaps, he wanted to demonstrate that he did not want to be pushed around simply because he was a minority on the Council. In any case, this councilman has moderated his approach and began to see himself very much like the "loyal opposition" as in the British Parliamentary system. That notwithstanding, he always pursued with great enthusiasm and passion the interest of his constituency in the Council.

Decision Making

Matters to be discussed on the agenda by the Council are submitted by individuals or an interest group. The issue could be brought to the attention of the Council either as a problem or a request for assistance. Institutionally, the Council has a Strategic Planning Committee (SPC). The SPC's function is basically to meet with the sole purpose of formulating important plans to guide the actions of the Timmonsville City Council (TCC). The SPC is composed of the TCC members, special members of the Timmonsville community, members of the business community and members of the school district. Obtaining ideas and drawing strength from this cross-section of the community is significant in that it promotes the legitimacy of whatever decision are made for the entire community. Moreover, such an involvement of a significant segment of the community in decision-making process mitigated the perception that only a few elite really made important decisions in Timmonsville. One major advantage in this process of governance is that it taps into the expertise of various informed groups in the polity, without placing major financial burden on the city itself. At the end of a SPC meeting recommendations in the form of comprehensive plans are made and presented to the Council.

Church Membership and Politics

The important role that most religions play in assuaging social problems in a society cannot be over-exaggerated. Oftentimes, it is useful to apply religious doctrines and philosophies to further good governance especially in cities in which the population identify closely with the Church. If race relations, in Timmonsville with a population ratio of approximately eight African Americans to two Whites, are to be promoted, it might be significant to start with a biracial Ministerial Alliance—one that brought together Black and White church ministers to confront some of the societal problems. Unfortunately, the infusion of politics into the structure of the Alliance rendered the movement ineffectual so much so that the group became moribund shortly after it was founded. In the end, the entire community was on the losing end because it was denied the political and especially social counseling that it could have received from such a powerful and influential organization.

The debate concerning the nature of the relationship between Church and State is likely to continue for sometime to come. The concept of, and attempts at, separation of the social and political functions of the Church and State has been difficult to implement in the body politic of most rural communities and the republic itself. The difficulty in separating the activities of State and Church flows from the numerous and overlapping interests that these important entities share in common. The State and Church are unique to the extent that their institutions shape individual's life and behavior patterns in many complementary ways. It is citizens who operate and interact within these institutions that make them "organic." In other words, a Church may not be a Church, philosophically speaking, unless and until it has a congregation of believers, and a State may not be a State unless it is inhabited by people or citizens who share some common interests, boundaries and autonomous government. Since "men" tend to be political actors who may belong to a church, synagogue, mosque, and so on, their activities related to the State and wherever they worship are bound to overlap from time to time.

It was the above realities in Timmonsville that prompted Reverend Peoples to suggest that political issues should be discussed in churches. Historically, for African Americans, the church was one important rendezvous that was relatively immunized from intrusion by the plantation masters. So, for the African Americans the church not only remained the most significant center for worship, it was also the focal point for organizing political activities intended to address their needs and interests. Additionally, it was the center from which they planned protests and raised campaign funds for political activities in society. Therefore, it is useful for the church to continue educating the citizenry not only on how the political system works, but also other social issues that can enhance the quality of life for African Americans. Indeed, there will always exist a relationship between politics and quality of life issues in a political system.

Race Relations

Cornell West in one of his acclaimed books, *Race Matters,* suggested that in American polity no matter the guise in which decisions are made in Corporate America, Institutions of Higher Learning and Government, for example, race and racial considerations nearly always comes into the final outcome. Analogous to the above supposition on race in other democratic and non-democratic societies is the cliché that "ethnicity matters." Indeed, race and ethnicity shape the character of political governance in most multi-lingual, multi-ethnic/racial societies. What probably matters on racial issues are the racial epithets and perceptions that individuals invent in their psyche toward another race or ethnic group nurtured in an environment with tortured history of racism and ethnicity. But, increasingly, we see that manufactured perceptions of the other—as a "demon," "unfit," to govern a polity tend to be sharpened when the interactions between races and ethnic groups involve competition for resources—especially scarce resources. And, this is not to mention the impact of race and ethnicity in the struggle to control the apparatus of power with which to apportion goods and services in a political system.

There is little wonder, then, that issues concerning the need for good race relations in the society and government continue to persist. The issue of race and its political and social attributes in Timmonsville is very sensitive and yet its influence in the community's life cannot be wished away in spite of the open condemnation of racial vices. It was to this end, that Mayor Peoples insisted that the Council needed to come to grips with this reality, recognize the problem, and nip it in the bud. In order to confront racial prejudice of any kind (Blacks toward Whites or Whites toward Blacks), for instance, there was need to call a spade a spade and to tackle the issue with fairness and probity.

The paradox, one sees within the political and economic mix in Timmonsville is that despite the African American majority Whites wield economic power. They have easier access to bank loans, control the major businesses, and in general provide or generate more jobs for the population in Timmonsville than Blacks do. Since colloquially, whoever pays the piper may have to name the tune, these successful entrepreneurs are able to use their position of economic strength to control poor African American electorates. In factories, industries and other work places a sort of patron-client system has developed. In patron-client system the bosses could in a delicately skillful way "threaten" their clients (of course, illegally) that they might lose their job or their loans might not be renewed because of glitches on their credit records as a way to control their political behavior. In other words, clients might be told in a subtle way that their (financial and other forms of) problems could be straightened out if "clients" voted a certain way—usually a way that represented the interest of the patron or boss.

Suffice it to say that this complex interaction between wealth and politics is not peculiar to the politics of Timmonsville or rural America; indeed, patron-client politics is played out in virtually all societies (Africa, Latin America, Asia, the Middle East, and so on). Some might argue that patron-client politics is alive and well in urban or inner city politics, too.

In the case of Timmonsville, however, mayor Peoples noted that African Americans were sometimes paid not to go to the polls. This is a clever strategy that can militate against the voting bloc of African Americans since the voting pattern in the city tended to be along racial lines—Blacks voting for black candidates and Whites for white candidates. The above strategy that is aimed at suppressing African American votes is popular in the area—notwithstanding its illegality.

By way of comparison, in the 1994 South African case, Nelson Mandela instructed Blacks to accept gifts or bribe if given by the opponents of African National Congress (ANC). He, nevertheless, urged them to vote for ANC since they were going to vote by secret ballot in a booth. This was particularly smart since there was no way of telling how Blacks voted. The moral of the story is very clear; the electorates did not have to sell their vote, but if they have to, they were to do it at the expense to those who had given them money for their vote.

In the Timmonsville case, however, by asking voters to stay at home or go to the park, the patrons or bosses do not want to take chances. In short, patrons did not wish to allow those they had paid off to go to the polls for fear that they might take the "gift" and yet vote for their opponents, who are generally, but not always, African American candidates. This "vote killing" scheme was relatively successful among the poor, ill-educated and often marginalized black electorates. Some of the "middlepersons" in this plot are themselves well-informed African Americans who connive with patrons to depress black voting power. These black political actors who work for patrons, I have sometimes referred to as "political entrepreneurs"—i.e. political risk takers.

Budget

The city needs money to run its day-to-day affairs. The Council votes on its annual budget. In order to further transparency and accountability in the way that the budget is written, council members are encouraged to attend a special budget workshop. At this workshop, issues relating to the annual budget are discussed and problems ironed out before the final budget is submitted and implemented for the year. The Council also consciously set aside discretionary funds that could be tapped into in cases of emergency and unforeseen budget crisis.

Discussion

In spite of the civil rights revolution that led to a number of sweeping legislation to address the marginalization of African Americans in the social, economic and political mainstream of the society, the overall results have been mixed in Timmonsville. To be sure, many African Americans regained their right to be full participants in the political landscape of America after the bitter struggle. The result was particularly delightful in a nation-state that was not only a strong advocate of "world-wide democracy" but also promoted human rights and espoused the powerful creed in her constitution that: "We hold these truths to be self-evident, that all men are created equal, that they are endowed by their Creator with certain unalienable rights, that among these are Life, Liberty, and the pursuit of Happiness."

It is generally true that a certain amount of satisfaction tend to flow from fighting a "just war"—especially for liberating a people whose histories are strongly linked to those of every single group that inhabited and built America. One problem, though, is that after such a battle was won that passion which united the "victims" in combat tended to peter out. By way of illustration and comparison, the history of African liberation movements against the colonial powers in the continent in the last half of the 20th century approximates the above conjecture. After emancipation, internal dissension and rivalries weakened the cohesiveness of the governing elite. It did not take much time before political comrades of yesteryears turned against each other in their struggle to control political and economic power.

In Timmonsville, as elsewhere in rural America, one of the many outcomes of the civil rights movement aimed at promoting social and political equality was the voting right. Following the voting rights legislation of the 1960s, African Americans could now participate actively in the system and by so doing furthered American democratic genre. Although political power was and is within grasp, the same could not be said of economic empowerment.

In the state of South Carolina, it would be an exaggeration to suggest that African Americans, at any given time, have owned and operated more than three statewide banks. In Florence County in which Timmonsville is located, not a single bank is owned and operated by an African American entrepreneur. To be sure, there are a few church-owned lending institutions in the area (such as Trinity Baptist Federal Credit Union) that were specifically developed to cater for African American needs in light of the problematic lending practices toward African Americans of the major banks.

The reason for the lack of ownership of major banks by African Americans might be historical and political. Historically, as a group, African Americans have not really controlled substantial wealth. Politically, it might be threatening to local power brokers for Blacks to control vast wealth. One powerful reason is definitely obvious: the group that controls wealth invariably controls politics and in most societies they tend to be relatively few; in rural America they tend to be even fewer. The few wealthy individuals influence policies in a city and even determine the character of leadership for the community. As noted in chapter 6, some political scientists have invented the phrase the "iron law of oligarchy" to explain this phenomenon. It was this development that probably prompted Mayor Peoples to affirm that on the one hand African Americans have made giant strides politically in the post-civil rights era, but on the other hand there are some vital areas in which they lag terribly behind, for instance, economic empowerment.

The economic stagnation, with a few exceptions, in the African American community, has, arguably, created a peculiar perception, and some might say reality, of social, economic and political malaise among poor Blacks that make them susceptible to political manipulations. In fact, in the words of Mayor Peoples "some people are hoodwinked into believing that Whites are better than Blacks." Sociologically, too, the evidences that could lead to this observation are conspicuous in the city. Some of the most expensive homes at the Country Clubs, impressive industries and banks owned and run by peoples other than African Americans are some examples. Blacks have a long way to go in order to generate wealth and become key political movers and shakers in the area. Whereas the above analyses and conjectures might represent an exaggeration of the situation, they nevertheless provide a caricature of the existing condition for much of black Americans in rural America.

All is not lost as one could witness the rising numbers of African American *noveau riche*. They are slowly but surely building and acquiring wealth and political power. They are moving ever so slightly toward the Country Clubs, too, and are doing so through their hard work.

Conclusion

It is hoped that this study would provide an insight into how politics are played out in this small city in rural America. Politics in such a setting must, in my view, be seen to be addressing the needs of the various groups and publics with the view to making positive contributions to the citizens' lives. Public office must not be seen as a source for amassing power and for pursuing self-interest, noted Mayor Peoples; indeed, to follow this route could lead to disastrous consequences for such political actors and society that they govern.

Conclusion: Looking Ahead

This study on grassroots politics in rural America was and is informed by the fact that there are more Americans who live in small cities than those who live in urban and metropolitan areas. Yet, no major studies of this kind or topic have been conducted on black politics in this area. Thus, the analyses in the pages of this book are very significant and should augment the literature in state and local government in particularly and national government in general.

Overall, there has been a mass exodus of some of African American best and brightest from rural America to urban America (e.g. Atlanta, New York, Chicago, Washington, DC and Los Angeles) in search of greater opportunities. Such a movement has often eroded black political influence in rural America. Moreover, the presence of African American intelligentsia and highly successful entrepreneurs in America's megalopolis has in part led to the outpouring of studies on their social, economic and political activities.

That the character of the environment in which politics are played out often affects the nature of interactions between the various groups and actors operating in the system is not lost in the analyses in the preceding chapters. This book serves, I hope, as a beginning or continuation of an area of study that has been largely neglected and at best dealt with marginally. State and local government texts generally concentrate on the major actors and how the institutions function. Not much is written in these texts to explain the peculiar character of the politics of minority groups—particularly African Americans political actors in rural America.

In writing this book, *African American Politics in Rural America: Theory, Practice and Case Studies from Florence County, South Carolina,* I attempted to blend theory with practice in the analyses. Thus attempts were made to visualize African American politics holistically drawing upon the impressive works of African American scholars and others in Chapter 2. Indeed, a deeper understanding of African American politics in rural America in the 21st century could only flow from the group's rich and yet turbulent political history, particularly from the period starting with the Emancipation Proclamation of the 1860s to what some scholars have referred to as the "Second Emancipation" in the 1960s. The Second Emancipation that followed the civil rights marches finally gave the vote to all Americans in the South without regards to race, wealth, education and so on. But, having been given the right to vote is one thing and actually using the power of the vote to change or alter the character of politics in the society in favor of those who were once politically victimized is another. In the same vein, student of democracy seldom fail to remind us and political actors that election in and of itself does not democracy make.

So, African Americans have the vote, but as this study suggests Blacks have not used it as effectively as they should. Nationally, the percentage of African Americans who go to the polls is lower than Whites. In the politics of rural America the percentage is even lower. Black voting habit needs to improve although it might be difficult because of inadequate education, high unemployment and unusually high number of black incarcerated youth. These are some of the young men to whom African American leadership could have been turned over to, when the older leaders retired.

The character of political leadership in all systems is often problematical as noted in Chapter 3. But if there is one area that students of black politics need to investigate more deeply, it is that of leadership. In fact, many have. Yet, because leadership means different thing to different people, the prodigious scholarship on leadership is still to yield a satisfactory result. Producing black political leaders at the national level has been tough, let alone in rural America.

An important agent of political socialization is the family. Hypothetically, children raised in families in which the parents are political tend to become politically active. Similarly, children raised in a household in which there have been political leaders are themselves likely to aspire toward leadership. The rise of George W. Bush, as the 43rd president of the United States, at the national level bears this hypothesis out.

In rural America, though, Blacks tend to be less politically active in part because a majority of families are so concerned about daily survival and therefore may not wish to be bordered by politics. Put another way, in the households of most African Americans there are few political leaders that children could emulate. This is one source of the difficulty in cultivating future black political leaders. To be sure, political leadership among Blacks has come from religious leaders, Dr. Martin Luther King, Jr., Reverend Jesse Jackson, for example. While some religious leaders have been effective in politically rallying African American votes for a candidate, their ability to transfer through socialization their political leadership function to their off-springs is not always easy. The bottom line is that there exists a "crisis" of African American political leadership at the national level, and this problem is even more prevalent in rural America.

The creation of Florence County in Chapter 4 and the developments that provided its political contours are illuminating. More important is the character of African American politics in the area historically. The impact of the changing political history in the republic and the region in particular is felt as the once proud black Republicans who at one time legislatively dominated the politics of South Carolina had their privileges taken away under the weight of racial politics. It was a politics that made strange bedfellows of white Republicans who migrated to the South with white Democrats leaving in its wake marginalized black Republicans—a political paradox, indeed. But as some political scientist would argue, individual interest nearly always trumps ideology in most human interactions. In the end, African American political leaders, confronted with political reality that they were losing their brief political gains, pleaded with other Blacks to embrace their white southern brothers with whom they shared more in common as farmers.

The instruments that were employed in changing the political and social fate of African Americans in the politics of South Carolina were contained in the tenets of the constitution of 1868 and 1895. The constitution of 1868 gave political franchise to all males and excluded property qualification for one to hold political office. The 1895 constitution stipulated, among other things, that only males over 21 years who had paid their taxes and could read and write the constitution could vote. The latter constitution literally killed African American political participation since most could not read or write in those days.

The politics of Lake City, Florence and Timmonsville as articulated by Councilmen Anderson, Jr. Robinson and Mayor Peoples are fundamental to this study. The theoretical and analytical contextualization of the responses to my questionnaire and the activities of these actors in the operation of their cities represent the real stuffs of which politics at the rural level of government are made. Indeed, as a political scientist with many years of teaching and writing, I can assert, unequivocally, that my dialogue with these political actors represented one of the finest moments in my career. Very often, many political scientists tend to write in great depth about their "glorious" encounters with national and state leaders. They also situate their political and theoretical analyses on the activities of these great political actors and the institutions that they direct and lead. There is nothing wrong about this intellectual approach. Indeed, these were the actors that we studied at some of the finest universities and colleges in America and elsewhere. But, one important question, out of several remains: are the activities of these national and state actors politically more important than those of rural City/County Council members and mayors? I contend that, in the governance of a society, presidents, prime ministers, governors and their cabinets are not more important than rural lawmakers who collectively provide most citizens with sufficient resources for their daily survival—education, industries, hospitals, roads, security, religious and moral support, and so on. This opinion might seem radical, but it was this political philosophy that informed my study of African American politics in rural America.

The issue, now, is what next in light of this study? As noted earlier, the political "activism" of African Americans in rural America has to be told piece by piece and in community after community in order to inform the future generations on how the political system developed in the society. That politics is the central activity of any community, especially in democratic societies, is a given. And since who gets what, when and how in most polities are determined by political actors, it is imperative for African Americans—particularly the youth to strive to understand how politics works in the society so that they could use their knowledge of it to further their group and community interests.

Appendix A

General Opinion Survey
No. 1

Conducted by: E. Ike Udogu
Date: 7.24.2002
City: Lake City
Position: Lake City Council Member

Demographic Issues
- Mr. Lorith Anderson
- From Lake City
- Part-time position (4 year terms)-serving his first term
- Candidate for Mayor in upcoming term

❖ <u>Father</u> was Mayor of the city of Andrews for 11 yrs./first African American to run for any office in Lake City (school board)/First African American to run for a City Council in Lake City
      ➢ Lost both elections, but was later elected to school board for 2 terms
❖ All lake City elections are nonpartisan
❖ In his election, four people ran for three seats; incumbent was ousted by the newcomer
❖ PLATFORM: "community-minded" and early involvement in politics
      ➢ Major issue: Drug/Alcohol abuse
      ➢ Began a recovery group at his church
          ▪ "All politics to me are local", so the recovery group kept him in touch with issues in the community
          ▪ As a former alcoholic himself, better able to relate and identify with improving this aspect of the community
          ▪ Communication is key/Community involvement, too

Interaction within the County/City government

❖ 6 City Council members + Mayor = 7
❖ 6 African Americans, 1 Caucasian

      ➢ PROBLEMS:
▪ Communication:
- Emphasizes the need for moral, godly men to be in office, which may not be the case
- Emphasizes the need for community minded individuals
- 2 Council Members and the Mayor "go their separate ways" from the other 4 Council Members (Mr. Anderson included)
▪ "Partisan politics:
- "Mayor+2 council members (CMS) go to the same church

> SOLUTIONS:
- Monthly or Quarterly workshop for CMS.
- Focus on defining how city govt. should organize itself: finances, hiring practices, fire/police, public works, etc. Discuss problems and potential projects.

❖ Mr. McAlister, Caucasian Mayor: impartial, god guy
  > No racial tension according to CM Anderson

❖ Strength of the Council is that issues are not voted on according to ideology, but by what is best for the community…even though CMS may have *different* ideologies
❖ Social, civic, etc. Organization Membership:
  > Lake City Coalition on Drug and Alcohol Abuse: Board Chair
  > Florence County Drug and Alcohol Commission
    - Both of the above majority white
    - In his personal experience, race is not a factor: general interest in the community needs overrides questions of race

Constituency

❖ Policies formulated are based on needs or desire to improve legal processes
❖ Major issues
  > Communications/Cellular Tower
  > Infrastructure, i.e. Water/Sewage
  > Fire Coverage/Training Center
  > Housing, Affordability and Repairs.
  > Education
  > City vehicles, Police Department, Garbage Disposal, etc.
  > Recreation
  > Industry
  > Health (esp. black males)
  > Single parent families

❖ Community involvement and interaction:

  > "The black community in rural America react to problems at an *ad hoc* basis
  > Many CMS are not proactive…Mr. Anderson prefers to deal with potential problems by disseminating information to the community before the potential problem becomes a real problem
  > Advice: get a library card and a voter registration certificate.
  > Importance of informed dialogue and communication with community

Government, Race Relations and New Direction

❖ Constituency Breakdown/Demographics:
  > Blue Collar: approximately 70%
    - Blue Collar (African-American): 90%
    - Blue Collar (Caucasian): 50%
  > White Collar: approximately 30%
    - White Collar (African-American): 10%
    - White Collar (Caucasian): 50%

❖ Desire for a Town Hall Meeting so that the community can express and discuss issues directly with the Town Council
❖ Emphasis on teamwork in the Council
❖ Mentoring of new Council Members (CMS)

Transparency of and accountability Council Budget should be improved
Responsibility of CMS to be good stewards

❖ **Race-Relations**:
   ➤ Mr. Anderson graduated from Lake City H.S. in 1971; the first integrated graduating class
   ➤ Race relations are "cordial", but not social; i.e., structured events are integrated without incidents, but little social interaction outside of that
   ➤ His opinion is that there is a race issue, but is not really talked about, and is not seen as a problem
      ▪ Generally a white male feels more comfortable in conversation with black females, but less comfortable with black males
❖ Critical of Affirmative Action, stressing the need for "level playing field", not a "special break"

New Directions
❖ Calls for a "City of character" to "enforce positive traits of our community"
   ➤ Desire to clean up drugs, gambling, prostitution because of detrimental effect on youth
   ➤ Build self-esteem in the youth

Post-civil Rights Era

❖ Lake City had an all-white Council until 8 years ago

❖ Lack of trust in the community towards politicians because of past corruption

❖ Because of the civil rights struggle, the community should demand moral, principled leaders
   ➤ The struggle for good leadership crosses racial lines

❖ Will not compromise ideals because he wants to be elected;   i.e. will not receive outside support from "big wigs" in the community who may demand a lot from him for their support

❖ Talks about the antagonism between "old money" and Progressive ideas
   ➤ Makes a point that his concerns on Southern politics will continue to exist until successful African Americans return to reinvest in the community

Conclusion

❖ Potential political agendas for rural America:
   ➤ Education
   ➤ Health
   ➤ Affordable Housing/Ownership
   ➤ Social programs for youth

- ➤ Employment/Job Development
- ➤ Accountability by elected officials
  - ▪ Strong, moral leadership

General Opinion Survey
No. 2

Conducted by: E. Ike Udogu
Date: 10.16.2003
City: Florence City
Position: Florence City Council Member

Demographic Issues

- o Mr. Edward. Robinson
- o Part-time position (4 years term)
- o Has served for 13 years (didn't plan to serve this long at first)
- o First member of family to hold political office
- o Mid-1970s first African American candidate for office
- o First election Mr. Robinson won 76% of vote in his Ward
- o Democrat, never been any Republican opposition in District 2
- o District 2 is made up 90% African American and overwhelmingly democrat, cites lack of Republican sensitivity to minor issues as a reason
- o In the 70s he taught in a Drivers training School...says he basically taught the youth in the area on how to drive. So, he was well-known

Interaction within the County/City Government

- ❖ 6 City Council members + Mayor = 7
- ❖ 2CMS are African American
  - ➢ PROBLEMS:
    - ▪ Gaining respect for other CMS
    - ▪ Addressing African American issues such as housing (low income) and transportation
  - ➢ SOLUTIONS:
    - ▪ Challenged the power of the Mayor
    - ▪ Marched with supporters in protests against "disparages that the City Council had shown against minority needs and concerns"
    - ▪ Created an environment in which people had to listen

- ❖ Has received much support from the African American community (especially as voters), but has realized that he can't please everyone all of the time
  - ➢ He cites *fear* as a prime factor for any lack of involvement within the African American community: e.g., fear of losing their job, fear of exposure due to involvement in "criminal activities"

- ❖ Pleasures from serving in Council:
  - ➢ Beginning to see results from earlier struggles
  - ➢ Satisfaction of knowing that he is "fighting for freedom"
  - ➢ Victories in financing housing development, higher income jobs for African American

- ❖ Displeasures from serving in Council

> ➢ Trying to convince African American community to become more involved
>   - ▪ "Now that the door is unlocked, all you have to do is twist the knob and push a little bit and you can get in"

- ❖ Present council is very convivial
  - ➢ Gets along well with other African American CMS
  - ➢ Satisfied with relations with white CMS

- ❖ Policy problems with White CMs:
  - ➢ Insensitivity to the needs of African American community
  - ➢ Non-acceptance of Mr. Robinson as a community leader
    - ▪ Tried to ignore and discredit his leadership position

- ❖ Some decisions are made along racial lines
  - ➢ When a project is formulated without direct input of African American interest in the planning process, it holds the entire community back

Activities in Constituency

- ❖ Formulating Policies
  - ➢ Community meetings
  - ➢ Day-to-day interactions
  - ➢ Conferences (to share ideas)

- ❖ Problem convincing constituents of their rights and privileges
  - ➢ Again emphasizes actual interactions with people for guidance

Race-Relations and Government

- ❖ City council is "very much aware that there is a serious racial problem in Florence"
  - ➢ Race-relations committee exists, but has not made much progress
  - ➢ Black community should come together to correct social injustices
  - ➢ Has worked on a black agenda and organizing a mass rally to examine problems and proffer solutions

- ❖ Cites instance of an African American woman in a white neighborhood who is being harassed
  - ➢ He plans on bringing the problem to the Council

- ❖ Makes the point that racial tension hurts the economy
- ❖ Making racial biases public is not a good strategy
  - ➢ Good example: Maurice's BBQ Sauce boycotted by all grocery stores except Piggly Wiggly because Maurice is an advocate of separatism
    - ▪ So community boycotted Piggly Wiggly and won

City Budget

- ❖ City of Florence is well-off financially
  - ➢ It has money on reserve
    - ▪ There is transparency and accountability on budget matters

Post-Civil Rights Era

❖ Believes that African Americans have retrogressed (community has become politically lax)
  ➢ Politics are still top-down
  ➢ Calls for more activism
    ▪ But, "You can't fight a '90s war with '60s weapons"
  ➢ Calls for strong leadership in the black community
  ➢ Calls for general support of citizens

Political Strategies

❖ "I'm a different kind of politician than most"
  ➢ Not concerned about being reelected
  ➢ Focused on doing the will of the people

❖ Emphasized more community involvement by politicians as for example, his interactions with constituents at the local public parks
❖ Passed out voter registration cards and offers chances to win prizes to people who registered
❖ Helped the community understand the "power of politics" and the power of voting
❖ Helped the community understand that even if they can't see immediate results, they are making a difference by being involved

Conclusion

❖ Reemphasized his involvement at the park on Sunday afternoons
  ➢ Politicians need to go where the people are:
    ▪ Park on Sunday (even if the activities are church-related)
    ▪ Nightclubs
    ▪ Public Housing schemes

❖ Noted that white folk tended to respect his position as an elected official more than black folk do

❖ Stressed the bottom-up approach to creating a strong foundation to build on
  ➢ Emphasized the need for grass-roots politics

❖ Set an agenda and set goals
  ➢ Planning and evaluation of programs aimed at improving society are important

❖ Encouraged the need for regularly scheduled meetings to discuss issues in the community

❖ Politicians must put the people first

❖ Exhorted ministers to become involved in political issues because of the powerful influence that they wield in the community

General Opinion Survey
No. 3

Conducted by: E. Ike Udogu
Date: 12.12.02
City: Timmonsville
Position: Mayor

Demographic Issues

- ❖ Reverend Henry Peoples
- ❖ Mayor of the City of Timmonsville
- ❖ Population 2,400
- ❖ 60% African American
- ❖ 70% of pop. registered to vote
- ❖ Of registered voters, 25-30% actually vote
- ❖ Part-time position
- ❖ Salary: $7,300 annually-also works as a pastor
- ❖ 10 years as a mayor, 8 years previously as a City Council Member
- ❖ First black Mayor of Timmonsville elected in 1984, Rev. Peoples is the second (elected in1993)
- ❖ Rev. Peoples ran as a non-partisan
  - o Election in 2000, 4 candidates, Rev. Peoples won 50% (not the needed 51%). In the runoff (against a white opponent), he won 2 to 1.
  - ➢ STRATEGIES?
    - o "Sticking with the issues that concern the people"

Interaction within the City Government

- ➢ 6 City Council members + Mayor = 7
- ➢ 5 CMS and the mayor are African Americans
  - ▪ # of Whites/Blacks fluctuates on city council from one election to another

- ➢ POLITICAL PROBLEMS
  - ▪ Lack of adequate Housing
  - ▪ Lack of recreational facilities
  - ▪ Inadequate Police protection

- ➢ Deals with problems from the perspective of the needs of the community

  - ▪ Tries to be fair in dealing with issues of both the white and black communities
  - ▪ Even though the black community has been left behind in many ways, Rev. Peoples does not feel that it is right to take advantage of others (white minority) in order to right those wrongs

- ❖ Constituency Breakdown
  - ➢ More Blue Collar African Americans than White Collar

- When the lower class (Blue Collar) became more involved politically, the upper class (White Collar) took flight our of the city
- The increased awareness and involvement by Blue Collar in the political system was good, but lack of experience and knowledge about how system worked was a problem
  - ➢ The first African American Mayor resigned after two years
    - Believed that the reasons for his resignation was weight of the job and because not enough African American citizens understood how the government worked

- ❖ Pleasures from serving on Council:
  - ➢ Making a difference for his people
  - ➢ Success in his goal of creating jobs, creating a better law, enforcement team, and in bettering race relations

- ❖ **Displeasures**:
  - ➢ To see the lack of knowledge about how municipal government is run
    - Wanted to address the problem
  - ➢ Criticism arising from the lack of understanding of what you are trying to accomplish
  - ➢ Some people either because of envy or disagreements on certain issues have tried to discredit him

- ❖ Rev. Peoples has had differences with all CMS, but some have been more antagonistic than others
  - ➢ Good rapport with white CM now, but at first he was a political opponent
  - ➢ Council in general got along very well

- ❖ During Rev. Peoples' first term, a bi-racial Ministerial Alliance was created (of which he was a member) in the community, but the white members eventually drifted away. Now all members are African American.

Constituency
- ❖ Issues are brought to the attention of the Council by individuals. This might be problems or request for assistance

- ❖ There is also a committee that meets and formulates a Strategic Plan
  - ➢ The committee consists of CMS, general members of the community, members of business community, and members of the school district
  - ➢ Information is gathered from different sources in the community with which decisions and policies are made

- ❖ Stated that citizens are not well-informed on the issues
  - ➢ This is the major problem he faces
- ❖ Disagreed with the notion that political issues should not be discussed in churches
  - ➢ Noted that churches and other social organizations could be valuable spaces for discussing political issues
  - ➢ "If we are going to be effective leaders as ministers, we must be concerned about everything that concerns individuals".
  - ➢ "Jesus was concerned about the total person, and that's what we must be about."

- But, the Ministerial Alliance kept themselves away from the political arena

❖ Policy Formulation:
  ➤ Issues are discussed in Council and then voted upon
  ➤ Also, the mayor, other CMS, and a consultant hired for research and grant-writing can all make recommendations that the Council then votes upon

Race-Relations and Government
❖ Problems exist
  ➤ Council needed to recognize and accept that there is a problem
  ➤ Must be up-front and fair when confronting racial issues
  ➤ Must find ways to show that racism is destructive to the community, both Blacks and Whites

❖ Even though the community has a majority African American population, the white minority group controlled the economy
  ➤ Blacks are intimidated not to speak out or vote
  ➤ People, often African Americans, were actually paid by their employers not to go to the polls

City Budget
❖ City Council votes on annual budget
  ➤ All CMS are encouraged to attend a Budget Workshop
  ➤ Discretionary allowances exist for unforeseen expenses

Post-Civil Rights Era

❖ In some areas African American have made significant progress, but in some areas they have not

❖ He was proud of the progress in Timmonsville, especially in the areas of employment and community involvement
  ➤ Reemphasized the problem of lack of knowledge and understanding of how the political system worked in the City Council
    - Stated that some people are "hoodwinked" into believing that Whites are somehow better than Blacks
    - Noted that citizens must address the concerns and need to improve race-relations in the community

Conclusion

❖ Expressed hope that this study can be used as a tool for people in similar leadership positions as himself

❖ Emphasized that people should be in public office to make a difference and not for the prestige that flows from the position.

Sample Questionnaire∗

Demographic Issues
Name...
Age: 24-25 .... 36-45 .... 46-55 .... Over 55 ....
Occupation: Educator...Self-employed...Business (Other than self-employed)
What district/area do you represent?
What is the approximate population of your ward/city?
African American population...%...White population...%...
What is the percentage of eligible voters in your district?
Generally, what is the percentage of registered voters that actually vote?
What is the salary or pay for serving on the Council?
$5,000-10,000; $10,001-15,000; $15,001-20,000; Over $20,000
Is your legislative function on the city council a part time job?
How long have you served in city government?
Has any member of your family (before) you held a political office in the community?
When was the first time you had an African American represent your district?
Did you run for office along party line?
Who were your political opponents?
What political strategy or political strategies did you employ to win your seat in office?
Has your district or ward been always represented by an African American?

Interaction with the City Government
What is the number of council members on the city council?
How many African Americans serve on the city council?
What are some of the political problems that you have encountered as a member of the Council?
What did you do to overcome these difficulties?
How do you deal with black and white members of the Council to promote the interest of your district?
What is the approximate percentage of "blue collar" workers in your district?
What is the approximate percentage of "white collar" workers in your district?
What pleasures have you had from serving on the Council?
What displeasures have you had from serving on the Council?
How well do you get along with African American members on the Council regarding issues that affect your district?
How well do you get along with white members on the Council regarding issues that affect your district?
How well do you get along with white members on the Council on issues affecting the larger community?
What are the major problems that you have had with African American members of the Council?
What are the major problems that you have had with white members on the Council?
What are the minor problems that your have had with African American members on the Council?
Are the formulation and implementation of policies by members of the City Council government done along racial lines and interests?

Do you belong to any social, civic, religious and other non-governmental organizations with white members on the Council?

Constituency

How do you formulate policies that represent the interest of your district?

What are the major issues confronting your district?

How are these issues brought to your attention?

How do you bring major issues concerning and confronting your district in the city council to the attention of your constituents?

How well informed are citizens in your district on political issues affecting the interest of the community?

Race-Relations and Government

How well has the City Council dealt with race-relations in the community?

What is your opinion on what City Council should do to improve race-relations in the community?

What is the city budget for this fiscal year?

How is the city budget allocated to the various wards or districts in the city?

Are you satisfied with the current budget allocation formula?

Do you want to see the current budget allocation formula changed?

What could the city council do to promote (more) development in the predominantly African American ward or district?

Post-Civil Rights Era

How would you characterize the progress that African Americans have made since the 1960s in city politics?

What direction should the city move in order to address the needs of African Americans in the 21st century?

Do you foresee a time when one's race, ethnicity and gender would not matter politically in the city and America?

Conclusion

What issues should political actors in the politics of rural America address in order to confront the social, economic and political problems of a majority of African Americans in hopes of promoting the concept of the "melting pot" in America?

Are there issues regarding this study that you might like to comment on?

Thank you very much.

*This is not a scientific survey. The councilmen and mayor interviewed for this study had the option of either answering a question or ignoring it. In other words, there was no effort made to insist that they answer all of the questions. The outcomes of the tape-recorded interviews are briefly summarized in the general opinion surveys 1-3 and theoretically and contextually analyzed in the text itself.

Appendix B

Florence County Council Members
With Dates

Year: **2004**

Rev. Terry Alexander, Chairman
Thomas E. Smith, Jr., Vice Chairman
Mitchell Kirby, Secretary
Rev. Waymon Mumford, Chaplain
K.B. 'Rusty' Smith
Russell W. Culberson
John E. Floyd, Jr.
Johnnie D. Rodgers, Jr.
Jennie F. O'Bryan

Year: **2003**

John E. Floyd, Chairman
Rev. Waymon Mumford,, Vice Chair
Mitchell Kirby, Secretary/Chaplain
Rev. Terry Alexander
K.B. 'Rusty' Smith
Russell W. Culberson
Johnnie D. Rodgers, Jr.
Jennie F. O'Bryan
Thomas E. Smith, Jr.

Year: **2002**

Rev. Terry Alexander, Chairman
Herbert Ames, Vice Chairman
Mitchell Kirby, Secretary/Chaplain
Thomas E. Smith, Jr.
Rev. Waymon Mumford
K.B. 'Rusty' Smith
Russell W. Culberson
John E. Floyd, Jr.
Johnnie D. Rodgers, Jr.

Year: **2001**

Thomas E. Smith, Jr. Chairman
Herbert Ames, Vice Chairman
Mitchell Kirby, Secretary/Chaplain
K.B. 'Rusty' Smith

Rev. Terry Alexander
Rev. Waymon Mumford
Russell W. Culberson
John E. Floyd, Jr.

Year: **2000**

Thomas E. Smith, Jr. Chairman
Herbert Ames, Vice Chairman
Mitchell Kirby, Secretary/Chaplain
J.L. Dinky Miles
K.B. 'Rusty' Smith
Terry Alexander
Waymon Mumford
Russell W. Culberson
John E. Floyd, Jr.

Year **1999**

Thomas E. Smith, Jr. Chairman
Herbert Ames, Vice Chairman
Mitchell Kirby, Secretary/Chaplain
J.L. Dinky Miles
K.B. 'Rusty' Smith
Terry Alexander
Waymon Mumford
Russell W. Culberson
John E. Floyd, Jr.

Year **1998**

K.B. 'Rusty' Smith, Jr., Chairman
Waymon Mumford, Vice Chairman
Mitchell Kirby, Secretary/Chaplain
J.L. Dinky Miles
Russell W. Culberson
Herbert F. Ames
Tom Smith
Terry Alexander

Year **1997**

Herbert F. Ames, Chairman
J.L. Dinky Miles, Vice Chairman
Waymon Mumford, Sec./Chairman
K.G. 'Rusty' Smith
Joe W. King
Terry Alexander
Russell W. Culberson
Mitchell Kirby
John A. Hyman

Year: **1996**

Herbert F. Ames, Chairman
J.L. Dinky Miles, Vice Chairman
John A. Hyman, Secretary /Chaplain
K.G. 'Rusty' Smith
Joe W. King
Terry Alexander
Russell W. Culberson
Mitchell Kirby
Waymon Mumford

Year: **1995**

K.G. 'Rusty' Smith, Chairman
Joe W. King, Vice Chairman
John A. Hyman, Secretary /Chaplain
J.L. Dinky Miles
Terry Alexander
Russell W. Culberson
Mitchell Kirby
Waymon Mumford
Herbert F. Ames

Year 1994
K.G. 'Rusty' Smith, Chairman
Terry Alexander, Vice Chairman
J.L. Dinky Miles, Secretary/Chaplain
Grady L. Greer
Mitchell Kirby
Ralph Hunt
Russell W. Culberson

Year: **1993**

Grady L. Greer, Chairman
Terry Alexander, Vice Chairman
Jerry M. Kerry, Secretary/Chaplain
James R. Harwell

J.L. Dinky Miles
K.G. 'Rusty' Smith
Joseph W. King
Ralph Hunt
Mitchell Kirby

Year: **1992**

Grady L. Greer, Chairman
Terry Alexander, Vice Chairman
Jerry M. Kerry, Secretary/Chaplain
James R. Harwell
J.L. Dinky Miles
K.G. 'Rusty' Smith
Joseph W. King
Ralph Hunt
Mitchell Kirby

Year: **1991**

Joseph W. King, Chairman
J. Ted Vause, Jr., Vice Chairman
Jerry M. Keith, Secretary/Chaplain
James R. Harwell
J.L. Dinky Miles
Shirley T. Corbett
Grady L. Greer
Terry Alexander

Year: **1990**

J.L. Dinky Miles, Chairman
J. Ted Vause, Jr., Vice-Chairman
Vandroth Backus, Secretary/Chaplain
Jerry M. Keith
James R. Harwell
Shirley T. Corbett
John J. Powers
K.G. 'Rusty' Smith, Jr.
Joseph W. King

Year: **1989**

James R. Harwell, Chairman
J. Ted Vause, Jr., Vice-Chairman
Vandroth Backus, Secretary/Chaplain
Jerry M. Keith
Shirley T. Corbett
John J. Powers
J.L. Dinky Miles
K.G. 'Rusty' Smith, Jr.

Year: **1988**

R. L. Poston, Chairman
J. Ted Vause, Jr., Vice Chairman
Vandroth Backus, Secretary/Chaplain
Jerry M. Keith
Shirley T. Corbett
John J. Powers
James R. Harwell
J.L. Dinky Miles
K.G. 'Rusty' Smith, Jr.

Year: **1987**

R. L. Poston, Chairman
J. Ted Vause, Jr., Vice Chairman
Vandroth Backus, Secretary/Chaplain
Jerry M. Keith
Shirley T. Corbett
John J. Powers
James R. Harwell
J.L. Dinky Miles
K.G. 'Rusty' Smith, Jr.

Year: **1986**

R. L. Poston, Chairman
J. Ted Vause, Jr., Vice Chairman
Vandroth Backus, Secretary/Chaplain
Jerry M. Keith
John J. Powers
James R. Harwell
L. O. Lamb
Shirley T. Corbett
J.L. Dinky Miles

Year: **1985**

Jerry M. Keith, Chairman
L. O. Lamb, Vice Chairman
Vandroth Backus, Secretary/Chaplain
R. L. Poston
J. Ted Vause, Jr.
James R. Harwell
Shirley T. Corbett
J.L. Dinky Miles

Year: **1984**

Herbert G. Ham, Chairman
L. O. Lamb, Vice Chairman
Jerry M. Keith, Secretary/Chaplain
R.L. Poson
J. Ted Vause, Jr.
James R. Harwell
John J. Powers
A. C. Allen
Vandroth Backus

Year: **1983**

Herbert G. Ames, Chairman
L. O. Lamb, Vice Chairman
Jerry M. Keith, Secretary/Chaplain
R.L. Poson
J. Ted Vause, Jr.
James R. Harwell
John J. Powers
A. C. Allen
Vandroth Backus

Year: **1982**

John J. Powers, Chairman
R. L. Poston, Vice Chairman
Jerry M. Keith, Secretary/Chaplain
A. C. Allen
James R. Harwell
J. Ted Vause
Herbert G. Ham
L. O. Lamb

Year: **1981**

John J. Powers, Jr., Chairman
R.L. Poston, Vice Chairman
Jerry M. Keith, Secretary/Chaplain
Jim Harwell
J. Ted Vause
Herbert G. Ham
L. O. Lamb
A.C. Allen

Year: **1980**

Robert H. Rhodes, Chairman
John J. Powers, Jr., Vice-Chairman
Jerry M. Keith, Secretary/Chaplain
Jim Harwell
J. Ted Vause, Jr.
L. O. Lamb
F. M. Lynch, III-R.L. Poston
Wylie H. Caldwell, Jr.

Year: **1979**

R.L. Poston, Chairman
Robert H. Rhodes, Vice-Chairman
Jerry M. Keith, Secretary/Chaplain
Wylie H. Caldwell, Jr.
Jim Harwell
L. O. Lamb
J. Ted Vause, Jr.
John J. Powers, Jr

Year: **1978**

R.L. Poston, Chairman
Wylie H. Caldwell, Jr, Vice Chairman
Jerry M. Keith, Secretary/Chaplain
F. M. Lynch, III
Robert H. Rhodes
Jim Harwell

Year: **1977**

R.L. Poston, Chairman
Wylie H. Caldwell, Jr, Vice Chairman
Jerry M. Keith, Secretary/Chaplain
D. M. Bath
F. M. Lynch, III
Robert H. Rhodes
Cale Yarborough
K.G. Smith
Jim Harwell

Year: **1976**

D. M. Bath, Chairman
R.L. Poston, Vice-Chairman
Jerry M. Keith, Secretary/Chaplain
Joe L. Griffin
K.G. Smith
Jim Harwell

Cale Yarborough
F. M. Lynch, III-died 1/6/76
G.B. Stokes, Jr.

Year: **1975**

G.B. "Bo" Stokes, Jr., Chairman
Joe L. Griffin, Vice-Chairman
R.L. Poston, Secretary/Chaplain
D. M. Bath
Jerry M. Keith
Cale Yarborough
Jim Harwell
F. M. Lynch, III
K.G. Smith

Year: **1974**

G.B. "Bo" Stokes, Jr., Chairman
J.B. McCutcheon, Vice-Chairman
R.L. Poston, Secretary/Chaplain
Joe L. Griffin, Vice-Secretary
F. M. Lynch, III
D. M. Bath
Cale Yarborough
Jerry M. Keith

Year: **1973**

D. M. Bath, Chairman
J.B. McCutcheon, Vice-Chairman
R.L. Poston, Secretary/Chaplain
Herbert T. Floyd
F.M. Lynch, Jr.
Cale Yarborough
G.B. "Bo" Stokes
Jerry M. Keith
Joe L. Griffin

Year: **1972**

D.M. Bath, Chairman
J.B. McCutcheon, Vice-Chairman
R.L. Poston
Jerry M. Keith
Ed. T. Fountain
F.M. Lynch, Jr.
Joe L. Griffin
G.B. Stokes
Herbert T. Floyd

Year: **1971**

F.H. Schipman, Chairman
R.L. Poston, Secretary
J.B. McCutcheon
D.M. Bath
G.B. Stokes
F.M. Lynch, Jr.
Ed. T. Fountain
Joe L. Griffin
Herbert T. Floyd

Year: **1970**

J.B. McCutcheon, Chairman
F.M. Lynch, Jr., Secretary
F.H. Schipman
D.M. Bath
G.B. Stokes
Joe L. Griffin
R.L. Poston
Herbert T. Floyd
Ed. T. Fountain

Year: **1969**

J.B. McCutcheon, Chairman
F.M. Lynch, Jr., Secretary
F.H. Shipman
D.M. Bath
G.B. Stokes
R.L. Poston
Ed. T. Fountain
Joe L. Griffin

Year: **1968**

J.B. McCutcheon, Chairman
F.M. Lynch, Jr., Secretary
F.H. Schipman
D.M. Bath
Joe L. Griffin
R.L. Poston
Herbert T. Floyd
Ed. T. Fountain

Year 1967

J.B. McCutcheon, Chairman
F.M. Lynch, Jr., Secretary
D.M. Bath

Herbert T. Floyd
F.H. Schipman
R.L. Poston
M.W. Poston
Ed. T. Fountain
R. L. O'Harra

Year: **1966**

J.B. McCutcheon, Chairman
F.M. Lynch, Jr., Secretary
F.H. Schipman
Herbert T. Floyd
Ed. T. Fountain
D.M. Bath
R.L. O'Harra
R.L. Poston
M.W. Poston

Governing Commission Members

Year: **1965**

J.B. McCutcheon, Chairman
F.M. Lynch, Jr., Secretary
F.H. Schipman
Ed. T. Fountain
M.W. Poston

Year: **1964**

J.B. McCutcheon, Chairman
F.M. Lynch, Jr., Secretary
Ed. T. Fountain
Willis G. Hyman
M.W. Poston
F.H. Schipman

Year: **1963**

J.B. McCutcheon, Chairman
F.M. Lynch, Jr., Secretary
Ed. T. Fountain
Willis G. Hyman
Herbert T. Floyd
M.W. Poston

Year: **1962**

F.H. Schipman, Chairman
F.M. Lynch, Jr., Secretary
J.B. McCutcheon
Herbert T. Floyd
Ed. T. Fountain
W.H. Meng
Willis G. Hyman

Year: **1961**

J.B. McCutcheon, Chairman
F.M. Lynch, Jr., Secretary
F.H. Schipman
Herbert T. Floyd
Ed. T. Fountain
Willis G. Hyman

Year: **1960**

J.B. McCutcheon, Chairman
F.M. Lynch, Jr., Secretary
F.H. Schipman
Willis G. Hyman
Herbert T. Floyd
Ed. T. Fountain
W.H. Meng

Year: **1959**

J.B. McCutcheon, Chairman
F.M. Lynch, Jr., Secretary
F.H. Schipman
W.H. Meng
Ed. T. Fountain
Willis G. Hyman
Herbert T. Floyd

Year: **1958**

F.H. Schipman, Chairman
F.M. Lynch, Jr., Secretary
J.B. McCutcheon
Euford Godwin
Herbert T. Floyd
Ed. T. Fountain
W.H. Meng

Year: **1957**

J.B. McCutcheon, Chairman
F.M. Lynch, Jr., Secretary
K.R. Ward
Freddie Schipman
Bert Calcutt
J.E. Godwin
W.H. Meng

Year: **1956**

J.B. McCutcheon, Chairman
F.M. Lynch, Jr., Secretary
W.H. Meng
Freddie Schipman
K.R. Ward
J.E. Godwin
Bert Calcutt

Year: **1955**

Freddie Schipman, Chairman
W.H. Meng, Secretary
K.R. Ward
J.E. Godwin
Bert Calcutt
J.B. McCutcheon
F.M. Lynch

Year: **1954**

Freddie Schipman, Chairman
W.H. Meng, Secretary
K.R. Ward
Bert Calcutt
A.W. Brown
P.B. Mixon
C. Epps McCutcheon

Year: **1953**

Freddie Schipman, Chairman
W.H. Meng, Secretary
Bert Calcutt
A.W. Brown
K.R. Ward
P.B. Mixon
J.B.McCutcheon

Year: **1952**

Freddie Schipman, Chairman
C. Epps McCutcheon, Secretary
(Died 6/8/52)
W.H. Meng
Bert Calcutt
A.W. Brown
K.R. Ward
P.B. Mixon

Year: **1951**

Freddie Schipman, Chairman
C. Epps McCutcheon, Secretary
W.H. Meng
Bert Calcutt
A.W. Brown
K.R. Ward
P.B. Mixon

Year: **1950**

Freddie Schipman, Chairman
C. Epps McCutcheon, Secretary
W.H. Meng
Bert Calcutt
A.W. Brown
K.R. Ward
P. B. Mixon

Year: **1949**

Freddie Schipman, Chairman
C. Epps McCutcheon, Secretary
W.H. Meng
Bert Calcutt
A.W. Brown
K.R. Ward
P.B. Mixon

Year: **1948**

A.W. Brown, Chairman
C. Epps McCutcheon, Secretary
Bert Calcutt
Freddie Schipman
K.R. Ward
W.H. Meng
P.B. Mixon

Year: **1947**

H.M. Thomas, Chairman
C. Epps McCutcheon, Secretary
A.W. Brown
Bert Calcutt
K.R. Ward
W.H. Meng
P.B. Mixon

Year: **1946**

H.M. Thomas, Chairman
C. Epps McCutcheon, Secretary
A.W. Brown
S.B. Davis
K.R. Ward
W.H. Meng
P.B. Mixon

Year: **1945**

H.M. Thomas, Chairman
C. Epps McCutcheon, Secretary
A.W. Brown
S.B. Davis
K.R. Ward
W.H. Meng
P.B. Mixon

Year: **1944**

H.M. Thomas, Chairman
C. Epps McCutcheon, Secretary
A.W. Brown
S.B. Davis
K.R. Ward
W.H. Meng
P.B. Mixon

Year: **1943**

H.M. Thomas, Chairman
C. Epps McCutcheon, Secretary
A.W. Brown
S.B. Davis
K.R. Ward
W.H. Meng
P.B. Mixon

Year: **1942**

P.C. Brown, Chairman
T.M. Gregg, Secretary
A.W. Brown
K.R. Ward
C.A. Waters
C. Epps McCutcheon, Secretary

Year: **1941**

P.C. Brown, Chairman
C. Epps McCutcheon, Secretary
T.M. Gregg
R. Kemper Ward
A.W. Brown
Cyril A. Waters

Year: **1940**

P.C. Brown, Chairman
C. Epps McCutcheon, Secretary
T.M. Gregg
R. Kemper Ward
A.W. Brown
Cyril A. Waters

Year: **1939**

P.C. Brown, Chairman
C. Epps McCutcheon, Secretary
T.M. Gregg (Died 2/18/39)
R. Kemper Ward
A.W. Brown
Cyril A. Waters

Year: **1938**

J.A. Carter, Chairman
Cyril A. Waters, Secretary
P.C. Brown
A.W. Brown
J.C. Lee
T.M. Gregg

Year: **1937**

J.A. Carter, Chairman
Cyril A. Waters, Secretary
P.C. Brown
A.W. Brown
J.C. Lee
T.M. Gregg

Year: **1936**

J.A. Carter, Chairman
Cyril A. Waters, Secretary
P.C. Brown
A.W. Brown
J.C. Lee
T.M. Gregg
Year: **1935**

J.A. Carter, Chairman
Cyril A. Waters, Secretary
P.C. Brown
A.W. Brown
J.C. Lee
T.M. Gregg

Year: **1934**

J.A. Carter, Chairman
Cyril A. Waters, Secretary
P.C. Brown
A.W. Brown
J.C. Lee
T.M. Gregg

Year: **1933**

J.A. Carter, Chairman
Cyril A. Waters, Secretary
P.C. Brown
A.W. Brown
J.C. Lee
T.M. Gregg

Year: **1932**

J.F. Robertson, Chairman
T.R. Miller, Secretary
P.C. Brown
J.A. Carter
W.W. Purvis
R.S. Wilson

Year: **1931**

J.F. Robertson, Chairman
T.R. Miller, Secretary
P.C. Brown
J.A. Carter
W.W. Purvis
R.S. Wilson

Year **1930**

J.F. Robertson, Chairman
T.H. Harllee, Secretary
A.W. Rodgers
R.S. Wilson
B.F. Turner

Year: **1929**

J.F. Robertson, Chairman
T.H. Harllee, Secretary
A.W. Rodgers
R.S. Wilson

Year: **1928**

J.F. Robertson, Chairman
T.H. Harllee, Secretary
A.W. Rodgers
Caswell Rhinehart
B.F. Turner
W.W. Purvis

Year: **1927**

J.F. Robertson, Chairman
T.H. Harllee, Secretary
A.W. Rodgers
Caswell Rhinehart
B.F. Turner
W.W. Purvis

Year: **1926**

C.G. Brown, Chairman
W.J. Revell, Secretary
S.R. Floyd
B.F. Turner
W.W. Purvis
M.B. Huggins

Year: **1925**

E.M Matthews, Chairman
G.R. Gaskins, Secretary
S.R. Floyd
B.F. Turner
W.L. Copeland

Year: **1924**

E.D. Sallenger, Chairman
E.M. Matthews, Secretary
W.L. Copeland
S.R. Floyd
G.R. Gaskins
B.F. Turner

Appendix C
City of Florence Mayors and Council Members 1879-2004

April 21, 1879
Mayor: W.J. Norris
Wardens: McMillian;* Wilson; *Day;*Kuker.* (*no first name listed)

April 14, 1880
Mayor: W.A. Brunson
Wardens: J.P. Gayle; J.E. Wilson; C. Phillips; G.F. Buchheit.

April 11, 1881
Mayor: W.A. Brunson
Wardens: J.E. Schouboe; Cronenburg*; J.E. Wilson; G.F. Buchheit.

April 10, 1883
Mayor: W.H. Day
Wardens: J.E. Wilson; L.S. Phillips; W.J. Norris; S. Sternberger; G.F. Buchheit

April 14, 1884
Mayor: W.H. Day
Wardens: A.A. Cohen; John Kuker; E. Crawford; J.E. Wilson.

April 16, 1885
Mayor: W.H. Day
Wardens:_   John Kuker; A.A. Cohen; W.A. Brunson; E.W. Lloyd;
                J.E. Schouboe; G.F. Buchheit.

January 5, 1900
Mayor: W.H. Malloy
Aldermen: J.J. Brown; J.F. Stackley; E.J. Pendergrass; B. Rutledge; W.J. Brown;
                T.N. Jones; E.M. Matthews; J.B. Douglas.

May 13, 1901
Mayor: W.H. Malloy
Aldermen: T.N. Timmerman; J.J. Brown; E.M. Matthews; E.J. Pendergrass;
                B. Rutledge; W.J. Brown; J.L. Jacobi; H.K. Gilbert.

January 23, 1902
Mayor: W.H. Malloy
Aldermen: J.J. Brown; H.K. Gilbert; E.M. Matthews; J.B. Douglas;
                E.J. Pendergrass; B. Rutledge; W.J. Brown. Election
                held February, 10, 1902 to fill unexpired term of T.N. Timmerman.
                W.H. Waters was elected to fill this vacancy.

May 7, 1903
Mayor: W.H. Malloy
Aldermen: J.J. Brown; J.E. Edwards; W.M. Waters; A.L. Sessoms;
                E.J. Pendergrass; J.B. Douglas; B. Rutledge; W.J. Brown.

October 15, 1903: Walter H. Wells elected to City Council.
November 15, 1904: E.H. Tomlinson is elected as an Alderman till May 4, 1905.
December 5, 1904: W.H. Malloy resigns. W.J. Brown elected Mayor.
January 30, 1905: R.B. Hare and J.P. McNeill were elected as Aldermen.

May 4, 1905
Mayor: W.J. Brown
Aldermen: J.E. Edward; F. Koopman; A.L. Sessoms;R.C. Commander;
                    R.B. Hare; J.B. Douglas; B. Rutledge; J.P. McNeill.
May 13, 1907
Mayor: H.K. Gilbert
Aldermen: A.A. Cohen; T.J. Smith; A.L. Sessoms; J.C. McClenaghan;
                    R.B. Hare; T.B. Haynesworth; E.J. Pendergrass; L.C. Jones.
March 3, 1908: Alderman C.L. Johnson elected; serves till May 13, 1909.

May 13, 1909
Mayor: H.K. Gilbert
Aldermen: A.A. Cohen; J.W. Ivey; J.C. McClenaghan; A.L. Sessoms ;
                    A.C. Ellerbe; R.B. Hare; E.J. Pendergrass; B.A. Early, Jr.
                    Mr. A.C. Ellerbe resigned December 1909.
                    L.B. Gregory elected December 21, 1909.
May 4, 1911
Mayor: H.K. Gilbert
Aldermen: A.A. Cohen; C.E. Houston; J.C. Mc Clenaghan; W.H. Berry;
                    C.F. Gilchrist; E.J. Pendergrass; D.G. Baker.
May 13, 1913
Mayor: Wm. R. Barringer
Commissioners: C.E. Commander; T.P. Spenser; S.I. Sulzbacher (resigned 10-1-14)
                    Newton Johnston appointed 10- 9, 1914.

May 9, 1914:
Mayor: W.R. Barringer
Councilmen: Frank H. Barnwell; B.S. Meeks
                    J.F. Stackley; E.J. Smith

May 9, 1923
Mayor: W.M. Waters
Councilmen: Frank H. Barnwell; J. C. Kendall; B.S. Meeks; S. I. Sulzbacher.
City Manager: C.G. Brown (appointed 6-4-1923; resigned 5-9-1924)
                    T.W. Sparrow (appointed 5-24-1924).

May 9, 1925 to May 5, 1927:
Mayor: Herbert K. Gilbert
Councilmen: R.F. Zeigler; R.C. King; F.K. Rhodes; R.L. Reed.
City Manager: D.L. Husbands (appointed April 22, 1926)

May 3, 1927:
Mayor: Herbert K. Gilbert
Councilmen: R.C. King; B.W. Covington; F.K. Rhodes; F.H. Barnwell.

May 9, 1927 to April 25, 1929:
Mayor: Herbert K. Gilbert
Councilmen: F.H. Barnwell; B.W. Covington; R.C. King; F.K. Rhodes.
City Manager: D.L. Husbands

May 9, 1929 to April 15, 1931:
Mayor: Herbert K. Gilbert
Councilmen: F.H. Barnwell; R.C. King; B.W. Covington; R.F. Zeigler.
City Manager: D.L. Husbands

April 30 1931 to April 14, 1932:
Mayor: H. K. Gilbert
Councilmen: R.C. King; R.F. Zeigler; F.H. Barnwell; Harry E. Thomas.
City Manager: D.L. Husbands

May 12, 1932 to April 25, 1935:
Mayor: H. K. Gilbert
Councilmen: R.C. King; F.H. Barnwell; Harry E. Thomas; R.F. Zeigler.
City Manager: D.L. Husbands

May 9, 1933:
Mayor: Herbert K. Gilbert
Councilmen: R.C. King; Harry E. Thomas; F.K. Rhodes; D.E. Ellerbe.
City Manager: D.L. Husbands; David G. Adams appointed May 25, 1933.

May 10, 1935 to April 25, 1940:
Mayor: D.E. Ellerbe
Councilmen: T.R. Miller; D.J. Ratley; R.L. Reed; F.K. Rhodes.
City Manager: D.G. Adams

May 10, 1937:
Councilman: James R. Schipman, Sr.

May 10, 1939:
Mayor: D.E. Ellerbe
Councilmen: T.R. Miller; Thomas E. Wolfe; R.F. Zeigler; R.L. Reed.
City Manager: David G. Adams

May 7, 1940 to March 31, 1942:
Mayor: D.E. Ellerbe
Councilmen: T.R. Miller; R.L. Reed; Thomas E. Wolfe; R.F. Zeigler.
City Manager: David G. Adams

May 10, 1941:
Mayor: D.E. Ellerbe (resigned January 31, 1942)
Councilmen: T.R. Miller; R.F. Zeigler ; W.L. Collins; Tomas E. Wolfe.
City Manager: David G. Adams

April 6, 1942 to April 26, 1945:
Mayor: R.F. Zeigler
Councilmen: T.R. Miller; Thomas E. Wolfe; W.L. Collins.
City Manager: David G. Adams

April 30, 1942:
Mayor:　　　　　J. R. Schipman
Councilmen:　　W.L. Collins; T.R. Miller; Thomas E. Wolfe; R.F. Zeigler.
City Manager:　David G. Adams

May 10, 1943:
Mayor:　　　　　R.F. Zeigler
Councilmen:　　H.M. Gilbert; Harry Stokes; Thomas E. Wolfe; W.L. Collins.
City Manager:　David G. Adams

May 10, 1945 to April 25, 1947:
Mayor:　　　　　R.F. Zeigler
Councilmen:　　H.M. Gilbert; J.R. Schipman; Harry Stokes; Walter D. Tyler.
City Manager:　David G. Adams

May 8, 1947 to February 8, 1950:
Mayor:　　　　　H. M. Thomas
Councilmen:　　V.C. Cox; James Maxwell; James T. Rice; James R. Schipman.
City Manager:　E.L. Blackwell (elected November 20, 1946)

May 10, 1949:
Mayor:　　　　　Haskell M. Thomas
Councilmen:　　James R. Schipman; V.C. Burrell; James Maxwell; C.D. Cox.
City Manager:　E.L. Blackwell

March 30, 1950 to December 21, 1950:
Mayor:　　　　　Haskell M. Thomas
Councilmen:　　James R. Schipman (resigned 3-22-51; effective 5-10-5);
　　　　　　　　　V.C. Burrell; James Maxwell; C.D. Cox.
City Manager:　D.C. Barbot (elected October 13, 1949)

May 10, 1951:
Mayor:　　　　　James R. Schipman
Councilmen:　　V.C. Burrell; Henry F. Dragan, Jr.; Julian West; E.E. Stone.
City Manager:　D.C. Barbot

January 7, 1952-December 30, 1952:
Mayor:　　　　　James R. Schipman
Councilmen:　　V.C. Burrell; Henry F. Dragan, Jr.; Julian Weston; E.E. Stone.
City Manager:　D.C. Barbot

January 19, 1953 to December 21, 1953:
Mayor:　　　　　James R. Schipman
Councilmen:　　Henry F. Dragan, Jr.; Julian Weston; E.E. Stone; V.C. Burrell.
City Manager:　D.C. Barbot

May 11, 1953:
Mayor:　　　　　James R. Schipman
Councilmen:　　Mrs. Maye Stevenson; David H. McLeod; H. F. Dragan, Jr.; E. E. Stone.
City Manager:　D.C. Barbot

May 10, 1955:
Mayor: David H. McLeod
Councilmen: Mrs. Maye Stevenson; Maitland S. Chase, Jr.; Louis O. Yarbororough;
                     B.B. Gilbert (elected 5-24-55 to complete McLeod's term).
City Manager: D.C. Barbot

January 4, 1956 to December 17, 1956:
Mayor: David H. McLeod
Councilmen: Louis O. Yarbororough; Mrs. Maye Stevenson; Maitland S. Chase, Jr.;
                     B.B. Gilbert.
City Manager: D.C. Barbot (dismissed 5-28-56). Howard McCall appointed.

May 10, 1956:
Mayor: David H. McLeod
Councilmen: James R. Schipman; R. Weston Patterson; Louis O. Yarbororough;
                     Maitland S. Chase, Jr.
City Manager: Aaron Marsh (appointed 12-17-56).

January 16, 1957 to December 27, 1957:
Mayor: David H. McLeod
Councilmen: B.B. Gilbert; Mrs. Maye Stevenson; Maitland S. Chase, Jr.;
                     Louis O. Yarbororough.
City Manager: Aaron Marsh

January 17, 1958 to December 19, 1958:
Mayor: David H. McLeod
Councilmen: Maitland S. Chase, Jr.; James R. Schipman; R. Weston Patterson;
                     Louis O. Yarbororough.
City Manager: Aaron Marsh

January 6, 1959 to December 21, 1959:
Mayor: David H. McLeod
Councilmen: Louis O. Yarbororough; James R. Schipman;
                     R. Weston Patterson; Maitland S. Chase, Jr.
City Manager: Aaron Marsh

January 5, 1960 to December 19, 1960:
Mayor: David H. McLeod
Councilmen: R. Weston Patterson; Louis O. Yarbororough;
                     James R. Schipman; Maitland S. Chase, Jr.
City Manager: Aaron Marsh

May 16, 1960:
Mayor: David H. McLeod
Councilmen: Louis O. Yarbororough; Maitland S. Chase, Jr.;
                     Dennis D. O'Brian; R. Weston Patterson.
City Manager: Aaron Marsh

January 14, 1961 to December 18, 1961:
Mayor: David H. McLeod
Councilmen: Louis O. Yarbororough; Maitland S. Chase, Jr.;
                    Dennis D. O'Brian; R. Weston Patterson.
City Manager: Powell Black (appointed 11-21-60)

January 22, 1962 to December 21, 1962:
Mayor: David H. McLeod
Councilmen: Louis O. Yarbororough; Maitland S. Chase, Jr.;
                    Dennis D. O'Brian; R. Weston Patterson.
City Manager: Powell Black

January 4, 1963 to December 16, 1963:
Mayor: David H. McLeod
Councilmen: Dennis D. O'Brian; Louis O. Yarbororough;
                    Maitland S. Chase, Jr.; R. Weston Patterson.
City Manager: Powell Black

January 20, 1964 to December 21, 1964:
Mayor: David H. McLeod
Councilmen: Louis O. Yarbororough (passed away March 20, 1964);
                    Maitland S. Chase; Dennis D. O'Brian; R. Weston Patterson.
City Manager: Powell Black

May 29, 1964:
Mayor: David H. McLeod
Councilmen: J. Madison Rainwater; Maitland S. Chase, Jr.;
                    Dennis D. O'Brian; R. Weston Patterson.
City Manager: Powell Black

January 8, 1965 to December 20, 1965:
Mayor: David H. McLeod
Councilmen: Dennis D. O'Brian; R. Weston Patterson;
                    J. Madison Rainwater; Maitland S. Chase, Jr.
City Manager: Powell Black

January 17, 1966 to December 19, 1966:
Mayor: David H. McLeod
Councilmen: Maitland S. Chase, Jr.; Dennis D. O'Brian;
                    R. Weston Patterson; J. Madison Rainwater.
City Manager: Powell Black

January 9, 1967 to December 28, 1967:
Mayor: David H. McLeod
Councilmen: Maitland S. Chase, Jr.; Dennis D. O'Brian;
                    R. Weston Patterson; J. Madison Rainwater.
City Manager: Powell Black

January 15, 1968 to December 30, 1968:
Mayor: David H. McLeod
Councilmen: Maitland S. Chase, Jr.; Dennis D. O'Brian;
                    R. Weston Patterson; J. Madison Reinwater.

City Manager: Powell Black

January 6, 1969 to December 29, 1969:
Mayor: David H. McLeod
Councilmen: Maitland S. Chase, Jr.; Dennis D. O'Brian;
     R. Weston Patterson; J. Madison Rainwater.
City Manager: Powell Black

May 12, 1969:
Mayor: David H. McLeod
Councilmen: Maitland S. Chase, Jr.; R. Weston Patterson;
     Joe P. Waters, Jr.; J. Madison Rainwater.
City Manager: Powell Black

January 19, 1970 to December 28, 1970:
Mayor: David H. McLeod
Councilmen: Maitland S. Chase, Jr. (passed away July 22, 1970);
     R. Weston Patterson; Joe P. Waters, Jr.; J. Madison Rainwater.
City Manager: Powell Black

October 13, 1970:
Mayor: David H. McLeod
Councilmen: R. Weston Patterson; Joe P. Waters, Jr.;
     J. Madison Reinwater; A.P. Skinner.
City Manager: Powell Black

January 17, 1971 to December 15, 1971:
Mayor: David H. McLeod
Councilmen: R. Weston Patterson; Joe P. Waters, Jr.;
     J. Madison Rainwater; A.P. Skinner.
City Manager: Powell Black

May 5, 1971:
Mayor: C. Cooper Tedder
Councilmen: R. Weston Patterson; J. Madison Rainwater;
     A.P. Skinner; Joe P. Waters, Jr.
City Manager: Powell Black

January 17, 1972 to December 18, 1972:
Mayor: C. Cooper Tedder
Councilmen: R. Weston Patterson;J. Madison Rainwater;
     A.P. Skinner; Joe P. Waters, Jr.
City Manager: Powell Black

January 3, 1973 to December 31 1973:
Mayor: C. Cooper Tedder
Councilmen: R. Weston Patterson; J. Madison Rainwater;
     A.P. Skinner;Joe P. Waters, Jr.
City Manager: Powell Black

May 8, 1973:
Mayor: C. Cooper Tedder
Councilmen: Simons L. Chase; Herbert G. Ham; J. Madison Rainwater; A.P. Skinner.
City Manager: Powell Black (resigned October 1, 1973).
                Douglas J. Watson appointed October 31, 1973

January 9, 1974 to December 16, 1974:
Mayor: C. Cooper Tedder
Councilmen: J. Madison Rainwater; A.P. Skinner; Simons L. Chase; Herbert G. Ham.
City Manager: Douglas J. Watson

January 14, 1975 to December 9, 1975:
Mayor: C. Cooper Tedder
Councilmen: J. Madison Rainwater; A.P. Skinner; Simons L. Chase; Herbert G. Ham.
City Manager: Douglas J. Watson

May 9, 1975:
Mayor: C. Cooper Tedder
Councilmen: J. Madison Rainwater; Simons L. Chase; Herbert G. Ham;
                William P. Campbell.
City Manager: Douglas J. Watson

January 5, 1976 to December 20, 1976:
Mayor: C. Cooper Tedder
Councilmen: J. Madison Rainwater; Simons L. Chase; Herbert G. Ham.
City Manager: Douglas J. Watson (resigned May 1, 1976)
                J. Guy Smith (appointed August 1, 1976)

January 17, 1977 to December 19, 1977:
Mayor: C. Cooper Tedder
Councilmen: J. Madison Rainwater; Simons L. Chase; Herbert G. Ham;
                William P. Campbell
City Manager: J. Guy Smith

May 10, 1977:
Mayor: C. Cooper Tedder
Councilmen: J. Madison Rainwater; Simons L. Chase; Herbert G. Ham;
                William P. Campbell; John A. Sellers; Mordecai C. Johnson.
City Manager: J. Guy Smith (passed away in mid 1977)
                Thomas W. Edwards, Jr. (appointed September 6, 1977)

January 9, 1978 to December 19, 1978:
Mayor: C. Cooper Tedder
Councilmen: J. Madison Rainwater; Simons L. Chase; Herbert G. Ham;
                William P. Campbell; John A. Sellers; Mordecai C. Johnson
City Manager: Thomas W. Edwards, Jr.

January 8, 1979 to June 30, 1980:
Mayor: C. Cooper Tedder
Councilmen: J. Madison Rainwater;
                Herbert G. Ham (resigned 4-80; Ben Dozier appointed 8-80);
                William P. Campbell; John A. Sellers ; Simons L. Chase;

Mordecai C. Johnson.

City Manager: Thomas W. Edwards, Jr.

January 12, 1981 to June 19, 1981:

Mayor: C. Cooper Tedder

Councilmen: J. Madison Rainwater; William P. Campbell; Mordecai C. Johnson;
                   Ben Dozier; John A. Sellers.

City Manager: Thomas W. Edwards, Jr.

January 26, 1981:

Mayor: C. Cooper Tedder

Councilmen: J. Madison Rainwater; William P. Campbell; John A. Sellers;
                   Haigh Porter (sworn in January 21, 1981); Mordecai C. Johnson;
                   Ben Dozier.

City Manager: Thomas W. Edwards, Jr.

May 11, 1981 to December 20, 1982:

Mayor: C. Cooper Tedder

Councilmen: J. Madison Rainwater; William P. Campbell; John A. Sellers;
                   Mordecai C. Johnson; Ben Dozier; Edward J. McIver
                   (sworn in May 11, 1981).

January 10, 1983 to May 9, 1983:

Mayor: Joe W. Pearce, Jr.

Councilmen: John A. Sellers; Ben Dozier; Haigh Porter; Edward J. McIver;
                   James T. Schofield; K. Fred Samra.

City Manager: T. W. Edwards, Jr.

June 27, 1983 to May 13, 1985:

Mayor: Joe W. Pearce, Jr.

Councilmen: John A. Sellers; Ben Dozier; Haigh Porter; Edward J. McIver;
                   James T. Schofield; K. Fred Samra.

City Manager: Thomas W. Edwards, Jr.

May 13, 1988 to November 17, 1988:

Mayor: Joe W. Pearce, Jr.

Councilmen: John A. Sellers; Ben Dozier; James T. Schofield; K. Fred Samra;
                   Herbert G. Ham; James L. Daniels (passed away July 15, 1988;
                   Billy D. Williams completes term).

City Manager: Thomas W. Edwards, Jr.

November 17, 1988 to May 2, 1989:

Mayor: Joe W. Pearce, Jr.

Councilmen: John A. Sellers; Ben Dozier; Herbert G. Ham; James T. Schofield;
                   K. Fred Samra; Billy D. Williams.

City Manager: T. W. Edwards, Jr.

May 2, 1989 to June 1, 1990:

Mayor: Joe W. Pearce, Jr.

Councilmen: Ben Dozier; James T. Schofield; K. Fred Samra;
                   Billy D. Williams; Edward Robinson; Herbert G. Ham.

City Manager: Thomas W. Edwards, Jr.

June 11, 1990 to May 10, 1991:
Mayor: Joe W. Pearce, Jr.
Councilmen: Ben Dozier; James T. Schofield; K. Fred Samra;
                    Billy D. Williams; Edward Robinson; J. Ray Turner.
City Manager: Thomas W. Edwards, Jr.

May 10, 1991 to May 15 , 1995:
Mayor: Haigh Porter
Councilmen: John R. Chase; John R. Outlaw; Ben Dozier; J. Ray Turner;
                    Billy D. Williams; Edward Robinson.
City Manager: Thomas W. Edwards, Jr.

May 17, 1995 to May 29, 1995:
Mayor: Frank E. Willis
Councilmen: Ben Dozier; J. Ray Turner; John R. Outlaw; John R. Chase;
                    Billy D. William; Edward Robinson.
City Manager: Thomas W. Edwards, Jr.

May 29, 1995 to May 12, 1997:
Mayor: Frank E. Willis
Councilmen: Ben Dozier; J. Ray Turner; Rick Woodard; Bobby Holland;
                    Billy D. Williams; Edward Robinson.
City Manager: Thomas W. Edwards, Jr. resigned as effective December 2, 1995.
David N. Williams appointed interim City Manager December 1, 1995 to May 1996
Mr. Ed Burchins appointed City Manager May 1996 until February 1997.

May 12, 1997 to May, 1999:
Mayor: Frank E. Willis
Councilmen: Ben Dozier; J. Ray Turner; Rick Woodard; Bobby Holland;
                    Billy D. Williams; Edward Robinson.
City Manager: David N. Williams (appointed interim February to June 1997).

May 1999 to May 14, 2001:
Mayor: Frank E. Willis
Councilmen: Billy D. Williams; Edward Robinson; Bobby Holland;
                    Maitland S. Chase, III; Bill Bradham
City Manager: David N. Williams

May 14, 2001 to May 9, 2003:
Mayor: Frank E. Willis
Councilmen: Billy D. Williams; Edward Robinson; Bobby Holland;
                    Rick Woodard; Maitland S. Chase, III; Bill Bradham.
City Manager: David N. Williams

May 9, 2003 to May 2, 2005:
Mayor: Frank E. Willis
Councilmen: Billy D. Williams; Edward Robinson; Bobby Holland;
                    Rick Woodard; Maitland S. Chase, III; Bill Bradham.
City Manager: David N. Williams

Appendix D

Lake City

Mayors since Incorporation (1/7/64)

C. LaRue Alford (1/1/03 – 11/30/06)
Ralph Singletary
James C. Brown
Wilford Barr
William J. Sebnick
Wilbur Brown
Carlton J. Gaskins
C. J. Evans

**Council members since
Incorporation (1/7/64)**

C. LaRue Alford
Lovith Anderson, Jr
Edward C. Brown
James C. Brown
William P. Campbell, Jr
Warren Carter
Perry D. Cockfield
L. M. Coleman III
Wyman Eaddy
Harrison Ervin
J. Wesley Floyd, Jr.
Carlton J. Gaskins
Kevin Gaskins
Haile S. Green
Bert Godwin
Lawrence D. Guerry

Jim McEveen
R. L. McEveen
Rogers R. Nettles
Paul D. Poston
Yvonne Scott
William J. Sebnick
George E. Simmons
Ralph Singletary.
Allen Timmons
Charles F. Tomlinson
John M. Truluck
Michael Rhodes.
Archie P. Webb
R. T. Whitehead, Sr.
W. Leon Whitehead, Jr.

**Council members at the time the
research was conducted**

Jean G. Lee
Joseph Singletary (Mayor Pro Tem)
A. Russ Martin
Kenneth Feagins
Franklin D. McAllister
Gloria C. Tisdale

Appendix E

Timmonsville

Elections are held on the first Tuesday after the first Monday in November of each odd numbered year. The term of newly elected officers shall begin on January 1st immediately following such election.

Mayor and Council Representatives
2005

Henry B. Peoples   Office Expires 12/31/05
Mayor

Jeanette Friday Timmons   Office Expires 12/31/05
Councilmember

Clarence Joe   Office Expires 12/31/05
Councilmember

King D. Lowery   Office Expires 12/31/05
Councilmember

James D. Pigate   Office Expires 12/31/07
Councilmember

Joseph L. Graham   Office Expires 12/31/07
Councilmember

Johnny E. Wright   Office Expires 12/31/07
Council Member

Appendix F

African American History
Time-Line of Major Events 1525-1997

1525: First arrival. Spanish explorer Ayllon brings a few enslaved Africans to the South Carolina coast. The attempt to build a colony fails. Before the survivors leave, some Africans may have escaped and then intermarried with native Americans in the area.

1670: Settlement. A group of about 100 English settlers and at least one enslaved African create the first permanent colony near present-day Charleston. Soon after, the governor brings a family of enslaved Africans, known only as John Senior, John Junior, and Elizabeth, to the colony. In the following years enslaved Africans help establish the first colony in many ways, building homes and performing such tasks as the cooking, sewing and gardening required on plantations and in towns. They also use their African-learned cattle raising and driving skills--they are the first American cowboys. Around one in three of the early settlers are African.

1685: Rice Culture. Seed rice arrives in Charleston as a gift from a sea captain whose boat was under repair. Efforts by the English to grow rice fail. Enslaved Africans, who grew rice in Africa, show the English how to grow rice in wet areas--the rice culture, which creates great wealth for the colony, begins.

1708: Population growth. The growth of indigo and cotton requires more and more labor, which leads to the importation of more and more enslaved Africans. By 1708 the numbers of whites and blacks in South Carolina are equal at about 4,000 each, according to British census figures. For most of the next two centuries (except a brief period between 1790 and 1820) blacks will outnumber whites in the state.

1730-39: About 20,000 enslaved Africans are brought to the state. Enslaved people resist in a wide range of ways, from acting lazy or stupid or breaking tools in order to minimize the work that is being forced upon them, to theft, running away, and even individual violent resistance.

1739: The Stono Rebellion. Although enslaved people have periodically fought back, this is the first large-scale rebellion. Roughly 100 enslaved Africans, led by "Jemmy," capture firearms about 20 miles south of Charles Town, and attempt to rally more people to join them. They plan to fight their way to St. Augustine where the Spanish promise freedom. They accidentally run into a group of whites led by the Lt. Governor of the state, who alerts white authorities before the group has time to grow into an overwhelming force. The revolt is forcefully put down and some sixty of the rebels are executed.

1740: Slave Codes. In reaction to the Stono Rebellion, the legislature passes slave codes which forbid travel without written permission, group meetings without the presence of whites, raising their own food, possessing money, learning to read, and the use of drums, horns, and other "loud instruments," that might be used by enslaved Africans to communicate with each other.

1790: The Brown Fellowship Society is formed. It is one of many self-help groups formed by free African-Americans to help with education, burial costs, and support of widows and orphans of members. Others include the Human Brotherhood and the Unity and Friendship Society. The Brown Fellowship Society reflects the prejudice of the day, restricting its membership to those who are racially mixed and whose skin color is brown rather than black.

1792: Restrictions are placed on free African-Americans. South Carolina passes a law requiring all free African-Americans between the ages of 16 and 50 to pay a yearly "head tax" of $2.00, a significant sum of money in that day. This is but one of a number of laws that make life very difficult for the relatively few African-Americans who are free. In 1790 they number only 1,801 of the 109,000 African-Americans who live in the state.

1793: Invention of the cotton gin makes the growing of cotton profitable in coastal areas where only cotton with a lot of seeds in the bolls will grow. This greatly increases the need for labor and once again increases the number of enslaved Africans brought to the state.

1803: The Minors Moralist Society founded. A purely charitable organization founded by free African-Americans for the purpose of caring for free African-American orphans.

1810: Tom Molyneux, who had won his freedom in Georgetown as a reward for his boxing skills following eight straight wins, boxes against the world heavyweight champion in England. He loses this match when he hits his head on the ring post and fractures his skull. No other major boxing matches take place between blacks and whites until 1891.

1816: Camden Revolt. Few records exist about this revolt, but it is stopped before it really takes place. Local enslaved Africans are plotting a violent revolt in order to take revenge upon those who had enslaved them.

1817: Morris Brown, wealthy free African-American, starts an AME church in Charleston. The church is closed forcibly after the Vesey Rebellion.

1820-1860: Edgefield Pottery: During the early 1800s, a number of enslaved people became famous for their beautiful and useful pottery made in this area. The most famous is known as Dave the Potter. Scholars estimate that some 140 potters were plying their craft in this area during this period.

1822: Denmark Vesey Rebellion. Led by Denmark Vesey, an African-Methodist church founder and former enslaved person who had bought his freedom, the rebellion is well-planned and widespread. It involves about 9,000 people. However, two house servants tell their masters before the planned date. Vesey and about 100 others are arrested. Vesey refuses to reveal any names, and he and thirty-three others are hanged.

1829:   The Georgetown Conspiracy. Details are sketchy, but a plot is uncovered and at least 20 enslaved people are arrested. Written documents suggest that many were hanged.

1839:   The Christian Benevolent Society is formed by free African-Americans to provide for the poor.

1850:   Fugitive Slave Law. This law, passed by Congress as part of a compromise to keep the nation together, is designed to help southern whites recapture enslaved people who flee to the northern "free" states. However, the law does not work very well because of abolitionists such as Robert Purvis. Born in Charleston to an enslaved mother and a white father, he is lucky in that his wealthy father sends him to school in the North. He settles in Philadelphia and helps organize the American Anti-Slavery Society and raises money for the underground railway.

1861:   Union forces take control of the Sea Islands. Enslaved African-Americans flee to the area where Union troops consider blacks to be free because they are the "contraband of war." That is, they were the property of the enemy which is forfeited. Formal freedom comes more than a year later with the Emancipation Proclamation.

1862, May 12:   Robert Smalls sails *The Planter* through Confederate lines and delivers it and its cargo to Union forces off the South Carolina coast. He volunteers to help the Union Navy guide its ships through the dangerous South Carolina coastal waters for the rest of the war.

1862:   Two Northern Quakers create the Penn School on St. Helens Island after the Union captures the area and thousands of former enslaved people flee to safety there. The school survives as the Penn Center, serving as a conference center for the civil rights movement and a center for self-help and historical preservation today.

1862:   The First Regiment of South Carolina Volunteers is formed. African-Americans in the Sea Islands area volunteer for the first black unit to fight in the war as part of a Union experiment. The unit proves to be a great success. Throughout the war over 5,400 South Carolina African-Americans serve in the Union Army. They are a small but important part of the 200,000 African-Americans from all over America who serve in the Union Army and fight in over 400 different engagements.

1864:   Spirituals. The *Atlantic Monthly* publishes a collection of African-American spiritual hymns collected by Charlotte Forten, a free African-American from the North who comes to live and teach on St. Helena Island.

1865:   New Constitution and Black Codes. Following the war, white South Carolinians rewrite the state constitution in order to return to the union. They restrict the right to vote and elect an all-white legislature that then passes the "Black Codes," which restrict rights of the newly freed people. Congress responds by passing the

Reconstruction Acts, which require that the state rewrite the Constitution. African-Americans participate under federal military supervision.

1867:   The Howard School is opened in Columbia. This is the only public school to serve African-Americans in Columbia until 1916. It serves all grades.

1867:   An African-American teacher, Francis Cardozo, founds the Avery Normal Institute in Charleston, a comprehensive school. No longer a school today, it exists as the Avery Research Center for African-American History and Culture.

1868:   New Constitution. A convention of 48 whites and 76 blacks meet and write a very progressive constitution that includes representation based on population, a complete bill of rights, protection of a married woman's property rights, a homestead exemption, and a right to a public education.

1868:   A northern missionary, Martha Schofield, founds the Schofield Normal and Industrial School in Aiken. It later becomes a public high school for African-Americans and finally an integrated middle school.

1868:   State Senator and presidential elector B.F. Randolph is murdered by radical whites in Abbeville County.

1869:   Joseph Rainey becomes the first African-American in South Carolina to become a U.S. Representative in Congress. He is followed by seven others before African-Americans are driven out of elected office: Robert C. DeLarge, Robert Brown Elliott, Richard H. Cain, Alonzo Ransier, Robert Smalls, Thomas E. Miller, and George W. Murray.

1869:   The South Carolina Land Commission is created by the new legislature. Though troubled by corruption, the commission does sell farms to about 14,000 African-Americans.

1869:   The legislature grants a charter that creates Claflin College in Orangeburg.

1869:   Black and white workers form the Longshoreman's Protective Union Association. The Union is relatively successful until 1890 when whites break away to form their own separate group. After that the union declines.

1870:   Public Education. The state legislature, with African-Americans in control, passes a law to create a state-wide public school system. Although insufficient funds are available, this is the first such effort in the history of the state.

1870:   The self-sufficient farming community of Promised Land is formed on land in Greenwood County bought from the S.C. Land Commission. Residents survive by avoiding the cotton based crop lien system and instead grow the food they need and avoid contact with whites during the difficult decades after Reconstruction.

1870:   James Webster Smith of Columbia becomes the first African-American to enter West Point. He survives the vows of silence taken by other cadets, having to drill alone, eating after all the other cadets, being screamed at by instructors until 1874 when he is failed on an oral exam that is given to him in secret by a hostile philosophy professor and is dismissed from the academy. In 1996 President Clinton awarded him his West Point Commission posthumously.

1870, November: Alonzo J. Ransier becomes the first African-American elected Lt. Governor. He is followed by Richard H. Gleaves in 1872.

1871:   With much support from African-American Baptists all over the state, the American Baptist Home Mission Society creates Benedict Institute, which later evolves into Benedict College.

1871:   The AME church founds Payne Institute in Abbeville, which in 1880 is moved to Columbia and becomes what is today Allen University.

1872:   The state legislature creates the S.C. Agricultural College and Mechanics Institute near Orangeburg, which later grows into S.C. State.

1873:   The first African-American enters the University of South Carolina. All white students and faculty leave, but the school remains open with the help of white faculty from the North. After Reconstruction, USC is reopened as an all-white school.

1876:   The Hamburg Massacre takes place near Aiken in a battle between Democratic private para-military groups and the African-American state militia. After forcefully disarming the militia unit, whites execute five of their prisoners.

1876:   November. Fraud, violence, and intimidation enable white Democrats to claim a victory, to try and take control of state government after the election, and to begin to dismantle Reconstruction.

1877:   Both parties claim to have won the election, and for several months the state has two governors and two sitting legislatures. The withdrawal of federal troops in April spells doom for the Republicans, who cannot match the firepower of the Democrats, led by Governor Wade Hampton.

1877:   Knowing that whites will soon force him off the bench, State Supreme Court Justice Jonathan Jasper Wright resigns from the court.

1878:   About 200 African-Americans from South Carolina, following the advice of Reverend Richard H. Cain, a member of Congress from South Carolina and a newspaper publisher, emigrate to Liberia. Despite Cain's call for a million people to go, few others do.

1879:   P.B. Morris founds a newspaper for African-Americans, the *Sea Island News*, later replaced by the *New South* after his death in 1891.

1880-1900: As conditions worsen in the state following the end of Reconstruction, about 20,000 African-Americans leave the state, many moving west as the frontier opens to opportunity. Out-migration accelerates after the turn of the century.

1881: Reverend Alexander Bettis, a former enslaved person, creates the Bettis Academy in Trenton in Edgefield County to teach basic academic skills and trades and crafts.

1882: White Democrats use the Eight Ballot Box law to disenfranchise African-American voters and pass laws to allow white registrars to strike African-Americans from the voting registration lists.

1885-6: Columbia native Clarissa Thompson has her book *Treading the Winepress: A Mountain of Misfortune*, published as a serial in a Boston newspaper, making her the first female African-American from South Carolina to have her work published.

1886: Arthur MacBeth opens a photographic studio in Charleston, winning many awards for his pioneering work.

1887: The United Methodist Church founds the Mather Academy in Camden, the only African-American secondary school to be accredited during this period.

1890: The Colored Farmers' Alliance reaches a membership of 30,000 members in South Carolina and prints its own newspaper. However, a failed strike effort by cotton pickers a year later marks the decline of this self-help group.

1892: The Jenkins Orphanage is begun in Charleston by Rev. Daniel Jenkins, the only orphanage for African-Americans in the state. The band formed by Jenkins to help support the enterprise becomes famous, makes European tours, and produces many professional musicians.

1895: Governor Ben Tillman leads a state constitutional convention to rewrite the state constitution to eliminate virtually all African-American influence in state politics. Six African-American politicians attend the convention (Robert Smalls, Thomas Miller, William Whipper, James Wigg, Isaiah Reed, and Robert Anderson) and speak out against the proceedings but are outvoted.

1896: African-Americans, now comprising about sixty percent of the population, are relegated to less than five percent of the voters in South Carolina.

1897: Elizabeth Evelyn Wright and Jessie Dorsey open the Denmark Industrial School, which later becomes Vorhees Industrial School and then Vorhees College, one of many examples of African-American self-help in education.

1898: Battle of San Juan Hill, in which two African-American Cavalry units, the Ninth and Tenth, which include South Carolinians, help take the hill. According to some reports, they may have saved Teddy Roosevelt's "Rough Riders" from defeat.

1900:   The number of African-American owned general stores, the business centers in the communities across the rural state, reaches nearly 500, about ten times the number in 1880.

1900:   African-Americans own or operate more than half the farms in the state, but these are smaller farms, comprising only twenty-seven percent of the farmland in the state. However these farms are relatively productive, producing thirty-nine per cent of agricultural output.

1900:   The Colored Agricultural and Mechanical Association, begun by A.E. Hampton about a decade earlier, is holding county fairs all over the state to improve farmer education and self-sufficiency.

1900:   Simon Brown moves to Society Hill to work on the family farm of young William Faulkner. As an adult, Faulkner remembers Brown's stories about Brer Rabbit and Brer Fox and publishes them under the title *The Days When Animals Talked*. These tales preserved some of the trickster stories told by enslaved people.

1900-1950:   An estimated half million African-Americans leave the state, mainly for northern cities during WWI and WWII when industrial opportunities are the greatest.

1902:   John William Bolts of Georgetown leaves office as a member of the state house, the last African-American to serve there after Reconstruction.

1904:   The Penn School begins teaching the African craft of basketmaking, which had once been a vital part of the rice culture.

1906:   Isaac Samuel Leevy returns to his home state to teach and help the African-American community, building many businesses, helping organize a state fair for African-Americans, helping found Booker T. Washington High School in Columbia, working for higher education, promoting many charities, helping organize the Columbia branch of the NAACP, and running for city council and the state legislature as a Republican. He helps lay the foundation for the next generation, including his grandson, I.S. Leevy Johnson, who is elected to the state legislature in 1971.

1909:   Georgetown native, William A. Sinclair who was born enslaved in 1858 and who later earned a theology degree from Howard University and a medical degree, helps create the NAACP. Another South Carolina native, Archibald Grimke, is among the first African-Americans to attend Harvard Law School, and is also an important figure in the early NAACP.

1911:   Former Civil War hero and Reconstruction politician Robert Smalls foils a lynch mob by spreading rumors that Charleston would be burned if the jailed African-Americans are harmed.

1916:   Septima Poinsette Clark begins her teaching career on Johns Island, receiving $25 a month for pay and supplies for teaching over 130 pupils. She is fired for helping organize the NAACP in Charleston in the 1920s. In the 1960s she helps organize the

Southern Christian Leadership Conference, Martin Luther King's organization, in the state. Throughout the drive to win the vote she runs "citizenship schools" that help overcome illiteracy. She is remembered as the "grandmother of the civil rights movement" in South Carolina.

1916:   Booker T. Washington High School opens its doors in Columbia, the second public school in the city to serve African-Americans. It remains the only public high school for African-Americans in the city until 1948.

1917:   John Birks "Dizzy Gillespie," who will become probably the state's most famous musician, is born in Cheraw.

1917:   The 371st Infantry Regiment, an all African American unit composed of many South Carolinians, trains at Ft. Jackson. A year later it was attached to the famous "Red Hand Division" of the French army in Europe, earning the nicknames of "black devils" and "hell fighters" from their German adversaries. Almost half of all South Carolinians serving in the first World War were African-American.

1917:   Chapters of the NAACP are organized in Charleston and Columbia.

1918:   Corporal Freddie Stowers of Anderson County dies while rallying his men in the 371st Infantry in the successful capture of a hill in France. In 1991 he is posthumously awarded the Congressional Medal of Honor.

1920:   Using a petition signed by nearly three-fourths of all African-American families in the city, the NAACP has its first significant victory in the state in convincing white Charleston leaders to hire blacks to teach in black public schools in the city.

1920:   Richard Samuel Roberts moves to Columbia and builds his photography business. He is later recognized as a great photographer for his portraits.

1920s: African-American art, music and literature flourishes in cities around the country. In South Carolina, there is a cultural flowering in the city of Charleston that later becomes known as the "Charleston Renaissance." Dubose Heyward explores African-American culture from a white perspective, writing the play Porgy. Elise Forrest Harleston becomes a portrait photographer, and her husband Edwin Harleston, a painter.

1921:   The Mutual Savings Bank is begun in Charleston, but it only survives for twenty years.

1921:   Dr. H.D. Monteith creates the Victory Savings Bank in Columbia, which still exists today.

1927:   Susan Dart Butler opens a free library for African-Americans in her own home in Charleston.

1932:   Dr. Matilda Evans, the state's first native-born female African-American doctor, trained at Schofield Industrial School and at Oberlin College in Ohio, opens the Evans Clinic in Columbia. Reportedly she worked 25 years without taking a vacation.

1935:   Mayesville native Mary McLeod Bethune, who in 1920 had founded what later became Bethune-Cookman College in Daytona, Florida, is named as head of the Division of Negro Affairs of the National Youth Administration. She becomes the first African-American woman to run a federal agency.

1938:   Painter and Florence native William H. Johnson returns from Europe to escape the Nazis. Most of his work was done in the 1920s and 1930s while living in Europe.

1939:   NAACP forms its first state organization, headed by Reverend A.W. Wright as president. Other leaders include Levi S. Byrd of Cheraw and Reverend James M. Hinton of Columbia.

1941:   The 99th Pursuit Squadron, the first African-American air fighting unit, begins training in Tuskegee, Alabama. The unit, whose pilots are known as the Tuskegee Airmen, includes Ernest Henderson of Laurens County, South Carolina. The unit and Henderson go on to win many air battles, and Henderson goes on to train other flying units, including the Black Eagles, who are formed and trained in Columbia in 1949.

1941, December 7:   Dorie Miller, assigned to a menial job in ship mess on a naval ship in Pearl Harbor, mans a gun and shoots down several attacking Japanese planes, winning the Navy Cross. Had he not been African-American, he probably would have been awarded the Congressional Medal of Honor.

1942:   South Carolina Civil Rights leader Mary McLeod Bethune uses her friendship with Eleanor Roosevelt to persuade President Roosevelt to create opportunities for African-Americans in the military, which is still totally segregated.

1942:   After decades of distinguished work in public school teaching and with the state tuberculosis association, Modjeska Montieth Simpkins becomes Secretary of the S.C. NAACP, serving in that capacity until 1956, when she steps down to do bookkeeping for her brother's Victory Savings Bank. In the 1960s she becomes an advocate for improved treatment of the mentally ill of all races.

1942:   Columbia native Edwin R. Russell is one of two African-American scientists helping develop nuclear weapons. He later receives a citation from President Roosevelt and works until retirement at the Savannah River Plant near Aiken.

1942:   Darlington County native Annie Greene Nelson publishes her first novel, *After the Storm.*

1944:   November. "Ossie" McKaine, a World War I military hero, businessman, journalist, and civil rights leader, runs under the Progressive Democratic Party label against Governor Olin Johnston for the U.S. Senate, invigorating the drive to win voting rights in the state.

1945: Columbia native Charity Edna Adams completes her tour of service in Europe after winning the highest rank in the army of any African-American woman, Lt. Colonel, serving as a Battalion Commander in the European Theater of Operations. Nearly fifty years later, after a lifetime of public service in voluntary and charitable organizations, she is named by the Smithsonian as one of the top 100 women in Black History.

1946: George Elmore tries to vote in the August Democratic primary, is refused, and becomes plaintiff in a suit filed by the NAACP. The next year he wins his case against the all-white primary (*Elmore v. Rice*).

1947, July: Moved by a plea from state NAACP president James Hinton, Reverend J.A. DeLaine convinces his friend Levi Pearson, father of three children, to file a petition with the public schools in Clarendon County, asking that his children and other Negro school children be provided public school transportation. Thus begins the case that will evolve into *Briggs v. Eliot* that will eventually be joined with *Brown v. Board of Education.* Pearson loses the initial case, becomes president of the local NAACP, but is punished by local white businessmen who refuse to buy the timber he cuts to make a living.

1947, July: Camden Native Larry Doby pitch hits for the Cleveland Indians, becoming the first African-American to play in the American League, eleven weeks after Jackie Robinson breaks the color barrier in the National League. Doby later becomes the first African-American to hit a home run in an All-Star game.

1948: Strom Thurmond temporarily bolts from the Democratic Party in protest over the civil rights plank in the national platform and runs for president under the State's Rights or Dixiecrat banner, carrying South Carolina in the electoral college.

1949, November: Harry Briggs is the first name on a list of more than a hundred petitioners in a test case filed with Clarendon County by the state NAACP, that goes beyond the earlier request for equal transportation by asking for total educational equality. Modjeska Montieth Simpkins writes the petition. Briggs and others in the case, including Reverend J.A. DeLaine, who was a school principal, are fired from their jobs. The case is filed in federal court the next year.

1951: Governor James Byrnes supports a three cent sales tax for eduction, mainly to improve African-American schools in hopes of avoiding integration.

1954: Following the Supreme Court's order that public schools be desegregated in *Brown v. Board of Education* and the attached cases, including *Briggs v. Elliot*, Reverend J.A. DeLaine's church is burned and his life is threatened. He escapes from the state and spends the rest of his working life in New York where he founds a new church, later retiring in Charlotte, N.C.

1959: Popular singer Camden native "Brook" Benton begins having success, recording twenty-one gold records over the next five years.

1960:   Due West native Charlayne Hunter (later Hunter-Gault), is one of the first two African-Americans to integrate the University of Georgia. She later wins fame as a co-anchor reporter on the PBS McNeil/Lehrer Report.

1960:   Lancaster native Maurice Williams and his group the Zodiacs produce a gold record with the song "Stay," to which South Carolinians dance the shag, the official state dance. The shag was partly based on dances developed by African-Americans at a nightclub in Columbia in the 1930s, the Big Apple.

1962:   The all-white legislature votes to fly the Confederate Naval Jack over the capitol dome to mark the hundredth anniversary of the Confederate secession.

1963, January: Governor Ernest Hollings leaves office warning the state that segregation can no longer be maintained and that it is time to move on. Incoming Governor Donald Russell has a barbecue at the governor's residence for both races.

1960:   Harvey Gantt becomes the first African-American to enroll in Clemson University, with little vocal opposition. Years later Gantt becomes mayor of Charlotte and runs for the U.S. Senate in North Carolina.

1960, September: James Solomon and Henri Monteith, grand niece of Modjeska Montieth Simpkins, enroll at the University of South Carolina.

1964:   The Civil Rights Act of 1964 is passed under the leadership of Democratic President Lyndon Johnson, ending segregation laws in all public facilities and easing voting restrictions somewhat. The percentage of African-Americans registered to vote in the state more than doubles from the previous presidential election, rising to nearly thirty-nine percent. Strom Thurmond moves to the Republican Party for good in support of Barry Goldwater's anti-civil rights law position, and the state votes for Goldwater in the presidential election.

1965:   The Voting Rights Act of 1965 is passed, which leads to further gains in African-American voter participation all over the South.

1967, October 15: Winnsboro native Sergeant First Class Webster Anderson of the 101st Airborne Division, suffering multiple wounds that result in the loss of both legs and part of an arm, successfully defends his artillery position from a sustained enemy attack. His many heroics include throwing an exploding hand grenade that otherwise would have harmed the men under his command. He is awarded the Congressional Medal of Honor.

1968, February: The Orangeburg Massacre takes place when a year of student protests at the S.C. State campus culminate in white highway patrol officers shooting into a crowd of students who were throwing objects at the officers, killing three students and wounding twenty-eight more. The state unfairly pins the blame on Cleveland Sellers, a young civil rights organizer, who serves a year in prison, but who is finally granted a full pardon in 1993.

1969, March 5:   Nineteen year old Marine Corps Private First Class Ralph Johnson of Charleston throws himself on a hand grenade to save the lives of his fellow soldiers in a foxhole in Vietnam. He is awarded the Congressional Medal of Honor, posthumously.

1969:   300 female workers at the Medical University of South Carolina hospital go on strike with the support of labor and civil rights groups protesting poor working conditions and low wages. After confrontations with police and the arrival of National Guard troops, the mostly African-American workers win a settlement--violence is narrowly averted.

1969:   Rev. I.D. Newman takes Sen. Ernest Hollings on a tour of poor areas in the state and Hollings calls for programs to help the poor and hungry.

1970:   Beaufort County native "Smokin'" Joe Frazier beats Muhammad Ali for the world heavyweight boxing title in one of the best matches of all time. In 1964 he had been the first American to win the heavyweight gold medal Olympic match.

1970:   Angry whites overturn a school bus that is taking young black school children to integrate local schools in Lamar. The state restores order and enforces the rule of law.

1970:   African-American voter registration reaches fifty-seven percent of the voting age population, sixteen percentage points behind the white figure.

1970, November: I.S. Leevy Johnson, James Felder, and Herbert Fielding are elected to the S.C. House in the General Assembly, the first African-Americans since 1902. County-wide at-large elections make winning difficult for African-Americans. Republican Albert Watson, basing his campaign for governor on opposition to the civil rights movement and integration, loses to Democrat John West, but Watson wins nearly three-fifths of the white vote.

1971:   Newly elected Governor John West creates the state Human Affairs Commission, headed by James Clyburn, who holds the position until he runs for Congress in 1992.

1973:   After winning international fame as a civil rights leader, Greenville native Rev. Jesse Jackson returns home to a dinner held in his honor by the local citizens.

1974:   Under pressure from the federal courts, the S.C. General Assembly rewrites election laws to end at-large election of legislators from counties and create single member districts. This enables an additional ten African-Americans to be elected to the S.C. House.

1974:   African-American voter registration nearly equals that of whites and will remain within a few percentage points of the white figures.

1975:   African-American legislators in the S.C. House form the Legislative Black Caucus in order to promote cooperative legislative action. It is headed by Ernest Finney, Jr.

1975:   Sen. Strom Thurmond votes for extension of the Voting Rights Act, his first pro-civil rights vote.

1976:   Matthew J. Perry becomes a federal judge with the support of Senator Strom Thurmond. Perry had been chief counsel for the S.C. NAACP for twenty years, helping in key cases like the integration of Clemson.

1978:   Republican gubernatorial candidate Ed Young openly seeks votes of African-Americans, but loses badly to Richard Riley.

1978:   Janie Glymph Goree, daughter of a sharecropper in Newberry County who graduated from Benedict and taught mathematics for over three decades in Union and who was an adult literacy volunteer teacher, is elected mayor of Carlisle, the first female African-American mayor in South Carolina.

1980:   Columbia native and Annapolis graduate Charles Bolden becomes an astronaut. He will pilot two space shuttle flights and command a third flight.

1980:   Governor Richard Riley awards Dr. Benjamin Mayes, a nationally renowned scholar, author, and civil rights leader from Epworth, the Order of the Palmetto Award.

1983:   Columbia native and USC graduate Alex English wins the NBA scoring title. Before his career is over he plays in seven all-star games. He also writes three books of poetry and an autobiography, as well as raising a great deal of money for international aid to children.

1983:   The S.C. Athletic Hall of Fame inducts Silver native Althea Gibson, one of the best female athletes of all time. Gibson was the first African-American to play and win the U.S. Open and the first African-American winner of the Winbleton tennis title.

1983:   In a special election, long time civil rights leader Reverend I. DeQuincey Newman is elected to the S.C. State Senate, the first African-American since the 1800s.

1985:   Ernest Finney Jr. becomes the first African-American Associate Justice on the state Supreme Court since Reconstruction.

1986:   The Space Shuttle Challenger explodes on take-off, killing all astronauts aboard, including Lake City native and veteran astronaut and physicist Ron McNair.

1989:   North Charleston native and pro football hall of famer Art Shell becomes the first African-American NFL head coach, taking over the Oakland Raiders.

1990:   State Senator Theo Mitchell is nominated by the Democrats to run for governor. Though he loses to incumbent Carroll Campbell, he is the first African-American ever nominated by the Democrats for governor.

1990:   Census figures indicate that nearly twenty-nine percent of black families are below the poverty level, about five times the six percent rate for whites.

1990:   Dori Sanders publishes the award winning book, *Clover.*

1992:   Columbia native and pioneer heart and stroke researcher Dr. Edward Sawyer is elected president of the American Heart Association.

1992:   The infant mortality rate for blacks is more than twice the rate for whites in the state, 15.5 and 7.2 per thousand live births respectively.

1992:   African-American voter registration is fifty-five percent of the voting age population, six points behind the white rate.

1992:   James Clyburn becomes the first African-American to win a U.S. Congressional seat since the 1800s.

1992:   The number of African-Americans in the House and Senate of the General Assembly rises to 25 (7 in the Senate and 18 in the House), or about 15% of the total membership, which is about half the percentage of the population that is African-American.

1992:   In local offices around the state, over 250 African-Americans have been elected.

1993:   Aiken native Irene Trowell-Harris becomes the third female general and first African-American female general in the National Guard.

1993:   W. Melvin Brown becomes the first African-American to be named to the S.C. Business Hall of Fame for his work in building the American Development Corporation, a North Charleston company that made military equipment, some of which helped win the 1991 Persian Gulf War.

1993:   Columbia native Kimberly Aiken becomes the first African-American to win the Miss American title.

1994:   Legislative Black Caucus members torpedo a compromise proposal to move the Confederate Naval Jack from over the capitol dome. Republicans place a straw poll question on whether to fly the banner on their primary ballot. Republicans, voting in record numbers, overwhelmingly vote by about four to one to continue to fly the banner.

1994:   A November state-wide survey shows that three-fourths of whites see job opportunities as equal while three-fifths of black citizens see continued racial bias in favor of whites.

1994:   The number of African-Americans in the S.C. House of Representatives increases from eighteen to twenty-four, but Republicans take over a majority of the body. Six African-Americans are elected to the state senate.

1995: Tim Scott wins a Charleston County Council seat in a special election, the first African-American to win public office in the state as a Republican in modern times.

1995: The U.S. Supreme Court rules in *Miller v. Johnson* that race cannot be the predominant factor in creating election districts at any level. This sets the stage for redrawing district lines in South Carolina and other states that had in recent years enabled African-Americans to win office.

1995: A November state-wide survey reveals that while most blacks and whites work with each other at their places of employment, they live separate lives socially and religiously.

1995: Gov. David Beasley creates a Commission on Race Relations to seek ways to combat racially motivated crimes (such as some of the church burnings that had taken place) and to improve educational and economic opportunities.

1997: Eartha Kitt, world famous singer and Broadway star, returns to her home state of South Carolina for a benefit performance at Benedict College, creating the Eartha Kitt Performing Arts Scholarship.

1997: Governor David Beasley reverses his previous position on flying the Confederate Naval Jack over the capitol dome and seeks a compromise to lower the banner. He loses to determined Republican opposition in the legislature.

1997: August. Special primary elections are held in legislative districts that have been redrawn to eliminate the advantage given to African-American candidates.

Source: *South Carolina-African American History and Resource: SC Black History*
http://www.usca.edu/aasc/timeline.htm

Appendix G

South Carolina: Demographic Information

People QuickFacts	South Carolina	USA
Population, 2000	4,012,012	281,421,906
Population, percent change, 1990 to 2000	15.1%	13.1%
Persons under 5 years old, percent, 2000	6.6%	6.8%
Persons under 18 years old, percent, 2000	25.2%	25.7%
Persons 65 years old and over, percent, 2000	12.1%	12.4%
White persons, percent (a)	67.2%	75.1%
Black and African-American persons, percent, 2000 (a)	29.5%	12.3%
American Indian and Alaska Native persons, percent 2000 (a)	0.3%	0.9%
Asian persons, percent, 2000 (a)	0.9%	3.6%
Native Hawaiian and Other Pacific Islander, percent 2000 (a)	Z	0.1%
Persons reporting some other race, percent, 2000 (a)	1.0%	5.5%
Persons reporting two or more races, percent, 2000	1.0%	2.4%
Female population, percent, 2000	51.4%	50.9%
Persons of Hispanic or Latino origin, percent, 2000 (b)	2.4%	12.5%
White persons, not of Hispanic/Latino origin, percent, 2000	66.1%	69.1%
High school graduates, persons 25 years and over, 1990	1,480,330	119,524,718
College graduates, persons 25 years old and over, 1990	360,833	32,310,253
Housing units, 2000	1,753,670	115,904,641
Homeownership rate, 2000	72.2%	66.2%
Households, 2000	1,533,854	105,480,101
Persons per household, 2000	2.53	2.59
Households with persons under 18 years, percent, 2000	36.5%	36.0%
Median household money income, 1997 model-based estimate	$33,325	$37,005
Persons below poverty, percent, 1997 model-based estimate	14.9%	13.3%
Children below poverty, percent, 1997, model-based estimate	23.0%	19.9%

Business QuickFacts	South Carolina	USA
Private nonfarm establishments with paid employees, 1998	94,985	6,941,822
Private nonfarm employment, 1998	1,526,106	108,117,731
Private nonfarm employment, percent change 1990-1998	20.5%	15.7%
Nonemployer establishments, 1997	188,081	15,439,609
Manufacturers shipments 1997 ($1000)	70,797,020	3,842,061,405
Retail sales, 1997 ($1000)	33,634,264	2,460,886,012
Retail sales per capita, 1997	$8,874	$9,190
Minority-owned firms, 1992	21,127	1,965,565
Women-owned firms, 1992	64,812	5,888,883
Housing units authorized by building permits, 1999	36,162	1,663,533
Federal funds and grants 1999 ($1000)	20,833,188	1,516,775,001
Local government employment-full time equivalent, 1997	143,952	10,227,429

Geography QuickFacts	South Carolina	USA
Land area, 2000 (square miles)	30,110	3,537,441
Persons per square mile, 2000	133.2	79.6

(a) Including persons reporting only one race.
(b) Hispanics may be of any race, so also are included in applicable race categories.

FN: Footnote on this item for this area in place of data
NA: Not available
D: Suppressed to avoid disclosure of confidential information
X: Not applicable
S: Suppressed; does no meet publication standards
Z: Value greater than zero, but less than half unit of measure shown

Source: U.S. Census Bureau: State and County QuickFacts. Data derived from Population estimates, 2000 Census of Population and Housing, 1990 Census of Population and Housing, Small Area Income and Poverty Estimates, County Business Patterns, 1997 Economic Census, Minority and Women-owned Business, Building Permits, Consolidated Federal Funds Report, 1997 Census of Governments.

Florence County

DP-1. Profile of General Demographic characteristics: 2000
Data Set: Census 2000 Summary File 1 (SF 1) 100-Percent Data

Subject	Number	Percent
Total population	125,761	100.0
SEX AND AGE		
Male	59,099	47.0
Female	66,662	53.0
Under 5 years	8,216	6.5
5 to 9 years	9,077	7.2
10 to 14 years	9,620	7.6
15 to 19 years	9,514	7.6
20 to 24 years	8,389	6.7
25 to 34 years	17,162	13.6
35 to 44 years	19,235	15.3
45 to 54 years	18,141	14.4
55 to 59 years	6,421	5.1
60 to 64 years	5,149	4.1
65 to 74 years	7,940	6.3
75 to 84 years	5,100	4.1
85 years and over	1,797	1.4
Median age (years)	35.5	(X)
18 years and over	93,160	74.1
Male	42,581	33.9
Female	50,579	40.2
21 years and over	87,534	69.6
62 years and over	17,743	14.1
65 years and over	14,837	11.8
Male	5,588	4.4
Female	9,249	7.4
RACE		
One race	124,909	99.3
White	73,760	58.7
Black or African American	49,474	39.3
American Indian and Alaska Native	282	0.2
Asian	881	0.7
Asian Indian	226	0.2

Subject	Number	Percent
Chinese	281	0.2
Filipino	98	0.1
Japanese	69	0.1
Korean	94	0.1
Vietnamese	43	0.0
Other Asian [1]	70	0.1
Native Hawaiian and Other Pacific Islander	21	0.0
Native Hawaiian	6	0.0
Guamanian or Chamorro	2	0.0
Samoan	5	0.0
Other Pacific Islander [2]	8	0.0
Some other race	491	0.4
Two or more races	852	0.7
Race alone or in combination with one or more other races [3]		
White	74,392	59.2
Black or African American	49,828	39.6
American Indian and Alaska Native	634	0.5
Asian	1,074	0.9
Native Hawaiian and Other Pacific Islander	63	0.1
Some other race	694	0.6

Florence County

U. S. Census Bureau

People QuickFacts	Florence County	South Carolina
Population, 2000	125,761	4,012,012
Population, percent change, 1990 to 2000	10.0%	15.1%
Persons under 5 years old, percent, 2000	6.5%	6.6%
Persons under 18 years old, percent, 2000	25.9%	25.2%
Persons 65 years old and over, percent, 2000	11.8%	12.1%
White persons, percent, 2000 (a)	58.7%	67.2%
Black or African American persons, percent, 2000 (a)	39.3%	29.5%
American Indian and Alaska Native persons, percent, 2000 (a)	0.2%	0.3%
Asian persons, percent, 2000 (a)	0.7%	0.9%
Native Hawaiian and Other Pacific Islander, percent, 2000 (a)	Z	Z
Persons reporting some other race, percent, 2000 (a)	0.4%	1.0%
Persons reporting two or more races, percent, 2000	0.7%	1.0%
Female population, percent, 2000	53.0%	51.4%
Persons of Hispanic or Latino origin, percent, 2000 (b)	1.1%	2.4%
White persons, not of Hispanic/Latino origin, percent, 2000	58.2%	66.1%
High school graduates, persons 25 years and over, 1990	45,020	1,480,330
College graduates, persons 25 years and over, 1990	10,358	360,833
Housing units, 2000	51,836	1,753,670
Homeownership rate, 2000	73.0%	72.2%
Households, 2000	47,147	1,533,854
Persons per household, 2000	2.59	2.53
Household with persons under 18 years, percent, 2000	38.7%	36.5%
Median household money income, model based estimate	$30,557	$33,325
Persons below poverty, percent, 1997 model –based estimate	19.4%	14.9%
Children below poverty, percent, 1997 model-based estimate	28.7%	
Business QuickFacts	Florence County	South Carolina
Private nonfarm establishments with paid employees, 1998	3,281	94.985
Private nonfarm employment, 1998	54,875	1,526,106
Private nonfarm employment, percent change 1990-1998	17.9%	20.5%
Nonemployer establishments, 1997	5,913	188,081
Manufacturers shipments, 1997 ($1000)	2,114,244	70,797,020

Retail sales, 1997 ($1000)	1,467,326	33,634,264
Retail sales per capita, 1997	$11,799	$8,874
Minority-owned firms, 1992	985	21,127
Women-owned firms, 1992	2,150	64,812
Housing units authorized by building permits, 1999	648	36,161
Federal funds and grants, 1999 ($1000)	564,713	20,833,188
Local government employment-full-time equivalent, 1997	4,123	143,952

Geography QuickFacts	*Florence County*	*South Carolina*
Land area, 2000 (square miles)	800	30,110
Persons per square mile, 2000	157.2	133.2
Metropolitan Area	Florence, SC MSA	

(a) Including persons reporting only one race.
(b) Hispanics may be of any race, so also are included in applicable race categories.

FN: Footnote on this item for this area in place of data
NA: Not available
D: Suppressed to avoid disclosure of confidential information
X: Not applicable
S: Suppressed; does no meet publication standards
Z: Value greater than zero, but less than half unit of measure shown

Source: U.S. Census Bureau: State and County QuickFacts. Data derived from Population estimates, 2000 Census of Population and Housing, 1990 Census of Population and Housing, Small Area Income and Poverty Estimates, County Business Patterns, 1997 Economic Census, Minority and Women-owned Business, Building Permits, Consolidated Federal Funds Report, 1997 Census of Governments.

Florence City

DP-1. Profile of General Demographic Characteristics: 2000
Data Set: Census 2000 Summary File 1 (SF 1) 100-Percent Data

Subject	Number	Percent
Total population	30.248	100.0
SEX AND AGE		
Male	13,701	45.3
Female	16,547	54.7
Under 5 years	1,936	6.4
5 to 9 years	2,116	7.0
10 to 14 years	2,222	7.3
15 to 19 years	2,025	6.7
20 to 24 years	1,896	6.3
25 to 34 years	4,104	13.6
35 to 44 years	4,425	14.6
45 to 54 years	4,289	14.2
55 to 59 years	1,498	5.0
60 to 64 years	1,180	3.9
65 to 74 years	2,227	7.4
75 to 84 years	1,732	5.7
85 years and over	598	2.0
Median age (years)	36.8	(X)
18 years and over	22,680	75.0
Male	9,902	32.7
Female	12,778	42.2
21 years and over	21,567	71.3
62 years and over	5,221	17.3
65 years and over	4,557	15.1
Male	1,611	5.3
Female	2,946	9.7
RACE		
One race	30,034	99.3
White	16,020	53.0
Black or African American	13,541	44.8
American Indian and Alaska Native	54	0.2
Asian	352	1.2
Asian Indian	45	0.1
Chinese	162	0.5

Subject	Number	Percent
Filipino	51	0.2
Japanese	35	0.1
Korean	26	0.1
Vietnamese	20	0.1
Other Asian [1]	13	0.0
Native Hawaiian and Other Pacific Islander	4	0.0
Native Hawaiian	4	0.0
Guamanian or Chamorro	0	0.0
Samoan	0	0.0
Other Pacific Islander [2]	0	0.0
Some other race	63	0.2
Two or more races	241	0.7
Race alone or in combination with one or more other races [3]		
White	16,183	53.5
Black or African American	13,621	45.0
American Indian and Alaska Native	131	0.4
Asian	400	1.3

Florence: Neighborhood Information

Demographics	Florence, SC 29506	National Average
Population of Florence	30944	8385
Median Age	34,67 years	36.00 years
Median Household Income	$34890	$36169.94
Percentage of Single Households	55.35%	40.55%
Percentage of Married Households	44.65%	59.40%
Percentage Families (households with children)	67.87%	72.14%
Average Household Size	2.50 people	4.05 people
Percentage College or Better	27.09%	20.37%
Percentage White Collar	56.71%	46.00%
Cost of Living	Florence, SC 29506	National Average
Cost of Living Index	105	100
Average Yearly Utility Cost	$2691.12	$2567.34
Average Household Total Consumer Expenditures	$38964.41 per year	$37034.21 per year
Average Household Education Expenditures	$408.26 per year	$359.07 per year
Average Household Entertainment Expenditures	$2043.10 per year	$1965.76 per year
Average Household Transportation Expenditures	$7702.85 per year	$7475.12 per year
Average Household Retail Expenditures	$17965.14 per year	$16934.35 per year
Average Household Non-Retail Expenditures	$20999.27 per year	$20096.54 per year

Housing Characteristics	Florence, NC	National Average
Single Family Home Sale Price Index	83	100
Percent Homes Owner Occupied	54.31%	64.61%
Average Dwelling Size	4 rooms	4.54 rooms

Lake City: Neighborhood Information

Demographics	Lake City, SC	National Average
Population of Lake City	7304	8385
Median Age	31.70 years	36.00 years
Median Household Income	$20796	$39169.94
Percentage of Single Households	58.13%	40.55%
Percentage of Married Households	41.87%	59.40%
Percentage Families (households with children)	73.30%	72.14%
Average Household Size	2.85 people	4.05 people
Percentage College or Better	18.13%	20.37%
Percentage White Collar	38.27%	46.00%
Cost of Living	*Lake City, SC 29560*	*National Average*
Cost of Living Index	79	100
Average Yearly Utility Cost	$2195.33	$2567.34
Average Household Total Consumer Expenditures	$29331.83 per year	$37034.21 per year
Average Household Education Expenditures	$309.20 per year	$359.07 per year
Average Household Entertainment Expenditures	$1441.48 per year	$1965.76 per year
Average Household Transportation Expenditures	$5656.66 per year	$7475.12 per year
Average Household Retail Expenditures	$13519.20 per year	$16934.35 per year
Average Household Non-Retail Expenditures	$15812.63 per year	$20096.54 per year
Quality of Life	*Lake City, SC*	*National Average*
Average Winter High Temperature	51.59 degrees	40.70 degrees
Average Winter Low Temperature	27.67 degrees	19.35 degrees
Average Summer High Temperature	90.34 degrees	86.40 degrees
Average Summer Low Temperature	67.40 degrees	62.48 degrees
Average Annual Precipitation	48.45 inches	37.69 inches
Air Quality Index	4	3.42
Total Crime Index	202	100(county average)
Personal Crime Index	273	100(county average)
Property Crime Index	175	100(county average)
Culture Index	97	86.95(national average)

Housing Characteristics	Florence, NC	National Average
Single Family Home Sale Price Index	67	100
Percent Homes Owner Occupied	61.15%	64.61%
Average Dwelling Size	4 rooms	4.54 rooms

Timmonsville: Neighborhood Information

Demographics	Timmonsville, SC	National Average
Population of Timmonsville	2238	8385
Median Age	31.14 years	36.00 years
Median Household Income	$22999	$36169.94
Percentage of Single Households	58.64%	40.55%
Percentage of Married Households	41.36%	59.40%
Percentage Families (households with children)	73.11%	72.14%
Average Household Size	2.85 people	4.05 people
Percentage College or Better	15%	20.37%
Percentage White Collar	37.51%	46.00%

Cost of Living	Timmonsville, SC 29161	National Average
Cost of Living Index	79	100
Average Yearly Utility Cost	$2183.45	$2567.34
Average Household Total Consumer Expenditures	$29374.76 per year	$37034.21 per year
Average Household Education Expenditures	$290.78 per year	$9.07 per year
Average Household Entertainment Expenditures	$1451.45 per year	$1965.76 per year
Average Household Transportation Expenditures	$5719.64 per year	$7475.12 per year
Average Household Retail Expenditures	$13427.66 per year	$16934.35 per year
Average Household Non-Retail Expenditures	$15947.10 per year	$20096.54 per year

Quality of Life	Timmonsville, SC 29161	National Average
Average Winter High Temperature	54.89 degrees	40.70 degrees
Average Winter Low Temperature	32.95 degrees	19.35 degrees
Average Summer High Temperature	90.79 degrees	86.40 degrees
Average Summer Low Temperature	69.79 degrees	62.48 degrees

Average Annual Precipitation	44.63 inches	37.69 inches
Air Quality Index	3	3.42
Total Crime Index	74	100 (county average)
Personal Crime Index	66	100 (county average)
Property Crime Index	77	100 (county average)
Culture Index	88	86.95 (national average)

Housing Characteristics	Florence, NC	National Average
Single Family Home Sale Price Index	58	100
Percent Homes Owner Occupied	60.71%	64.61%
Average Dwelling Size	4 rooms	4.54 rooms

Bibliography

Abbott, Martin (1967), *The Freedmen's Bureau in South Carolina, 1865-1872*, Chapel Hill: University of North Carolina Press.

Abramson, Paul R. (1977), *The Political Socialization of Black Americans: A Critical Evaluation of Research on Efficacy and Trust*, New York: Free Press.

Aikin, Charles (ed.) (1962), *The Negro Voter*, San Francisco, CA: Chandler Publishing Company.

Alex-Assensoh, Yvette and A. B. Assensoh (2001), "Inner City Context, Church Attendance and African American Political Participation," *The Journal of Politics*, Vol. 63, No. 3, pp. 886-901.

Alex-Assensoh, Yvette, and Lawrence J. Hanks (eds.) (2000), *Black and Multiracial Politics in America*, New York: New University Press.

Alexander, Raymond P. (1945), "The Upgrading of the Negro's Status by Supreme Court Decisions," *Journal of Negro History*, Vol. 30, pp. 117-149.

Alilunas, Leo (1940), "Legal Restrictions on the Negro in Politics," *Journal of Negro History*, Vol. 25, pp. 153-202.

Almond, Gabriel and Sidney Verba (1980), *The Civic Culture Revisited*, Boston, MA: Little Brown.

Altshuler, G., and G. Powell (1970), *Comparative Politics*, Boston, MA: Little Brown.

Amaker, Norman C. (1988), *Civil Rights and the Reagan Administration*, Washington, DC: Urban Institute Press.

Apter, D., and C. Andrain (eds.) (1972), *Contemporary Analytical Theory*, Englewood Cliff, NJ: Prentice Hall.

Auletta, K. (1982), *The Underclass*, New York: Random House.

Axelrod, R. (1972), "Where the Vote Comes From: An Analysis of Electoral Coalitions, 1952-1968," *American Political Science Review*, Vol. 66, pp. 11-20.

Axelrod, Robert (1970), *Conflict of Interest: A Theory of Divergent Goals with Applications to Politics*, Chicago: Marham Publishing Company.

Babchuck, N. and R. Thompson (1962), "The Voluntary Association of Negroes," *American Sociological Review*, Vol. 27, pp. 647-655.

Bailey, Harry Jr. (ed.) (1968), *Negro Politics in America*, Columbus, OH: Charles E. Merrill.

Bailey, H. (1968), "Negro Interest Group Strategies," *Urban Affairs Quarterly*, Vol. 4, pp. 27-38.

Bailis, L. (1974), *Bread or Justice: Grassroots Organizing in the Welfare Rights Movement*, Lexington, MA: Lexington Books.

Bardolph, R. (ed.) (1970), *The Civil Rights Record: Black Americans and the Law, 1849-1970*, New York: Thomas Y. Crowell.

Barker, Lucius J., and Jesse McCorry (1980), *Black Americans and the Political System*, Boston, MA: Little Brown.

Barnett, M. (1975), "A Theoretical Perspective on American Racial Public Policy," in M. Barnett and J. Hefner (eds), *Public Policy for the Black Community*, Port Washington, NY: Alfred Publisher.

Barth, E. and B. Abu-Laban (1959), "Power Structure in the Negro Sub-community," *American Sociological Review*, Vol. 24, pp. 69-76.

Bass, Jack, and DeVries Walter (1977), *The Transformation of Southern Politics*, New York: New American Library.

Bell, Inge (1968), *CORE and the Strategy of Non-violence*, New York: Random House.

Bennett, Lerone (1968), *Black Power, USA*, Chicago, IL: John Publishing Company.

Bennett, S. (1985), *Apathy in America*, New York: Transaction Publishers, Inc.

Berenson, W., K. Elifson, and T. Tollerson (1976), "Preachers in Politics: A Study of Political Activism among Black Ministry," *Journal of Black Studies*, Vol. 6, pp. 373-392.

Black, E. and M. Black (1987), *Politics and Society in the South*, Cambridge: Harvard University Press.

Blaustern, Albert, and Robert Zangrando (1968), *Civil Rights and the American Negro*, New York: Washington Square Press.

Bleser, Carol and K. Rothrock (1969), *The Promised Land: The History of the South Carolina Land Commission, 1869-1890*, Columbia, SC: University of South Carolina Press.

Blumenthal, Henry (1963), "Woodrow Wilson and the Race Question," *Journal of Negro History*, Vol. 48, pp. 1-21.

Bolce, L. and S. Gray (1979), "Blacks, Whites and Race Politics," *The Public Interest*, Winter Issue, pp. 61-76.

Botsch, C. S., and R. E. Botsch (1996), "African Americans in South Carolina Politics," *SC Journal of Political Science*, Vol. 24, pp. 63-101.

Bracey, J., A. Meier, and E. Rudwick, E. (1970), *Black Nationalism in America*, Indianapolis, IN: Bobbs-Merril.

Brady, Patrick S. (1972), "The Slave Trade and Sectionalism in South Carolina, 1787-1808," *Journal of Southern History*, Vol. XXXVIII, pp. 601-620.

Braxton, G. (1994), "African American Women and Politics: Research Trends and Directions," *National Political Science Review*, Vol. 4, pp. 281-296.

Brewer, William M. (1944), "The Poll Tax and the Poll Taxers," *Journal of Negro History*, Vol. 29, pp. 260-299.

Brown, Ronald, and Monica Wolford (1994), "Religious Resources and African-American Political Action," *Political Science Review*, Vol. 4, pp. 30-48.

Brown, George Tindall (1952), *South Carolina Negroes, 1877-1900*, Columbia, SC: University of South Carolina Press

Browning, R., D. Marshall, and D. Tabb (1984), *Protest is not Enough*, Berkeley, CA: University of California Press.

Brownnell, Baline (1975), *Urban Ethos in the South, 1920-1930*, Baton Rouge, LA: Louisiana State University Press.

Brunson, W. A. (1940), *Reminiscences of Reconstruction in Darlington*, Hartsville, S.C: Hartsville Publishing Company.

Bullock, C. (1975), "The Election of Blacks in the South: Preconditions and Consequences," *American Journal of Political Science*, Vol. 10, pp. 727-739.

Bullock, Henry Allan (1967), *A History of Negro Education in the South*, Cambridge, MA: Harvard University Book Press.

Bunche, Ralph J. (1941), "The Negro in the Political Life of the United States," *Journal of Negro Education*, Vol. 10, pp. 567-584.

Burns, J. (1978), *Leadership*, New York: Harper and Row.

Burns, S. (1995), *The Black Progress Question: Explaining the African American Predicament*, Newbury Park, CA: Sage Publications.

Burns, W. Hayword (1963), *The Voices of Negro Protest in America*, New York: Oxford University Press.

Button, J. (1980), *Black Violence: Political Impact of the 1960s Riots*, Princeton, NJ: Princeton University Press.

Caffey, Francis G. (1905), "Suffrage Limitations at the South," *Political Science Quarterly*, Vol. 20, pp. 53-67.

Campbell, A. (1970), *White Attitude Toward Black People*, Ann Arbor, MI: University of Michigan Institute for Social Research.

Campbell, Angus, Philip E. Converse, Warren E. Miller and Donald E. Stokes (1960), *The American Voter*, New York: John Will Press.

Campbell, D. and J. Feagin (1975), Black Politics in the South: A Descriptive Analysis," *Journal of Politics*, Vol. 37, pp. 129-162.

Carmichael, Stokely S. and Charles V. Hamilton (1968), *Black Power: The Politics of Liberation in America*, New York: Random House.

Carmichael, S. and C, Hamilton (1992), *Black Power*, New York: Vintage Books.

Carmines, Edward G. and James A. Stimson (1982), "Racial Issues and the Structure of Mass Belief Systems," *Journal of Politics*, Vol. 44, pp. 2-20.

Carson, C. (1981), *In Struggle: SNCC and the Black Awakening of the 1960s*, Cambridge, MA: Harvard University Press.

Carter, Margaret (1976), *History of Lake City, South Carolina*, New York: Carleton Press.

Cartwright, J. R. (1983), *Political Leadership in Africa*, New York: St. Martin's Press.

Cash, Wilbur Joseph (1941), *The Mind of the South*, New York: A. A. Knopf.

Childs, J. (1989), *Leadership, Conflict, and Cooperation in Afro-American Social Thought*, Philadelphia, PA: Temple University Press.

Clark, Kenneth B. (1966), "The Civil Rights Movement: Momentums and Organization," *Daedalus*, Vol. 96, pp. 239-267.

Claude, Richard (1966), "Constitutional Voting Rights and Early U.S. Supreme Court Decisions," *Journal of Negro History*, Vol. 51, pp. 114-124.

Clayton, Edward T. (1964), *The Negro Politician: His Success and Failures*, Chicago, IL: Johnson Publishing Company.

Cobb, R. and C. Elder (1983), *Participation in American Politics*, Baltimore, MD: John Hopkins University Press.

Cobb, R. and C. Elder (1971), "The Politics of Agenda Building: An Alternative Perspective for Modern Democratic Theory," *Journal of Politics*, Vol. 33, pp. 893-915.

Cohen, C. and M. Dawson (1993), "Neighborhood Poverty and African American Politics," *American Political Science Review*, Vol. 87, No. 2, pp. 286-302.

Cole, L. (1976), *Blacks in Power: A Comparative Study of Black and White Elected Officials*, Princeton, NJ: Princeton University Press.

Congressional Black Caucus (1982), *The Black Leadership Family Program for the Survival and Progress of the Black Nation*, Washington, DC: Congressional Black Caucus Publication.

Conway, M. (2000), *Political Participation in the United States*, Washington, D.C: CQ Press.

Conyers, J. and W. Wallace (1976), *Black Elected Officials*, New York: Russell Sage.

Cook, Harvey Toliver (1926), *Rambles in the Pee Dee Basin, South Carolina*, Columbia, SC: University of South Carolina Press.

Cook, Samuel D. (1966), "The Tragic Myth of Black Power," *New South*, Summer Issue, pp. 58-64.

_____(1964), "Political Movements and Organization," *Journal of Politics*, Vol. 26, pp. 130-153.

Crawford, V., B. Woods and J. A. Rouse (1990), *Women in the Civil Rights Movement: Trailblazers and Torchbearers, 1941-1965*, Brooklyn, NY: Carlson Publishing.
Cruse, H. (1987), *Plural But Equal: Blacks and Minorities in America's Plural Society*, New York: William Morrow.
Cruse, H. (1968), *Rebellion or Revolution*, New York: William Morrow.

Dahl, R. (1961), *Who Governs?* New Haven, CT: Yale University Press.
Daniel, Johnie (1968), "Changes in Negro Political Mobilization and its Relationship to Community Socio-economic Structures," *Journal of Social and Behavioral Science*, Vol. 13, pp. 41-46.
Dawson, Michael C., C. Brown and Richard Allen (1990), "Racial Belief System, Religious Guidance, and African-American Participation," *National Political Science Review*, Vol. 2, pp. 22-44.
De Santis, Vincent P. (1960), "The Republican Party and the Southern Negro, 1877-1897, " *Journal of Negro History*, Vol. 45, pp. 71-87.
Dellums, R. V. (1993), "Black Leadership," in W. E. Rosenbach and R. L. Taylor (eds.), *Contemporary Issues in Leadership*, Boulder, CO: Westview Press.
Dollard, J. (1957), *Caste and Class in a Southern Town*, Garden City, NJ: Doubleday.
Douglas, Paul H. (1960), "Trends and Developments: The 1960 Voting Rights Bill: The Struggle, the Final Results, and the Reason," *Journal of Intergroup Relations*, Vol. 1, pp. 86-88.
Dubois, W. E. B. (1940), *Dusk of Dawn*, New York: Harcourt, Brace & World.
Dye, Thomas, R. (2003), *Politics in America*, Upper Saddle River, NJ: Prentice Hall.
Dye, Thomas, R. (1976), *Who's Running America*, Englewood Cliffs, NJ: Prentice Hall.
Dyer, Brainerd (1968), "One Hundred Years of Negro Suffrage," *Pacific Historical Review*, Vol. 37, pp. 1-20.
Dymally, Mervyn M. (ed.) (1971), *The Black Politician: His Struggle for Power*, Belmont, CA: Duxbury Press.

Edwards, D. V. (1982), *The American Political Experience*, Englewood, Cliffs, NJ: Prentice Hall.
Eisinger, P. (1980), *The Politics of Displacement: Racial and Ethnic Transition in Three American Cities*, New York: Academic Press.
_____(1974), "Racial Differences in Protest Participation," *American Political Science Review*, Vol. 68, pp. 592-607.
Elliot, J. (1986), *Black Voices in American Politics*, New York: Harcourt Brace Jovanovich.

Feagin, J. and H. Vera (1995), *White Racism*, New York: Routledge.
Feagin, J (1988), "A Slavery Unwilling to Die," *Journal of Black Studies*, Vol. 18, pp. 451-469.
Feagin, J. (1975), "The Black Church: Inspiration or Opiate," *Journal of Negro History*, Vol. 60, pp. 536-540.
Fendrich, J. (1993), *Ideal Citizens: The Legacy of the Civil Rights Movement*, Albany, NY: State University of New York Press.
Fix, M. and R. Struck (eds.) (1990), *Clear and Convincing Evidence: Measurement of Discrimination in America*, Washington, DC: Urban Institute Press.
Forsythe, D. (1972), "A Functional Definition of Black Leadership," *Black Scholar*, Vol. 3, pp. 18-26.
Franklin, V. P. (1984), *Black Self-determination*, Westport, CT: Lawrence Hill.
Frazier, E. F. (1964), *The Negro Church in America*, New York: Schocken Books.

Frederickson, G. (1981), *White Supremacy: A Comparative Study in American and South African History*, New York: Oxford University Press.

Froman, Jr., L. A. (1965), *People and Politics: An Analysis of the American Political System*, Englewood, NJ: Prentice Hall.

Frye, H. (1980), *Black Parties and Political Power: A Case Study*, Boston, MA: G. K. Hall.

Gaines, K. (1996), *Uplifting the Race: Black Leadership, Politics, and Culture in the Twentieth Century*, Chapel Hill, NC: University of North Carolina Press.

Garrow, D. (1978), *Protest at Selma: Martin Luther King, Jr. and the Voting Rights Act of 1965*, New Haven, CT: Yale University Press.

Gates, H. L. and C. West (1996), *The Future of the Race*, New York: Knopf.

Gatewood, Willard B. (1975), *Black Americans and the White Man's Burden, 1898-1903*, Urbana, IL: University of Illinois Press.

Gill, R. L. (1956), "The School Segregation Cases and State Racism, *Quarterly Review* of *Higher Education among Negroes*, Vol. 24, pp. 163-169.

Glasgow, D. (1980), *The Black Underclass*, San Francisco, CA: Jossey-Bass.

Glazer Nathan and Daniel P. Moynihan (eds.) (1975), *Ethnicity: Theory and Experience*, Cambridge, MA: Harvard University Press.

Glazer, N., and D. P. Moynihan (1970), *Beyond the Melting Pot*, Cambridge: MIT Press.

Golden, Harry (1964), *Mr. Kennedy and the Negroes*, Cleveland, OH: World Publishing Company.

Greenberg, S. (1980), *Race and State in Capitalist Development*, New Haven, CT: Yale University Press.

Greenstein, F. (1967), The Impact of Personality on Politics," *American Political Science Review*, Vol. 61, pp. 629-641.

Gregory, J. M. (1971), *Frederick Douglas: The Orator*, Chicago, IL: Apollo Edition.

Hacker, A. (1995), *Two Nations: Black and White, Separate, Hostile Unequal*, New York: Ballentine.

Hadden, Jeffrey, Louis Masottti and Victor Thiessen (1967), "The Making of the Negro Mayors," *Trans-Action*, Vol. 5, pp. 21-30.

Haines, H (1988), *Black Radicals and the Civil Rights Movements*, Knoxville, TN: University of Tennessee Press.

Hall, R. L. (ed.), (1979), *Ethnic Autonomy-Comparative Dynamics: The Americas, Europe, and the Developing World*, New York: Pergamon Press.

Hall, W., W. Cross and R. Freedle (1972) "Stages in Development of Black Awareness: An Exploratory Investigation," in R. L. Jones (ed.), *Black Psychology*, New York: Harper and Row.

Hamilton, C. and D. Hamilton (1997), *The Dual Agenda: Race and Social Welfare Policies of Civil Rights Organization*, New York: Columbia University Press.

Hamilton, C. (1973), *The Black Experience in American Politics*, New York: G. P. Putnam.

Hamilton, Charles V. (1962), *Minority Politics in Black Belt Alabama*, New York: McGraw-Hill Book Company.

Harmon-Martin, S. (1994), "Black Women in Politics: A Research Note," in H. Walton (ed.), *Black Politics and Black Political Behavior*, Westport, CT: Praeger.

Harris, Frederick (1994), "Something Within: Religion as a Mobilizer of African American Political Activism," *Journal of Politics*, Vol. 56, No. 1, pp. 42-68.

Hechter, M. (1972), "Toward a Theory of Ethnic Change," *Politics and Society*, Vol. 2, pp. 21-45.

Henderson, W. and L. Lewdebur (1972), *Economic Disparity: Problems and Strategies for Black America*, New York: The Free Press.
Higham, J. (1978), *Ethnic Leadership in America*, Baltimore, MD: John Hopkins University Press.
Higgins, W. Robert (1971), "The Geographical Origins of Negro Slaves in Colonial South Carolina," *South Atlantic Quarterly*, Vol. LXX, pp. 34-47.
Hirshson, Stanley P. (1962), *Farewell to the Shirt: Northern Republicans and the Southern Negro, 1877-1893*, Bloomington, IN: Indiana University Press.
Holden, M. (1973), *The Politics of the Black "Nation,"* New York: Chandler.
Holloway, Harry (1969), *The Politics of the Southern Negro*, New York: Random House.
Holt, Thomas (1977), *Black Over White: Negro Political Leadership in South Carolina During Reconstruction*, Urbana, IL: University of Illinois Press.
Huggins, N. (1971), "Afro-American History: Myths, Heroes, and Reality," in M. Kilson, D. Fox, and N. Huggins (eds.), *Key Issues in the Afro-American Experience*, New York: Harcourt Brace Jovanovich.

Jackson, J. (ed.) (1991), *Life in Black America*, Newbury Park, CA: Sage.
Jackson, John (1973), "Alienation and Black Political Participation," *Journal of Politics*, Vol. 35, pp. 850-859.
James, J. (1997), *Transcending the Talented Tenth: Black Leaders and American Intellectuals*, New York: Routeledge.
Jencks, C. (1989), "What is the Underclass—and is it growing?" *Focus*, Vol. 12, No. 1, pp. 14-31.
Joint Center for Political and Economic Studies (1983), *A Policy Framework for Racial Justice*, Washington, DC: JCPES Publication.
Jones, B. (ed.) (1989), *Leadership and Politics: New Perspective in Political Science*, Lawrence, KA: University of Kansas Press.
Jones, M. (1994), "Black Leadership and the Continuing Struggle for Racial Justice," in L. Barker, and M. Jones (eds.), *African Americans and the American Political System*, Englewood Cliffs, NJ: Prentice-Hall.
Jones, M. (1972), "A Framework of Reference for Black Politics," in L. Henderson (ed.), *Black Political Life in the United States*, New York: Chandler.

Keech, W. R. (1968), *The Impact of Negro Voting: The Role of the Vote in the Quest for Equality*, Chicago, IL: Rand McNally and Company.
Key, V. O. (1949), *Southern Politics in State and Nation*, New York: Vintage Books.
Killan, L. (1968), *The Impossible Revolution? Black Power and the American Dream*, New York: Random House.
Killan, L. and C. Smith (1960), "Negro Protest Leaders in a Southern Community," *Social Forces*, Vol. 38, pp. 253-257.
King, G. Wayne (1981), *Rise Up So Early, A History of Florence County, South Carolina*, Spartanburg, SC: The Reprint Company Publishers.
Kirby, Jack Temple (1972), *Darkness at the Dawning: Race and Reform in the Progressive South*, Philadelphia, PA: Lippincott Press.
Klingberg, Frank J. (1975), *An Appraisal of the Negro in Colonial South Carolina: A Study in Americanization*, Philadelphia, PA: Porcupine Press.
Kinfe, A. (1991), *Politics of Black Nationalism: From Harlem to Soweto*, Trenton, NJ: Africa World Press.
King, M. L. Jr. (1967), *Where Do We Go from Here: Chaos or Community?* Boston, MA: Beacon Press.

Kousser, J. Morgan (1974), *The Shaping of Southern Politics: Suffrage Restriction and the Establishment of the One-party South, 1880-1910*, New Haven, CT: Yale University Press.

Krug, Mark M. (1963), "The Republican Party and the Emancipation Proclamation," *Journal of Negro History*, Vol. 48, pp. 98-114.

Ladd, Everett C., Jr. (1966), *Negro Political Leadership in the South*, Ithaca, NY: Cornell University Press.

Lander, Jr. E. M (1960), A History of South Carolina, 1865-1960, Chapel Hill, NC: University of North Carolina Press.

Lane, E. (1962), *Political Ideology: Why the American Common Man Believes What He Does*, New York: The Free Press.

Lawson, Steven F. (1976), *Black Ballot: Voting Rights in the South, 1944-1969*, New York: Columbia University Press.

Leggett, John C. (1963), "Working, Class Consciousness, Race, and Political Choice," *American Journal of Sociology*, Vol. 69, pp. 171-176.

Levine, C. (1976), *Racial Conflict and the American Mayor*, Lexington, MA: D. C, Heath.

Levine, L. (1978), *Black Culture and Black Consciousness: Afro-American Folk Thought from Slavery to Freedom*, New York: Oxford University.

Levy, Mark R, and Michael S. Kramer (1972), *The Ethnic Factors: How America's Minorities Decide Elections*, New York: Simon and Schuster.

Lewis, Roscoe E. (1943), "The Role of Pressure Groups in Maintaining Morale among Negroes," *Journal of Negro Education*, Vol. 12, pp. 464-473.

Lewinson, Paul (1963), *Race, Class, and Party: A History of Negro Suffrage and White Politics in the South*, New York: Russell and Russell.

Lincoln, C. and L. Mamiya (1990), *The Black Church and the African American Experience*, Durham, NC: Duke University Press.

Lipsky, M. (1968), "Protest as a Political Resource," *American Political Science Review*, Vol. 62, pp. 1144-1158.

Loury, G. (1985), "The Moral Quandary of the Black Community," *The Public Interest*, Vol. 79, pp. 9-22.

Lubell, Samuel (1964), "The Negro and the Democratic Coalition," *Commentary*, Vol. 38, pp. 18-27.

_____(1963), *White and Black: Test of a Nation*, New York: Harper and Row.

Lyttle, Clifford M. (1966), "The History of the Civil Rights Bill of 1964," *Journal of Negro History*, Vol. 51, pp. 275-296.

MacDonald, A. (1975), "Black Power," *Journal of Negro Education*, Vol. 44, pp.547-554.

Marable, M. (1978), "Anatomy of Black Politics," *Review of Black Political Economy*, Summer Issue, pp. 68-83.

Marshall, Thurgood (1952), "An Evaluation of Recent Efforts to Achieve Racial Integration through Resort to the Courts," *Journal of Negro Education*, Vol. 21, pp. 316-326.

Marvick, Dwaine (1965), "The Political Socialization of the American Negro," *Annals of the American Academy of Political and Social Science*, Vol. 361, pp. 112-127.

Mathew, Donald and James Prothro (1966), *Negroes and the Southern Politics*, New York: Harcourt, Brace and World.

McClain, P. D and J. Stewart, Jr. (2006), *Can We All Get Along? Racial and Ethnic Minorities in American Politics*, Boulder, CO: Westview Press.

McLanahan, S. and I. Garfinkel (1989), "Single Mothers, the Underclass and Social Policy," *The Annals of American Academy of Political and Social Sciences*, Vol. 501, No. 22, pp. 92-104.

Meier, August (1965), "On the Role of Martin Luther King," *New Politics*, Vol. 4, pp. 52-59.

_____(1963), "Negro Protest Movements and Organizations," *Journal of Negro Education*, Vol. 32, pp. 437-450.

Middleton, Russell (1962), "Civil Rights Issue and Presidential Voting among Southern Negroes and Whites," *Social Forces*, Vol. 40, pp. 209-215.

Milbrath, L. W. (1969), *Political Participation*, Chicago, IL: Rand McNally.

Morris, M. (1975), *The Politics of Black America*, New York: Harper and Row.

Moynihan, P. D. (1965), *The Negro Family: The Case for National Action*, Washington, DC: Office of Policy Planning and Research, U. S. Department of Labor.

Murapa, Rukudzo (1969), "Race, Pride, and Black Political Thought," *Negro Digest*, Vol. 18, pp. 6-9.

Murray, R. and A. Vedlitz (1978), "Racial Voting Patterns in the South, *The Annals*, Vol. 439, pp. 29-39.

Nelson, W. and P. Meranto (1977), *Electing Black Mayors: Political Action in the Black Community*, Columbus, OH: Ohio State University Press.

Newby, Idus A. (1973), *Black Carolinians: A History of Blacks in South Carolina from 1895 to 1968,* Columbia, SC: University of Columbia Press.

Newman, Dorothy K. (1978), *Protest, Politics and Prosperity: Black Americans and White Institutions, 1940-1975*, New York: Pantheon Books.

Odgen, Frederick D. (1958), *The Poll Tax in the South*, Tuscaloosa, AL: University of Alabama Press.

Olsen, M. (1970), "Social and Political Participation of Blacks," *American Sociological Review*, Vol. 34, pp. 674-688.

Orum, M. (1966), "A Reappraisal of the Social and Political Participation of Blacks," *American Journal of Sociology*, Vol. 62, pp. 32-46.

Overacker, Louise (1945), "The Negro's Struggle for Participation in Primary Elections," *Journal of Negro History*, Vol. 30, pp. 54-61.

Paige, G. (1977), *The Scientific Study of Leadership*, New York: The Free Press.

Parent, Wayne and Paul Steckler (1985), "The Political Implications of Economic Stratification in the Black Community," *Western Political Quarterly*, Vol. 38, pp. 521-37.

Pateman, C. (1970), *Participation and Democratic Theory*, Cambridge: Cambridge University Press.

Patterson, E. (1974), *Black City Politics*, New York: Dodd, Mead.

Patterson, O. (1977), *Ethnic Chauvinism: The Reactionary Impulse*, New York: Stein and Day.

Perry, H. L. and W. Parent (eds.) (1995), *Blacks and the American Political System*, Gainesville, FL: University of Florida Press.

Perry, H. (1991), "Deracialization as an Analytic Construct," *Urban Affairs Quarterly*, Vol. 27, pp. 181-191.

Person, G. (1993), *Dilemmas of Black Politics: Issues of Leadership and Strategy*, New York: Harper Collins.

Peterson, P. (1979), "Organizational Imperatives and Ideological Change: The Case of Black Power," *Urban Affairs Quarterly*, Vol. 14, pp. 465-484.

Pittigrew, T. (1970), "Ethnicity in American Life: A Social Psychological Perspective,"
    In O. Fainstein (ed.), *Ethnic Groups in the City*, Lexington, MA: D. C. Heath
    Publishers.
Pinderhughes, D. (1995), "Black Interest Groups and the 1982 Extension of the Voting
    Rights Act," In H. Perry and W. Parent (eds.), *Blacks and the American
    Political System*, Tallahassee, FL: University Press of Florida
Poinsett, A. (1973), "Class Patterns in Black Politics," *Ebony Magazine*, August, pp. 36-
    40.
Preston, Michael B., Lenneal J. Henderson, Jr., and Paul L. Puryear (1987), *The New
    Black Politics: The Search for Political Power*, New York: Longman
    Publishers.
Price, Hugh D. (1957), *The Negro and Southern Politics*, New York: New York
    University Press.
Price, Margaret (1959), *The Negro and the Ballot in the South*, Atlanta, GA: Southern
    Regional Council.

Quarles, Benjamin (1962), *Lincoln and the Negro*, New York: Oxford University Press.

Rabinowitz, H. (1982), *Southern Black Leaders of the Reconstruction Era*, Urbana, IL:
    University of Illinois Press.
Rabushka, A. and K. A. Shepsle (1972), *Politics in Plural Societies: A Theory in
    Democratic Instability*, Columbus, OH: Charles E. Merrill Publishing
    Company.
Ransom, Roger L. and Richard Sutch (1977), *One King of Freedom: The Economic
    Consequences of Emancipation*, New York: Cambridge University Press.
Rapoport, A. (1958), "Varieties of Political Theory," *American Political Science Review*,
    Vol. 52, pp. 972-988.
Reed, A. (1986), *The Jesse Jackson Phenomenon*, New Haven, CT: Yale University
    Press.
Reese, Laura and Ronald Brown (1995), "The Effects of Religious Messages on Racial
    Identity and System Blame Among African Americans," *Journal of Politics*,
    Vol. 57, No.1, pp. 24-43.
Robnet, B. (1997), *How Long? How Long?: African American Women in the Struggle for
    Civil Rights*, New York: Oxford University Press.
Rogers, H. (1981), "Civil Rights: Another Myth of Popular Sovereignty," *Journal of
    Black Studies*, Vol. 12, pp. 53-70.
Rose, John C. (1906), "Negro Suffrage: The Constitutional Point of View," *American
    Political Science Review*, Vol. 1, pp. 17-43.
Rose, Harold (1965), "The All Negro Town: Its Evaluation and Future," *Geographical
    Review*, Vol. 65, pp. 362-381.
Roster of Black Elected Officials (1981), Washington, DC.: Joint Center for Political
    Studies Publication.

Sack, Karin (1988), "Gender and Grassroots Leadership," in A. Bookman and S. Morgan
    (eds.), *Women and the Politics of Empowerment*, Philadelphia, PA: Temple
    University Press.
Saint-James, Warren D. (1958), *The National Association for the Advancement of
    Colored People: A Case Study in Pressure Groups*, New York: Exposition
    Press.
Salamon, L. (1973), "Leadership and Modernization: The Emerging Black Political Elite
    in the American South," *Journal of Politics*, Vol. 35, pp. 615-646.

Scheiner, Seth M. (1962), "President Theodore Roosevelt and the Negro, 1901-1908," *Journal of Negro History*, Vol. 47, pp. 169-182.

Schuman, Howard, C. Steeh and L. Bobo (1985), *Racial Attitude in America: Trends* and *Interpretation*, Cambridge, MA: Harvard University Press.

Sellers, W. W. (1902), *A History of Marion County, South Carolina*, Columbia, SC: University of South Carolina Press.

Seligman, L. (1950), "The Study of Political Leadership," *American Political Science Review*, Vol. 44, pp. 904-915.

Shugg, Roger Wallace (1936), "Negro Voting in the Ante-Bellum South," *Journal of Negro History*, Vol. 21, pp. 357-364.

Shingles, Richard D. (1981), "Black Consciousness and Political Participation: The Missing Link," *American Political Science Review*, Vol. 75, pp. 76-91.

Silverman, Sondra (ed.) (1970), *The Black Revolt and Democratic Politics*, Boston, MA: D. C. Heath and Company.

Singh, R. (1997), *The Farrakhan Phenomenon: Race, Reaction and the Paranoid Style of American Politics*, Washington, DC: George Washington University Press.

Sirmans, M. Eugene (1966), *Colonial South Carolina: A Political History*, Chapel Hill, N.C: University of North Carolina Press.

Sitkoff, Harvard (1981), *The Struggle for Black Equality*, New York: Hill and Wang.

Smith R. (1996), *We Have No Leaders: African Americans in the Post-Civil Rights Era*, Albany, NY: State University of New York Press.

_____(1995), *Racism in the Post-Civil Rights Era: Now You Can See it, Now You Don't*, Albany, NY: State University of New York Press.

_____(1992), "Ideology as the Enduring Dilemma of Black Politics," in G. Persons (ed.), *Dilemmas of Black Politics*, New York: Harper Collins.

_____(1981), "Black Power and the Transformation from Protest to Politics," *Political Science Quarterly*, Vol. 96, pp. 431-445.

Smith, Robert C. (1984), *Black Leadership: A Survey of Theory and Research*, Washington, DC: Institute for Urban Affairs and Research, Howard University.

Smith, Robert (1981), "Black Power and the Transformation from Protest to Politics," *Political Science Quarterly*, Vol. 96, pp. 431-443.

Sniderman, Paul (1985), *Race and Inequality: A Study in American Values*, Chatham, NJ: Chatham House.

Sowell, T. (1981), *Ethnic America: A History*, New York: Basic Books.

_____(1975), *Race and Economics*, New York: Longman.

Stewart, James B. and Joyce E.Allen-Smith (1995) (eds.), *Blacks in Rural America*, New Brunswick, NJ: Transactions Publishers

Steinberg, Charles (1962), "The Southern Negro's Right to Vote," *American Federationist*, Vol. 69, pp. 1-6.

Stone, Chuck (1968), *Black Political Power in America*, New York: Dell Press.

Stone, P. (1980), "Ambition Theory and the Black Politician," *Western Political Quarterly*, Vol. 32, pp. 94-107.

_____(1978), Social Bias in the Recruitment of Black Elected Officials in the United States," *Review of Black Political Economy*, Vol. 9, pp. 384-404.

Stroud, Virgil (1961), "The Negro Voter in the South," *Quarterly Review of Higher Education among Negroes*, Vol. 29, pp. 9-39.

Tate, Katherine (1993), *From Protest to Politics: The New Black Voters in the American Electorate*, New York: Russell Sage Foundation.

Tate, K. (1992), "The Impact of Jackson's Presidential Bid on Blacks and the Democratic Party," *National Political Science Review*, Vol. 3, pp. 184-197.

Tollerson, Tandy (1976), Preachers in Politics: A Study of Political Activism among the Black Ministry," *Journal of Black Studies*, Vol. 7, pp. 373-392.

Udogu, E. I. (ed.) (2001), *The Issue of Political Ethnicity in Africa*, Aldershot, UK: Ashgate Publishers.
_____(1999), "The Issue of Ethnicity and Democratization in Africa: Toward the Millennium," *Journal of Black Studies*, Vol. 29, No. 6, pp. 790-808.
Underwood, J. L. (1994), *The Constitution of South Carolina, Volume IV: The Struggle for Political Equality*, Columbia, SC: University of South Carolina Press.

Verba, Sidney and Norman Nie (1972), *Participation in America*, New York: Harper and Row.
Vernon, Amelia Wallace (1993), *African Americans at Mars Bluff, South Carolina*, Baton Rouge, LA: Louisiana State University Press.

Walters, P. and R. Cleghorn (1967), *Climbing Jacob's Ladder: The Arrival of Negroes in Southern Politics*, New York: Harcourt, Brace and World.
Walters, R. W. and Smith, R. C. (1999), *African American Leadership*, Albany, NY: State University of New York Press.
_____(1992), "Two Political Traditions: Black Politics in the 1990s," *National Political Science Review*, Vol. 3, pp. 198-208.
_____(1981), "The Challenge of Black Leadership: An Analysis of the Problem of Strategy Shift," *Urban League Review*, Vol. 5, pp. 77-88.
_____(1980), "Black Presidential Politics: Bargaining or Begging?" *Black Scholar*, Vol. 11, No. 4, pp. 22-31.
_____(1972), "The New Black Political Culture," *Black World*, Vol. 22, pp. 4-17.
Walton, Hanes Jr. (1985), *Invisible Politics*, Albany, NY: State University of New York Press.
_____(1972a), *Black Politics: A Theoretical and Structural Analysis*, New York: J. B. Lippincott Company.
_____(1972b), *Black Political Parties*, New York: Free Press.
_____(1971), *The Political Philosophy of Martin Luther King*, Jr. Westport, CT: Greenwood Publishing Corporation.
_____(1968), "The Political Leadership of Martin Luther King, Jr." *Quarterly Review of Higher Education Among Negroes*, Vol. 36, pp. 163-171.
Washington, J. (ed.) (1992), *A Testament of Hope: The Essential Writings of Martin Luther King, Jr.*, New York: Harper and Row.
Welch, Susan and Michael Combs (1985), "Intra-Racial Differences in Attitudes of Blacks: Class or Consensus," *Phylon*, Vol. 2, pp. 91-97.
West, Cornel (1993), *Race Matters*, New York: Vintage Books.
White, J. (1990), *Black Leaderships in America: From Booker T. Washington to Jesse Jackson*, New York: Longman.
Williams, E. (1982), "Black Political Progress in the 1970s: The Electoral Arena," in M. Preston, L. Henderson, and P. Puryear (eds.), *The New Black Politics*, New York: Longman.
Williams, L. (1996), *Servants of the People: The 1960s Legacy of African American Leadership*, New York: St. Martin's Press.
Williams, Walter (1983), *The State against Blacks*, New York: McGraw-Hill.

Williamson, Joel (1965), *After Slavery: The Negro of South Carolina During Reconstruction*, 1861-1877, Chapel Hill, NC: University of North Carolina Press.

Wilson, James Q. (1973), *Political Organization*, New York: Basic Books.

_____(1961), "The Strategy of Protest," *Journal of Conflict Resolution*, Vol. 3, pp. 291-303.

_____(1960), *Negro Politics: The Search for Leadership*, New York: Free Press.

Wilson, William J. (1987), *The Truly Disadvantaged*, Chicago, IL: University of Chicago Press.

_____(1980), *The Declining Significance of Race*, Chicago, IL: University of Chicago Press.

_____(1972), "Black Demands and American Government Response," *Journal of Black Studies*, Vol. 1, pp. 7-28.

Wolfe, Deborah Partridge (1963), "Negroes in American Politics," *Negro Educational Review*, Vol. 14, pp. 64-71.

Wolfinger, R. E. (1980), *Who Votes?* New Haven, CT: Yale University Press.

Wolman, H. and N. Thomas (1970), "Black Interests, Black Groups, and Black Influence in the Federal Policy Process: The Cases of Housing and Education," *Journal of Politics*, Vol. 32, pp. 875-897.

Wood, Peter (1974), *Black Majority: Negroes in Colonial South Carolina from 1670 through the Stono Rebellion*, New York: Knopf.

Wright, B. (ed.) (1961), *Alexander Hamilton, James Madison, and Jon Jay, The Federalist*, Cambridge, MA: Harvard University Press.

Wright, Gerald, Jr. (1977), "Racism and Welfare Policy in America," *Social Science Quarterly*, Vol. 57, pp. 718-730.

Yvette, S. (1971), *The Choice: The Issue of Black Survival in America*, New York: G. P. Putnan Sons.

Zeigler, Eugene (1996), *Florence: A Renaissance Spirit*, Florence, SC.: Greater Florence Chamber of Commerce Publication.

Area News Papers

The Morning News, Florence, South Carolina

The News Journal: (Florence, Quimby, Darlington, Pamplico, Evergreen and Timmonsville).

The Community Times, Florence, South Carolina

News and Press, Darlington County, South Carolina

The News, Kingstree, Williamsburg County, South Carolina.

Index

Author Biography

E. Ike Udogu is professor of International, Comparative and African Politics at Appalachian State University, Boone, North Carolina, USA. He has lived in Florence, South Carolina since 1985. He taught at Francis Marion University, Florence, South Carolina until 2003. He has published extensively on African politics and presented scholarly papers at international conferences around the world.

Dr. Udogu is the author/editor of *Nigeria and the Politics of Survival as a Nation-state*; *Democracy and Democratization in Africa: Toward the 21st Century*; *The Issue of Political Ethnicity in Africa*; *An African Portrait: a Sociological and Political Fiction*; *Nigeria in the Twenty-First Century: Strategies for Political Stability and Peaceful Coexistence*. He has contributed numerous book chapters on African and Nigerian politics, and is working on a book entitled, *Africa in the New Millennium: Political and Economic Development Discourse*. His scholarly publications have appeared in the following journals: *Makerere Political Science Review; Journal of Asian and African Studies; African and Asian Studies; Africa Quarterly; African Studies Review; Ethnic and Racial Studies; Journal of Black Studies; The Review of Black Political Economy; Journal of Developing Societies; IN DEPTH: A Journal of Values and Public Policy; Canadian Review of Studies in Nationalism, Journal of Political Science; Journal of Third World Studies; Irinkerindo: A Journal of African Migration; Scandinavian Journal of Development Alternatives; International Journal of Comparative Sociology; Terrorism and Political Violence*, just to cite a few.

In addition, Dr. Udogu was a National Endowment for the Humanities Fellow and is listed in *Who's Who in American Education* and *2000 Outstanding Scholars of the 21st Century*. He is a recipient of the Africa Excellence in Research Award, Distinguished Leadership, Scholarship and Service Award, Excellence in Authorship Award, Decree of Merit for Outstanding contribution to Political Science Award and Francis Marion University 2000-2001 Award for Excellence in Research. He served on the editorial board of Collegiate Press, San Diego, California.

Presently, Dr. Udogu is the Director of Research and Publication, African Studies and Research Forum (ASRF) and Vice-President and President Elect of the Association of Third World Studies (ATWS), the world's largest organization dedicated to Third World Studies.